SPEED ACHIEVEMENTS

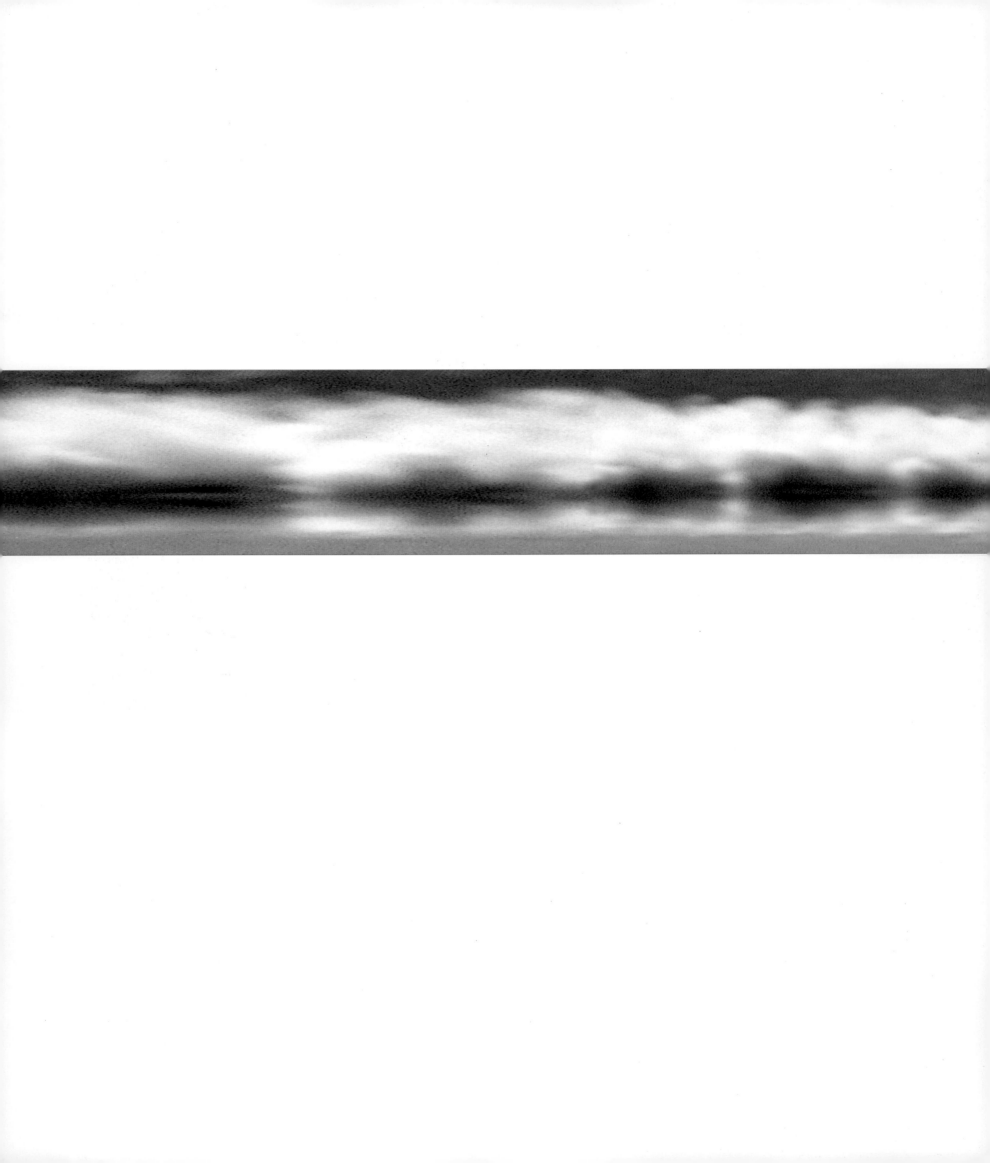

SPEED ACHIEVEMENTS

LAND SEA AND AIR: A CENTURY OF CONQUEST

RICHARD GRAVES

MBI Publishing Company

This edition first published in 1998 by MBI Publishing Company,
729 Prospect Avenue, PO Box 1, Osceola, WI 54020-0001 USA
Previously published by Bloomsbury Publishing Plc

Conceived and produced by Derek Forsyth
with Lucy Maw and Paul Stewart

Consultants: John Becklake, Tony Hall-Patch, Philip Jarrett,
John Robinson, Mick Walsh
Co-ordination: Linda Cripps, Jill Ridley, Castrol International
Editors: Richard Dawes, Ray Granger
Designer: Nigel Partridge
Picture Research: Dan Brooks/Brooks Krikler Research
Additional Reference: Jimmy Simpson
Additional Illustrative Material: Vana Skelley, Fran Hughes,
Burmah Castrol Archives
Commissioned Photography: Phil Sayer
Production: Polly Napper
Commissioning Editor: Sarah Polden

MBI Publishing Company books are also available at discounts in bulk quantity
for industrial or sales-promotional use. For details write to Special Sales
Manager at Motorbooks International Publishers & Wholesalers, 729 Prospect
Avenue, PO Box 1, Osceola, WI 54020-0001 USA.

Library of Congress Cataloging-in-Publication Data Available

ISBN 0-7603-0679-6

1 3 5 7 9 10 8 6 4 2

Printed by Artegrafica SPA, Verona, Italy

CONTENTS

FOREWORD

 Did you know that the first car ran in 1889 and that by 1904 the world land speed record had been raised by Louis Rigolly to 103.56mph (166.66kph). Did you know that the first non-stop transatlantic flight was made by Alcock and Brown in 1919 and that in October 1967 Major William J. Knight flew the X-15 rocket plane to Mach 6.7 – 4534mph (7297kph). And perhaps you already know that Dick Rutan and Jeana Yeager flew non-stop and without refuelling around the world in 1986.

In this age of global media we tend to take these achievements for granted; yet these are the very milestones by which we chart our technical progress. None of the records you read about in *Achievements* was easily won – they all required great personal risk and sacrifice, and also great foresight and a different order of courage from the people who backed them. Before today's powerful hardware and highly developed software, there was no sure way to predict performance – the only guide was the skills of the brave test pilots and test drivers. And by God they were brave!

The records included in this book serve two purposes: they help to develop technology and they inspire others to have a go in other fields. No one in their right mind would believe that Andy Green's supersonic runs in Thrust SSC are going to help today's traffic problems. Nevertheless, all over the world many millions of people have been deeply impressed with the Thrust SSC team's efforts and all kinds of new projects are emerging.

Please enjoy reading *Achievements* and remember the enormous efforts, huge personal courage and absolute dedication that were essential to achieve each record. Remember, too, Castrol's great heritage in record breaking. I can testify to that: Castrol were the first Thrust SSC sponsor, and without their help we might never have got started!

RICHARD NOBLE

World Land Speed Record 1983–97

Thrust SSC Project 1992–97

Farnborough, 1998

Charles Cheers

WAKEFIELD

Rarely can it be claimed that an individual played a direct and identifiable role in changing the course of history; but one figure who can rightfully be honoured in this way is Charles Cheers Wakefield, the founder of Castrol.

Wakefield, the son of a lay preacher from Liverpool, established his business in 1899, manufacturing lubricants for the railway, shipping and textile industries. In addition to his involvement with established technologies, Wakefield had the vision to see the great potential of the internal combustion engine in the development of 20th-century transport and introduced his now-famous Castrol Motor Oil in 1906. He worked closely with car manufacturers to help improve the engine and supported the efforts and activities of the pioneers who strove to push back the boundaries of mechanically aided travel in all its forms. This commitment to early endeavour was to see far-reaching results as motorized transport became more accessible to the general public as the century progressed, changing the character of daily life forever.

From 1912, Wakefield publicized the activities of the pioneers of land, sea and air in a booklet called *Achievements*. These records are still produced today by Castrol. It is fitting, therefore, that a book celebrating a century of human endeavour should bear the name of these historic publications which were the brainchild of a great and inspired innovator.

INTRODUCTION

The century now drawing to a close has witnessed more developments in transport than the whole of previous human history. As we have reached ever greater speeds on land, on sea and in the air, the world has become ever more accessible. At the same time we have begun to look beyond this planet towards the stars.

A handful of major achievements from recent decades illustrates just how far we have come in the past 100 years. In 1968 *Apollo 8* made the first manned orbit of the Moon. The following year Neil Armstrong, one of the three-man crew of *Apollo 11*, was the first person to walk on the Moon. In 1990, a French high-speed Atlantique train became the fastest in the world, reaching a speed of 320.2mph (515.3kph). Seven years later Andy Green set a new world land speed record in the jet-powered *Thrust SSC* by travelling at an average speed of 763.04mph (1227.98kph) over two runs, breaking the sound barrier for the first time on land.

Back in 1897, when our story begins, such feats could not have been foreseen – except perhaps by science-fiction writers. And none of them would ever have happened had it not been for the small band of pioneers and record-breakers who constantly challenged the idea of what was possible. It is on the extraordinary achievements of such figures during the 19th century that the technological advances of the present century were firmly founded.

On land, the horse-drawn wheeled vehicle was still the backbone of European transport, as it had been for almost four thousand years. However, with the substantial improvements to road surfaces in the early 19th century came two great advances. The 1860s saw the birth of the 'boneshaker' bicycle and, over the following decades, its more comfortable descendants confirmed the pedal cycle as an inexpensive and accessible mode of travel.

The bicycle is still with us, but the impact of the other great breakthrough in transport was immeasurably greater. In fact, the concept of the internal combustion engine dates from as early as 1673, when Christiaan Huygens constructed an 'engine' in which an

explosion of gunpowder pushed a piston up a cylinder. The explosion also created hot gases, and as these cooled they contracted, allowing the piston to drop back down. The Dutch scientist's device did not drive anything, but it did demonstrate the viability of the internal combustion engine.

Between 1800 and 1850 other engines were built on the same principle, but with gas rather than gunpowder providing the necessary explosions. Then, in 1860, J.J.E. Lenoir patented the first practical internal combustion engine, and two years later he drove an automobile with a gasoline engine for 7 miles (11.2km). Although he lost heart and abandoned his

experimentation, others took up the challenge, and in 1862 Alphonse Beau de Rochas discovered the four-stroke principle which is the basis of most modern car engines.

In 1876 Dr N.A. Otto built an engine using this four-stroke cycle; but it was Karl Benz and Gottlieb Daimler who, independently, applied the principle of internal combustion to the creation of a commercial powered road vehicle. By 1885 Benz had completed a motor-tricycle with a single-cylinder internal combustion engine. The following year Daimler modified a four-wheeled carriage so that it could be driven by a one-cylinder petrol engine. Then, in 1889, René Panhard and Émile Levassor, formerly Daimler's licensees in France, went into business on their own, building machines which were no longer converted carriages but true automobiles.

Alongside improvement to the roads came the birth of the railways. The first self-propelled steam vehicle had been built in China as early as 1681. But it was not until 1825 that George Stephenson opened a railway which ran from Stockton to Darlington, in north-east England, and not until 1830 that the Liverpool and Manchester Railway was inaugurated. The success of these lines sparked off a wave of railway construction, and by 1870 Britain would have some 13,500 miles (21,600km) of track.

The seas, rivers and canals had also long been important highways, and here steam was gradually taking over from sail. As early as 1801 William Symington had built the *Charlotte Dundas*, a steam-driven boat which worked as a tug on canals. Next Robert Fulton developed a boat which, by 1807, was regularly steaming between New York City and upstate Albany. Eighteen thirty-eight saw the first all-steam crossing of the Atlantic by Britain's *Sirius* and *Great Western*, in 17 and 15 days respectively.

As for the conquest of the air: it had fascinated thinkers as long ago as Roger Bacon in the 13th century and Leonardo da Vinci in the late 15th and early 16th centuries. But it was not until 1783 that Jean-François Pilâtre de Rozier and François Laurent made the first manned flight in a hot-air balloon developed by the Mongolfier brothers, Joseph-Michel and Jacques-Étienne, taking 23 minutes to fly over 7 miles (11.2km) at 3000 ft (914.4m) across Paris.

In 1852 came the first controlled flight. In a primitive airship which was carried aloft by a streamlined balloon, driven by a steam engine turning a propeller, and steered by a rudder, Frenchman Henri Giffard travelled 17 miles (27.2km). Attempts at powered flight in which wings rather than gas or hot air lifted flying machines were delayed partly because experimenters knew little about the mechanics of flight and partly because of the lack of a sufficiently light and powerful engine.

The basic principles of heavier-than-air flight had been laid down by George Cayley in 1799, who later built and tested both model and full-size, manned gliders. Most of those who flew in Cayley's machines were passive passengers, but the German aeronautical pioneer Otto Lilienthal realized that before he could attempt powered flight he would need to fly gliders in order to master control in the air. Between 1893 and 1896 he made more than two thousand flights in gliders which he had built himself, controlling them by moving his own body weight. When this arrangement proved unsatisfactory he experimented with an elevator controlled by head movements. Lilienthal, who was fatally injured in 1896, when his monoplane glider crashed, inspired other early aviators: in particular, two history-making brothers, Orville and Wilbur Wright.

From our vantage point on the threshold of a new millennium we look back with both pride and wonder at the remarkable progress of the past century. For this we must thank the innovative genius of figures like the Wright brothers, Frank Whittle, Robert Goddard and Christopher Cockerell; the immense bravery and determination of men and women like Louis Blériot, John Alcock, Arthur Whitten Brown, Malcolm and Donald Campbell, Amy Johnson, Chuck Yeager, Yuri Gagarin, Sheila Scott and Francis Chichester; the encouragement of sponsors like Charles Wakefield, Alfred Harmsworth, Jacques Schneider and James Gordon Bennett; as well as the unflagging efforts of the many other pioneers of land, sea and air transport whose stories fill these pages.

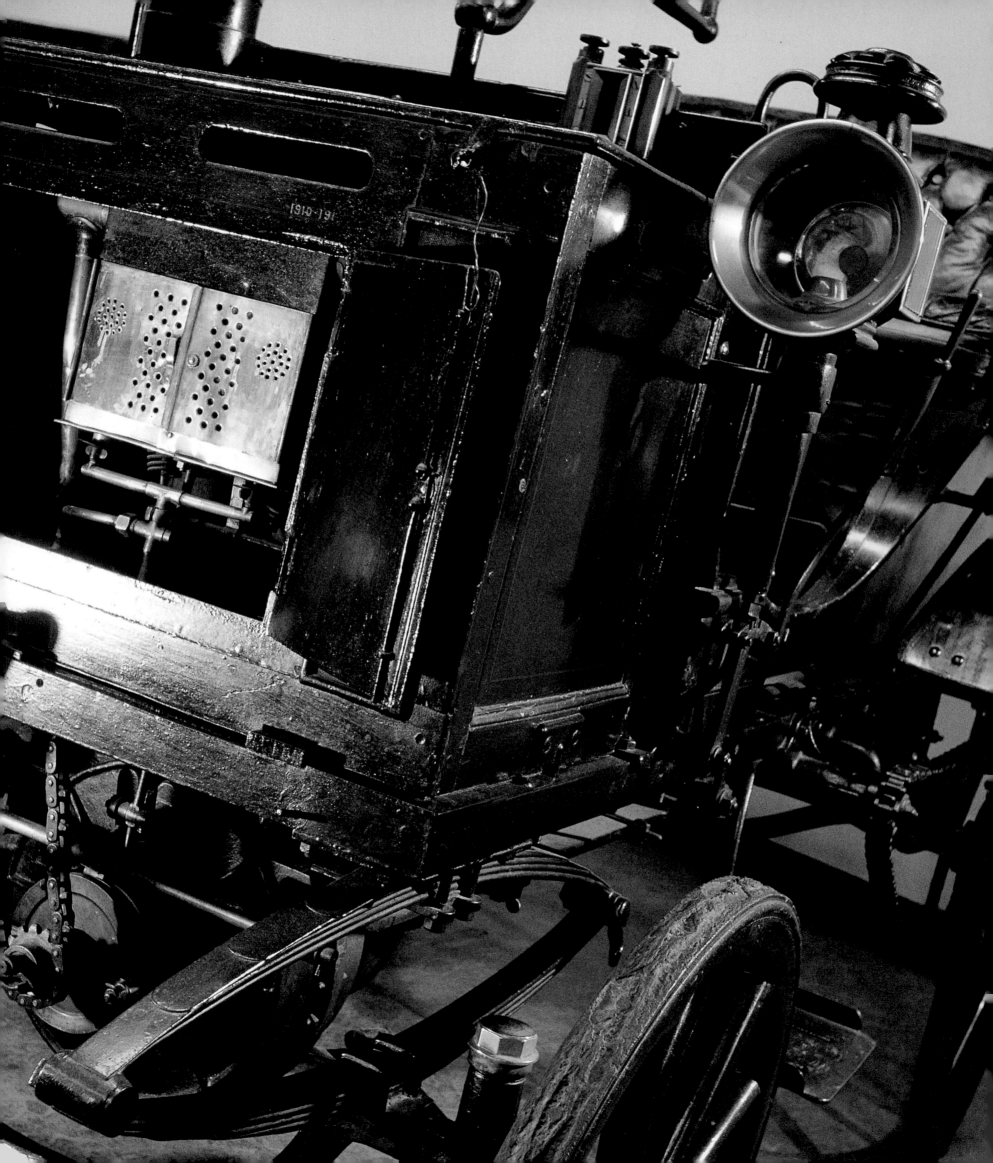

PIONEERS

1899–1918

The first two decades of the 20th century more properly belong, culturally and historically, to the 19th. They saw the end of many of the old empires, including Austria-Hungary, Russia, China and the Ottoman Turks. In the USA, the great cities of the East continued to grow as waves of immigrants arrived from central Europe, most of them crowded in the cramped holds of merchant ships.

Most people, if they travelled at all, did so by foot, on horseback or on bicycles. Mass transport relied on the motive power of the 19th century, the steam engine. The railway age had reached its peak, while at sea turbines were replacing pistons in steam engines.

Motor cars were an exciting, even alarming novelty, and motor races captured the popular imagination. Soon, purpose-made motor-racing circuits were drawing huge crowds, while pioneer motorists embarked on lengthy road races that could often involve cross-country driving. These pioneer drivers were usually wealthy men – often aristocrats – indulging their love of speed and machines. The demands of racing forced the design of cars to improve, and pioneer manufacturers such as Henry Ford began mass-producing motor cars for the ordinary man.

Other pioneers flew aeroplanes. Orville and Wilbur Wright conquered the air in 1903, and within a decade intrepid men and women were taking their flimsy machines all over the world, taking on mountain ranges and stretches of water as well as transcontinental challenges. Several of these pioneer flyers saw service in World War I, the crucible in which the world of the 20th century was forged, and the demands of war led to new innovations in aircraft design.

Left: A Panhard Levassor car, built around 1894–5. Its two-cylinder motor was invented by Otto Daimler in 1889 and gives a top speed of 15.5mph (25kph). This model was presented to the Science Museum in South Kensington, London, by the Royal Automobile Club in 1910.

At the turn of the 20th century, horse-drawn vehicles were still by far the most common form of road transport in the world. The historian and collector Lord Montagu of Beaulieu has estimated that, even in Great Britain, then in the vanguard of industrial and technological achievement, no more than 650 motor cars and motorcycles were in use at the time. Although they were few in number, the new vehicles had quite an impact, and led to a disproportionate amount of social friction. Tales circulated on both sides of the Atlantic of motorists being horsewhipped, stoned and shot at by testy horse riders and outraged rustics. The first motorist to drive up New York's Broadway, Philip Hagel in a De Dion-Bouton, found the excursion more expensive than he had planned; he had to pay $48,000 to owners of horses that had been terrified by their first sight of a horseless carriage.

Some early motorists remained unrepentant about the distress they caused to other road users. Writing in 1897, the Daimler-driving Briton Henry Sturmey describes how he put to flight a donkey carriage 'and we were all very much amused at the frantic efforts of the lady … to restrain her restive steed. I confess I could not resist the temptation of an occasional blast upon the horn to keep the fun going.'

However, the pioneer motorist also had to be prepared for the worst. In 1906, a typical motor tourist's kit weighed 18lb (8kg) and contained 38 wrenches and screwdrivers. The

Above: Early racing cars had a mechanic aboard to carry out running repairs. This painting shows the giant Panhard that won the first Vanderbilt Cup being chased by a Packard 'Grey Wolf'.

Emergency Motorist Kit sold by Saks and Company in the USA included emergency provisions of 4lb (1.8kg) of meat and 2lb (0.9kg) of chocolate, while in Milan, soon to become the centre of Italy's car industry, motorists had to apply in writing to the city authorities every time they wished to use their vehicle, giving details of the destination, the time of departure and the proposed route. Wear and tear to pneumatic tyres was a further, costly problem for early motorists. In 1902, it was calculated that a carefully driven light car might cover 2000 miles (3200km) on a set of tyres, while on a heavier, faster model a set might last for only half that distance.

Such legal and technical obstacles could not suppress the desire for speed for its own sake. The British had tried to curb this, first by requiring a man with a red flag to walk in front of all motor vehicles, then by imposing a speed limit of 12mph (19kph), but 'scorching' – the period's slang term for speeding – remained popular even after the limit was raised to 20mph (30kph).

Organized motor-racing was another symptom of this devotion to speed, and had its own beginnings before the turn of the century. France was the sport's spiritual home, but early in 1900 the French government legally discouraged it after a disastrous race from Paris to Roubaix injured dozens of spectators who wandered into the road for a better view. Before the year was out, though, the government had relented, and permitted an international contest promoted by James Gordon Bennett, the publisher of the *New York Herald*. Although he was

Right and below: Entrants in the first Gordon Bennett race, held in 1900, were given a specially commissioned map of the route. Although there were only five entrants, interest in the race was great, and crowds lined much of the route.

a keen supporter of racing on land, sea and air, the eccentric millionaire never drove a car himself, preferring his four-in-hand carriage, which he once drove up the Champs-Élysées at midnight, sitting naked in the coachman's box. Even though he promised a handsome silver trophy to the winner of the first Gordon Bennett race, he never once attended a race bearing his name.

The contest, which took place in 1900 and ran from Paris to Lyon, had only five entrants. Fernand Charron, in a 24hp Panhard Levassor, was the winner, despite having an accident not far from the finish.

In 1901, the newly formed Auto Club de France (ACF) combined the race with one from Paris to Bordeaux. Léonce Girardot, in a Panhard, won the Gordon Bennett Trophy, while the longer race was won by Henri Fournier in a Mors. That year, Fournier also won the Paris–Berlin race of 687 miles (1100km). However, his victory was overshadowed by the death of a young child who was knocked down by one of the racers. The result was a complete ban on road racing throughout France. This was not the first death related to driving; in Britain in 1899, a driver, a passenger and a motorcyclist had been killed in three separate incidents.

Top: The winner of the first Gordon Bennett race, Frenchman Fernand Charron, is seen here posing in the winning car.

Above: Early road racers – this shot shows a 15.5-litre Panhard Levassor in action in 1907 – had to contend with relatively poor road surfaces, as well as with the encroachment of overenthusiastic spectators, for whom the sight of an automobile was often still a novelty.

Right: The Paris–Madrid race of 1903, the first over unrestricted open roads, started amid a blaze of enthusiasm, with 216 cars and 59 motorcycles watched by a million spectators lining the route, but the race was abandoned at Bordeaux after five drivers were killed in a single day.

While other drivers were prepared to carry on, the death of Marcel Renault had vividly illustrated the dangers of racing on open roads. Racers switched their interest to closed roads and specially built racing circuits. On one such track, Britain's famous seaside sprint the Brighton Speed Trials, the formidable Dorothy Levitt stunned many of her male competitors by reaching a speed of 126.6kph (78.7mph).

THE FIRST GRAND PRIX

The Belgians had pioneered closed-road racing with the Circuit des Ardennes race in 1902, and the idea was taken up by the organizers of the Gordon Bennett races. Although this event was won by French drivers in 1904 and 1905, the Auto Club de France disliked the rules of

entry, under which the cup was contested by teams of just three cars nominated by each recognized national club. France, which had many automobile manufacturers, could enter no more cars than a country where the industry barely existed.

As a result of this, in 1906 the French effectively replaced the

Above: The Targa Florio, first run in 1906 over a beautiful but challenging mountainous route in Sicily, epitomized the romantic appeal of early motor-racing.

Right: The same year as the first Targa Florio, C. C. Wakefield & Co introduced an improved motor oil in Castrol Brand – a blend of castor oil and finest quality mineral oil. Soon, cars lubricated with Castrol were dominating the race.

Below: The 1907 Targa Florio was won by Felice Nazzaro's Fiat after eight hours' racing over three laps of the Grande Madonie circuit.

Above: The Renault brothers occupy a prominent place in the early history of motoring as both makers and drivers. This shot shows Marcel in the passenger seat of the De Dion tricycle, while Louis drives his 1898 prototype based on the tricycle (centre) and Paul Hugé drives the 1899 production model.

In 1902, the Auto Club de France persuaded the French Government to relent and allow a race from Paris to Vienna; the Gordon Bennett race was run concurrently, but finished at Innsbruck. The Gordon Bennett Cup was won by S. F. Edge, in a 35hp Napier, while the longer race was won in a 16hp motor by Marcel Renault, who had formed his own car-manufacturing company, Société Renault Frères, in 1898 with his brothers, Louis and Fernand.

Racing speeds rose quickly in the first few years of the century, as pioneer drivers and manufacturers vied for supremacy. Between 1900 and 1904, the winning speed of the Gordon Bennett race rose from 38.6mph (62.1kph) to 54.5mph (87.7kph), and the event became a major date in the international motor-racing calendar.

In 1903, 179 starters set out from Paris to race to Madrid. Three million spectators lined the route to watch the first stage to Bordeaux. The best cars were faster than ever before, with top speeds around 80mph (130kph). The problem was that improvements in braking power were lagging behind.

Louis Renault was the first to arrive in Bordeaux; he received an uproarious welcome, but his excitement turned to anguish as other drivers arrived with news of accidents in which five had died. The remainder of the race was cancelled. One of those who had been killed was Marcel Renault. When he heard of his brother's death, Louis fainted. He never raced again.

Gordon Bennett race with a Grand Prix open to any manufacturer, regardless of nationality. This first-ever Grand Prix was run over two days, 26 and 27 June. Each day, the competitors covered six laps of a 64-mile (103km) triangular circuit of closed roads near Le Mans, in northern France.

The competitors included a Mercedes team from Germany, Fiat and Itala teams from Italy and ten French teams, including Clément-Bayard, Panhard-Levassor, Lorraine-Dietrich and Renault. The surprise winner was François Szisz in a 13-litre Renault, which was by no means the fastest car.

Two other new popular races took place in 1906. First came the Targa Florio, named after Count Vincenzo Florio, who devised a gruelling 92-mile (148km) circuit through the most remote mountains of his native Sicily from the coastal town of Campofelice di Roccella. Only six of the ten cars which started the first race reached the finish 3600ft (1100m) up. The winner was Alessandro Cagno in an Itala. Then, in November, came the Coupe de l'Auto. This was a six-day event for voiturettes, smaller cars with one or two cylinder engines. The race was held in France and won by Georges Sizaire in his own Sizaire-Naudin.

BROOKLANDS

A purpose-built racetrack seemed an eccentric idea to most people, but in 1906 Mr H. F. Locke King set out to create one on his private estate at Brooklands, Surrey, just south of London. Working round the clock in shifts, 2000 men laid around 200,000 tons (203,000 tonnes) of concrete to build a course 2¾ miles (4.4km) long and 100ft (30m) wide, much of it banked to a height of 30ft (9m). By 28 June 1907, Brooklands was ready for its official opening, and Selwyn Edge marked the occasion by driving his Napier to a new world 24-hour distance record, travelling 1581 miles (2544km) at an average speed of almost 66mph (106kph).

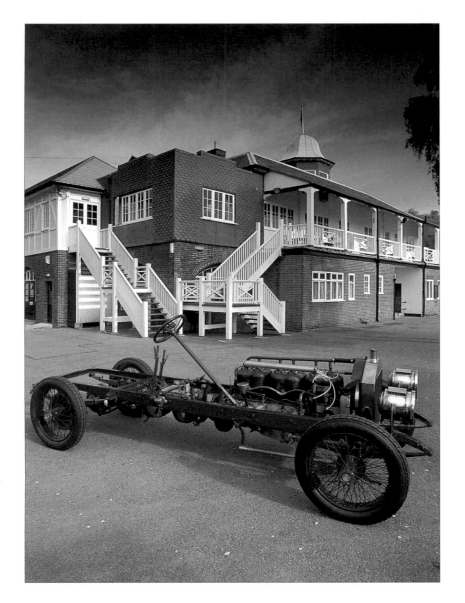

These new races and special racetracks had not, though, extinguished the epic spirit of the pioneering years. In 1907, the French newspaper *Le Matin* sponsored a road race of 9500 miles (15,289km) from Peking to Paris. There were only five entrants. The winning car, a 7.4-litre Itala driven by Prince Scipione Borghese with the help of his mechanic Ettore Guizzardi, took two months to complete the journey, and was first home by a margin of some three and a half weeks.

Right: Selwyn (S. F.) Edge, the manufacturer of the Napier marque, was a great salesman and propagandist for motoring. He was also a notable record-breaking driver and the winner of the Gordon Bennett Cup in 1902.

Above and left: The Napier in which Edge drove to a new world 24-hour distance record of 1582 miles (2545km) in 1907 to mark the opening of Brooklands is now preserved at the track's museum.

屏秀

EN SIBÉRIE
PEKIN - PARIS_1907   Le Prince Scipion Borghese Gagnant du Raid "PEKIN-PARIS" Sur sa Voiture "ITALA" 24 HP.

Above: The 1907 road race from Peking (Beijing) to Paris was the longest attempted at the time. Just five cars set out; this is a 10hp standard De Dion.

Left: The rough terrain encountered by the cars in the race – in many cases driving where no other automobile had gone before – was the main deciding factor in the contest.

Right: The race was won by Italian diplomat and explorer Prince Scipione Borghese. He is seen here with his mechanic Ettore Guizzardi in the 7.4-litre Itala in the Bois de Boulogne, on the outskirts of Paris, during the last leg of their epic journey.

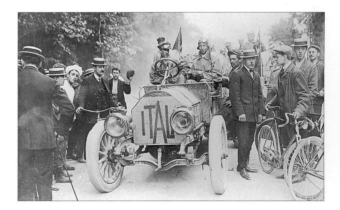

Right: On his arrival in Paris, Borghese sent a telegram to his main sponsor, Pirelli.

Right and below: The Itala car in which Borghese negotiated the Peking to Paris race is now on display in the auto museum in Turin.

Below: The Model T, which Henry Ford famously proclaimed was available in any colour so long as it was black, was the first car to be manufactured with the needs – and resources – of the less wealthy would-be motorist in mind.

MOTORING IN AMERICA

Motor-racing was just as popular in the USA as it was in Europe, but American businessmen seemed to grasp the commercial possibilities of motoring rather earlier than their European rivals.

On 12 August 1908, the first Model T rolled off the production line at Ford's factory in Detroit. Ford's new manufacturing method, which broke down the complex process of building a car into a succession of simple tasks that could be performed by relatively unskilled workers, allowed cars to be mass-produced at prices that the middle classes could afford. The Model T, or Tin Lizzie as it was affectionately known, greatly increased the appeal of motoring, particularly in rural areas.

It was in the rural Midwest that five businessmen involved in motor manufacture founded, on 9 February 1909, the Indianapolis Motor Speedway Corporation. They built a 2½-mile (4km) track of asphalt and crushed stone, to be used both for racing and for testing. There, on 19 August, Louis Schwitzer drove a Stoddard Dayton to win the first race (two laps) of the inaugural three-day meeting.

In 1910, race meetings were held at the Indianapolis Speedway on Memorial Day (30 May), Independence Day (4 July) and Labour Day (6 September). By holding races on public holidays the directors drew huge crowds, who watched numerous races of varying lengths. One of the directors, Carl Fisher, then suggested that the Speedway could be still more popular and profitable as the venue for just one race a year – provided that it was over a longer distance and carried heavier prize money than any other race in the country.

THE FIRST INDY 500

Fisher's co-directors agreed with him, and on Memorial Day 1911 the first Indianapolis 500 was run over 500 miles (805km). Some 77,000 people turned out to watch a field of 40 cars contest a dramatic race for a prize of $27,550. On the 13th of the 200 scheduled laps, Arthur Griener's Amplex spun out of control, and Griener's mechanic was killed. With 80 laps completed, the leader was 32-year-old American engineer and test driver Ray Harroun, driving a single-seater Marmon 'Wasp'.

At the close of the 87th lap the steering on another car broke just in front of the grandstands, causing a spectacular pile-up in which a mechanic was injured, but the race continued. Harroun was never overtaken and won in a time of 6 hours, 42 minutes and 8 seconds at an average speed of 74.6mph (120kph). This was the first of a legendary series of Indianapolis 500 races which – with intervals only for the war years of 1917–1918 and 1942–1945 – has lasted until modern times.

MOTOR RALLIES

Another kind of motoring event, the 'rally', grew in popularity alongside motor racing. The first true rally, for the Herkomer Trophy, took place in Germany in 1905. Competitors raced against the clock, aiming to achieve the best possible time between control points on a route set out over public roads. Although the regulations were too complex for many enthusiasts to follow, the Herkomer Trophy Rally was popular enough to last for several years.

In 1908, the Imperial Automobile Club of Germany persuaded Prince Heinrich of Bavaria to lend his name to a longer, more challenging rally, the Prinz Heinrich Fahrt. There were 130 starters, including two men bearing the great motoring names of Bugatti and Opel. After a week's hard rallying, the winner was Fritz Erle in a Benz. Two years later, the Austrians followed suit with their Internationale Alpenfahrt.

The popularity of these early rallies made a strong appeal to business interests in the principality of Monaco. Camille Blanc, the illegitimate son of the François Blanc who had helped to make Monaco a gambling paradise by founding the famous casino at Monte Carlo, approved an idea put forward by Alexander Noghues, President of Le Sport Automobile et Vélocipédique de Monaco, for a rally ending in the principality. So much the better, they reckoned, if the event could be held in January and attract some off-season visitors to Monte Carlo's hotel rooms and gaming tables.

MONTE CARLO OR BUST

The first Grand Tournoi Routier, which soon became universally known as the Monte Carlo Rally, was held in January 1911. A cup and a substantial prize of £400 were on offer for the best run from any one of a number of different starting-points scattered throughout Germany, Austria, Switzerland and France. The Rally attracted a gratifying 23 competitors, who were required to keep up

Above: The essential ingredients of rallying – rough roads and tracks, mud and mishaps – were all already present in the German Prinz Heinrich Fahrt of 1908.

Right and below: The Prinz Heinrich Fahrt of 1908 was the first long-distance motor rally in Europe, attracting a field of 130 competitors that included several famous names in motoring and a fair sprinkling of aristocrats, many of them carrying passengers as well as a mechanic.

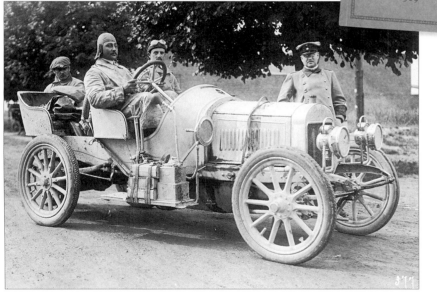

an average speed of at least 15mph (24kph) as they converged on Monte Carlo over mainly rough and uneven roads, often in distinctly unfriendly weather conditions.

The winner of the first rally was Henri Rougier, who had set out from Paris driving a 25hp Turcat-Mery. Second was M. Aspiague, in a 40hp Gobron tourer, complaining that he had been needlessly held for eight hours by the control point at Avignon. Third was Julius Beutler, who had started from Berlin in his 38hp Martini.

The following year, 87 drivers set out for Monte Carlo from starting-points in France, Germany, Austria, Russia and the Netherlands. For this rally, separate prizes were on offer for such variables as the number of passengers carried, the overall average speed and the total distance travelled. This time, Beutler, in a Berliet in which he had carried five passengers from Berlin, was the overall winner.

FLORAL TRIBUTE

At the end of the 1912 run to Monte Carlo, there was another innovation, which was to become a regular feature of future rallies. In the 'Battle of the Flowers', the competing cars that had reached Monaco paraded through the streets of Monte Carlo, decked from bonnet to rear bumper in a gorgeous array of flowers.

MOTORCYCLE MANIA

Although Henry Ford had begun mass-producing cheaper cars as early as 1908, motoring remained largely the preserve of the wealthy, in the USA as elsewhere, until after World War I. Pedal cycles were by far the most popular means of transport for the working man and woman. Before the end of the century, cycle manufacturers had turned their attention to producing powered bicycles and tricycles in an attempt to offer the less affluent a viable form of mechanized transport. Their efforts soon generated another new form of racing.

It began modestly as a separate 'class' within the early town-to-town European road races, such as the Paris–Marseilles race of 1896. In that race, a motor-tricycle powered by a 240cc De Dion-Bouton engine – the product of a collaboration between the artisan Georges Bouton and the aristocrat Count Albert de Dion – came third overall, with a top speed of some 25mph (40kph).

For a while in the late 1890s, motor-tricycles powered by De Dion-Bouton engines led the field, but later motorcycles, such as the Werner, on which M. Bucquet won the 1902 Paris–Vienna race, showed that racing on two wheels could be much more exciting than on three.

Above: Cyril Pullin, seen here on his Rudge at Brooklands in 1911, was one of many motorcyclists who took advantage of the introduction of Castrol C, introduced in 1909 and used by virtually all the winners of the Isle of Man TT races, including Pullin, in the following years.

INTERNATIONAL RACES

In the USA, motorcycle racing as an independent sport began in 1903, with the formation in New York City of the Federation of American Motorcyclists. The following year, representatives from Germany, Austria, France, Britain and Denmark formed the Fédération Internationale des Clubs Motocyclistes, which arranged an international cup race in 1905 at Dourdan, in France. The competing nations could each enter a team of three, riding machines wholly manufactured in the country for which they competed. The winner was an Austrian, Vondrich, on a Laurin-Klement.

THE TOURIST TROPHY

The most famous of all motorcycle races, the Tourist Trophy (TT) races on the Isle of Man in the Irish Sea, was first held on 28 May 1907. Rem Fowler, riding a British Norton with a Peugeot engine, won the twin cylinder category in the first race over the 15¾-mile (24.5km) circuit of public roads on the west of the island. Four years later, the Isle of Man Tourist Trophy races were moved to a far more demanding mountain circuit of 37½ miles (60.3km). Now as then, it climbs from sea level to 1400ft (427m) and down again in around 14 miles (22.5km). The circuit has some 200 bends and corners, most of them 'blind', which range from walking-pace hairpins to sweeping curves that can be taken at high speed.

The first of the Senior Tourist Trophy races, held in 1911 over five laps of this course, was won by Oliver Godfrey, riding an Indian machine. In 1912, Godfrey won the British Grand Prix on the same motorcycle, while Frank Applebee, on a Scott, won the Senior TT. In 1913 Tim Wood rode another Scott to victory, and the next year Cyril Pullin won the top prize on a Rudge.

Left: Oliver Godfrey is seen here in 1911 with the Indian machine on which he won that year's Senior TT race and the 1912 British Grand Prix.

Right: The Brooklands museum contains several of the motorcycles that won there and on the Isle of Man, including this Scott.

Below: The high-banked track at Brooklands provided a spectacular backdrop for motorcycle racing before World War I.

Above: This advertisement celebrates one of many motorcycle records achieved using Castrol. Australian Jack Booth, riding an Indian, covered the measured mile (1.6km) in 35 seconds, at an average speed of 102mph (164kph).

THE GRAND PRIX UNDER PRESSURE

In 1907 and 1908, the French Grand Prix was run over 10 laps of a 47-mile (75.6km) circuit near Dieppe. Felice Nazzaro won the first race in a Fiat, with François Szisz coming second in his Renault. This result was a huge disappointment to the French crowds, who had already been shocked by the deaths in practice of local favourites Marius Pin and Albert Clément.

In the 1908 race, half the 48 entrants were French, and at one point the field was led by two Brasiers, driven by Léon Théry and Paul Bablot, and Szisz's Renault. However, victory went to Christian Lautenschlager in a Mercedes. He was followed home by Victor Hémery and René Hanriot, each of them driving a Benz. The French motor manufacturers, dispirited by two years of recession and defeat, signed a document declaring that they would not participate in the following year's race.

So few entries were received that the 1909 Grand Prix was cancelled. The ACF did not decide to revive the race until 1912. Concerned that they would again be short of competitors, they decided to combine the Grand Prix with the increasingly popular Coupe de l'Auto (also known as the Coupe des Voiturettes) for cars with a maximum engine size of 3 litres. In the event, 14 Grand Prix cars and 33 voiturettes lined up on 25 June for the start of the two-day race of 956 miles (1538.5km).

OLD VERSUS NEW

The Grand Prix class was an exciting battle between the American David Bruce-Brown (who had won the US version of the Grand Prix, the Grand Prize, in 1910 and 1911) in a Fiat S74, and Frenchman Georges Boillot in a Peugeot L-76. It was a race of the old against the new. The Fiat S74 was a magnificent vehicle with good acceleration, a 14.3-litre engine running at 1600rpm and a top speed approaching 125mph (200kph), but had its disadvantages. Although it could outpace the Peugeot L-76 on an open road, it had to spend much longer in the pits, as its refuelling and wheel changing were outmoded; only the rims of the wheels were detachable.

The Peugeot was powered by a double-overhead-camshaft 16-valve engine with four cylinders, designed by the Swiss engineers Ernest Henry and Paul Zucarelli. This revolutionary design meant that the Peugeot, which had an engine capacity that was just over half that of the Fiat, at 7.6 litres, could yield 2200rpm. As the car could be refuelled under pressure, and had fully detachable wheels, it was also able to get by with comparatively brief pit stops.

The contest was close. At the end of the first day, Bruce-Brown was leading from Boillot by two minutes but the following day a fuel pipe

Above: Jean Chassagne, seen here in a 9-litre Sunbeam in 1914, was one of many Sunbeam drivers who set new records in 1912 at Brooklands. Sunbeam's chief engineer, Louis Coatalen, wrote to C. C. Wakefield & Co, attributing their success to Castrol lubricants.

broke on his Fiat after he hit a dog, and Boillot roared into the lead, more than 30 minutes ahead of Louis Wagner in another S74. Then a universal joint seized up in the Peugeot, and the gearbox jammed. After 20 minutes of frenzied work, Boillot and his mechanic somehow managed to get second and fourth gears working, and they managed to limp across the finishing-line just 13 minutes ahead of Wagner, who had suffered constant tyre trouble as a result of the Fiat's outdated detachable rims.

SUPREME SUNBEAMS

The British Sunbeams were the sensation of the 1912 Grand Prix in the 3-litre voiturette class. Victor Rigal took first place in the class, and came an impressive fourth overall, crossing the finishing-line just 40 minutes after Boillot in his much more powerful car. The other two Sunbeams in the race finished second and third in the class.

The Sunbeams had burst on to the scene the year before, when their chief engineer, Louis Coatalen, and T. H. Richards broke the world 12-hour record, driving at an average speed of 75.6mph (121.6kph) in a six-cylinder Sunbeam. In 1912, the company's test drivers broke no fewer than 44 time and distance records at Brooklands. The most prestigious of these was a new world one-hour record of 107.95 miles (173.73km), set by Jean Chassagne's 12-cylinder car.

The 1912 Grand Prix victory for Peugeot began a two-year period in which the French dominated the racetracks of Europe and the USA. Boillot went on to win the Grand Prix at Amiens in 1913, while his team-mate, Jules Goux, won the Indianapolis 500. Goux enjoyed a relatively easy cruise in his Peugeot as his rivals struggled with shredded tyres in their attempts to catch him. Goux and his mechanic fought dehydration in the heat by downing a pint of champagne at each of their six pit stops, and topped this off with plenty more in the winner's circle at the end of the race.

The 1914 Grand Prix took place over 20 laps of a new circuit at Lyon, at a time of mounting international tension. Although there were close to 40 cars in the race, the main interest was focused on the contest between the French Peugeot team, defending their 1912 and 1913 successes in three new cars with 4.5-litre double-overhead-camshaft engines, and the German Mercedes team.

TACTICAL VICTORY

The German cars, whose construction owed much to lessons which had been learned in the development of aeroplanes, were very light and fast on corners. They ran on single-overhead-camshaft engines made of four

separate forged steel (not cast-iron) cylinders, with welded valve ports and water jackets for a combination of precise engineering and extreme lightness. The Mercedes team not only had excellent machines, but had also made the most thorough preparations, examining the circuit well in advance, practising over it during the official practice periods and, perhaps most important of all, devising a tactical plan to help them outwit the competition.

When the race began, at 8a.m. on 5 July 1914, 'new boy' Max Sailer immediately began pushing his Mercedes to its very limits. In just five laps – two hours' racing – he had driven it to breakdown. However, his early sprint encouraged Georges Boillot and Jules Goux to push their own cars too hard. Boillot, who was in second place when Sailer was forced to retire, continued to drive brilliantly, and maintained his lead for much of the remainder of the race.

Eventually, though, with just one lap to go, Mercedes' Christian Lautenschlager, who had dogged Boillot relentlessly for most of the race, surged ahead of him. At the same time, Louis Wagner and Otto Salzer both overtook Goux. When Boillot's car expired with a failed valve, the Germans went on to take first, second and third places. Perhaps understandably, given the tensions of the period – France and

Top: The popularity of motor racing in France is reflected in posters such as this.

Right: Frenchman Georges Boillot's Peugeot won the 1913 French Grand Prix at Amiens. Tyres were the key to the victory; Boillot had to change only two in 569 miles (916km).

Below: This illustration from 1913 shows Boillot, the most famous racing driver of his time, at France's Circuit de Picardie.

Left: The *City of Truro,* designed by George Churchward, became famous in 1904 as the first steam locomotive to break the 100mph (160km) barrier, although there was no way of verifying the record.

Germany were to be at war within weeks – Lautenschlager crossed the finishing-line watched by silent and hostile crowds.

MASS MOVEMENTS

In the first decade or so of the century, the only impact the new automotive technology had on the great majority of people was provided by the spectacular entertainment value of races and rallies. Actually owning a car was still far beyond the means of the vast majority, who relied on bicycles and public transport. Horse-drawn omnibuses had been introduced in Paris and London in 1825 and 1829 respectively, while the first horse-drawn trams ran in New York in 1832. Steam was used to drive some urban trams in the 1880s, while the English seaside town of Blackpool introduced electrically driven trams in 1884. Electric trams, drawing power from a conduit in the rails or from overhead cables, appeared in London in 1901.

It was not until 1899 that the first scheduled passenger services using full-size petrol-driven buses were introduced, but as they were considered much cleaner and quieter than their horse-drawn counterparts, they steadily replaced them in the great cities of the world over the next 15 years. Electric trams and trolleybuses – which ran on electricity drawn from overhead cables, rather than tracks – were cleaner and quieter still, and remained the most popular form of public transport in many cities, although the restrictions on their mobility imposed by tracks and cables eventually counted against them.

The most convenient form of long-distance travel was the railways. The 19th century had been the great era of railway building in the industrialized world. The first steam railway carrying fare-paying passengers had opened in Britain in 1830, and in France in 1837. Where the railways had linked the industrial cities of Europe, they served to open up the country in the USA.

Safety rather than speed was the main concern in the early years of the railways, though a steam record of 90mph (144kph) had been set in Britain in 1897. In the early years of the century much improvement was made to the design of railway engines by George J. Churchward. His designs for Saint locomotives were the basis of all the mixed traffic used by Britain's railway companies and the Stanier Pacifics that followed in the 1930s; Churchward himself designed the first British Pacific-class (4-6-2) locomotive, *Great Bear*. His Star-class (4-6-0) engines were the precursors of several express passenger engines.

His most famous engine was the *City of Truro*, a City-class standard production model with no special preparation or modification, which was reported to have reached 102.4mph (164.8kph) in 1904. Though this top speed could not be verified, the engine certainly reached close to 100mph (161kph), a record for steam.

By this time, though, the rail speed record had passed to the German Siemens und Halske electric engine, which achieved 101mph (162.5kph) in tests in 1901 and raised the record in increments over the next two years to 130.6mph (210.2kph).

THE USES OF WAR

World War I was the first-ever motorized war. Dispatch riders rode motorcycles rather than pedal cycles or horses, trucks were used to transport soldiers and equipment, and cars were adapted or developed for military purposes. A motor vehicle had been used as a gun carrier as far back as 1899, when a powered quadricycle was fitted with a Maxim machine-gun, while John Fowler and Co. had armoured a steam traction engine for hauling supplies during the Boer War the following year. The start of the war accelerated the development of armoured cars.

The problem with armoured cars and trucks was that they could travel only on surfaces suitable for wheeled vehicles. They were useless on the front line, where the opposing forces were dug into defensive positions and the only way forward was over rough ground that had been pitted with shell holes, churned into mud and criss-crossed by trenches and barbed wire.

In 1912, an Australian engineer, Lancelot de Mole, had sent plans for a tracked fighting vehicle to the British War Office, which had, however, ignored him. Colonel Ernest Swinton, a staff officer in France, had a similar idea after seeing an American Holt caterpillar tractor towing guns across country, but again the War Office paid little attention to his idea. The next proposal came from the Armoured Car Division of the

Above: Tritton and Wilson's Mark 1 tank, known affectionately as 'Big Willie', was designed specifically to cope with the conditions on the Western front, where the terrain consisted largely of churned mud criss-crossed with earthworks and barbed wire, and progress was painstakingly slow.

Below: Horse-drawn or electric trams applied railway technology to the streets of cities, and were among the most popular forms of public transport before World War I. Although they were relatively quiet and efficient, they were eventually phased out as the need to run on tracks made them much less adaptable than petrol-driven buses.

Royal Naval Air Service, which was responsible for protecting advanced airfields. They advised that an armoured car placed on a tracked undercarriage would be a most powerful offensive weapon.

The Admiralty set up a committee to sponsor the building and testing of prototype 'landships' as they were called by the Navy. By July 1915, they had attached the body of an armoured car to the base of a specially lengthened tracked agricultural tractor, the Bullock Commercial. The result, designed by William Tritton and Major W. G. Wilson, was known as the Lincoln Machine No 1, or 'Little Willie'. Although it was top-heavy, and its tracks were not long enough to clear trenches, this was the world's first practical tank (the prototypes were called 'tanks' to hide their true, offensive nature from spies, and the code-name stuck).

Tritton and Wilson immediately began designing the Mark 1, 'Big Willie', which, with its lozenge shape and all-round tracks, proved immediately successful. On 15 September 1916, 49 were sent into action at Flers-Coucellette on the Somme, and 14 months later almost 10 times that number fought at Cambrai, where they achieved a dramatic victory. Their main drawback was that they had a top speed of just 4mph (6.4kph) and an average range of only 30 miles (48.3km). As a result, they were soon being superseded by new British and French tanks – the British Medium A and the French Renault FT – which could travel faster and further.

Until the arrival of the aeroplane, the only way for anyone, rich or poor, to cross the sea was by ship. Steam had surpassed sail in the 19th century, but there were technological problems with reciprocating steam engines with pistons. The massive cylinders and boilers needed to power the passenger ships that plied the Atlantic routes in the latter part of the 19th century were so large and heavy that steam power at sea appeared to be nearing the limits of its potential.

There was, however, an alternative form of power, the steam turbine, in which blades are set on a central revolving shaft and driven by steam being forced against them at high pressure in a confined space. In 1884 two engineers, the Swede Carl de Laval and the Irishman Charles Parsons, independently took out patents for turbine engines. After many years of work, Parsons's experimental ship, the *Turbinia,* a steel-plated craft 100ft (30m) long, astonished crowds at Queen Victoria's Diamond Jubilee Review of the Fleet on 27 June 1897 by racing between the other ships at more than 34 knots (63kph).

Above: The two-engined steam yacht *Arrow* was acknowledged as the fastest craft in the world in her time. In 1902, she covered a nautical mile (1.85km) in one minute 32 seconds, at a speed of approximately 45mph (72kph). Her overall length was 130⅓ ft (39.7m), her beam 12½ ft (3.8m) and her displacement 66 tons (67 tonnes). The hull was extremely light, and the frame, of composite construction, was made of steel beneath the water-line and of aluminium above it, apart from in the engine and boiler rooms.

Left: *Dreadnought,* a 17,900-ton (18,200 tonnes) battleship powered by steam turbines, was launched in 1906. Impressively equipped with ten big guns, she became the model for later heavily armed warships. The first vessel with this resonant name had been built some 400 years earlier, during the reign of Queen Elizabeth I.

Below: This bell and the accompanying postcard are all that are left of the Cunard liner *Lucania*, which won the Blue Riband for the fastest Atlantic crossing in 1894, when liners still ran on reciprocating piston engines.

Right and below: The first ship with a turbine engine, *Turbinia*, made its debut at Spithead, England, in 1897, when it sped through the assembled fleet, easily evading and outpacing the steam picket boats deployed to keep the area free of spectator craft. A model of the *Turbinia* is now on display in London's Science Museum.

This dramatic proof of the benefits of turbine engines led to the launching in 1901 of the *Cockerill*, the first merchant vessel to be driven by steam turbine machinery, and in 1906 steam turbines drove the four propellers of the pace-setting HMS *Dreadnought*, at that time by far the most powerful battleship ever built, with ten 12in (30cm) guns mounted in five turrets and a top speed of 21 knots (38.9kph).

Other developments in shipping technology were influenced by the internal combustion engine, and particularly the work of Rudolf Diesel, whose interest in engine technology dated back to a visit he made at the age of nine to the Paris World's Fair of 1867. Although it was large and heavy, Diesel's engine, which was patented in 1892 and 1893,

could burn low-grade liquid petroleum at a relatively slow rate. This offered obvious economic advantages over steam power, and 1903 saw the launch of the first boat to be powered by a diesel engine, the French canal barge *Petit-Pierre*, the first seagoing vessel using a diesel engine, the auxiliary cargo ship *Orion*, was launched in 1907, and in 1911 there were some 150 ships in the world powered by diesel engines.

SUBMARINES

Diesel engines were also used in the new generation of submarines which appeared between 1905 and 1914. Submarines had always been relatively ineffective because of the difficulty of finding a method of propulsion that worked underwater. The first, primitive submarines – such as that built by Cornelius van Drebel as long ago as 1620 – had been small craft that relied on hand-cranked propellers for motive power when they were submerged.

Advances had been made in the last quarter of the 19th century. The 1880s had seen the advent of steam-powered submarines – which were somewhat hampered by the need to shut down their fires when submerged – and then of craft such as *Nautilus*, launched in Britain in 1886 and powered by battery-driven electric motors. In 1899, the French launched *Narval*, which was powered by an electric motor when beneath the waves and a steam engine when above them. The German *Unterseeboot* No 1, produced in 1905, also depended on an electric motor when submerged but used a diesel engine for surface power.

SPEEDBOATS

Motor-boats were first raced on the River Seine during the Paris Exhibition of 1900, and in 1901 an unofficial world water speed record of 22.35mph (36kph) was set by a launch with a Mercedes-Daimler

Above: This photograph of Britain's first submarine of the A class was taken on its launch in 1901.

Right: This painting shows the turbine steamship and ferry *St Julien*, which ran between England's south coast and the Channel Islands.

Left: The engine that bears his name made Rudolf Diesel famous and was soon adapted to power ships.

Below: The ocean-going steam-turbine liners were among the most sophisticated ships ever built. This cutaway drawing shows the engines housed in the keel beneath the smokestacks, with the passenger quarters on the upper decks.

GREAT WESTERN RAILWAY

New Fast Turbine Steamers "S.T. Julien" and "S.T. Helier" now running between WEYMOUTH and the CHANNEL ISLANDS Accelerated Services

GREAT NORTHERN RAILWAY
BOOTH LINE
ROYAL MAIL STEAMERS
PARA & MANÁOS

TOURS
PORTUGAL SPAIN & MADEIRA
£12 £20

Left: This view of *Napier I* at Cowes Regatta, Isle of Wight, in August 1903 shows helmswoman Dorothy Levitt after winning the 26-mile (41.8kph) handicap for launches from scratch at 22 knots (40.7kph). On that occasion S. F. Edge was tending her engine.

Below: The Harmsworth Trophy is not a cup, but a mounted bronze of two speedboats rounding a marker.

engine. In November 1902, time trials on the Thames established an 34.5ft (11m) launch, *Vitesse*, as fastest on the river at 13.5mph (21.7kph). The success of this event encouraged eight men to establish the Marine Motoring Association to regulate the sport.

The following year, one of them persuaded his friend Alfred (later Lord) Harmsworth, publisher of the *Daily Mail*, to establish a new award, the British International Trophy for Motor Boats. To qualify for what soon came to be known as the Harmsworth Cup, competing boats had to be less than 40ft (12.2m) long and the hull, engine and two-man crew all had to originate in the country they were representing. There were no other restrictions on the construction of the boat as long as power was completely mechanical. The race was to be over three heats of 34.5 miles (56.3km).

The 1903 Trophy was won by S. F. Edge's *Napier I*, a boat in which, on another run, Edge set an unofficial world water speed record of 24.9mph (40.1kph) in Cork harbour, Ireland. A Frenchman, Henri Brasier, won the trophy the following year; England recovered it in 1905 and 1906, and in 1907 it went to the American boat, *Dixie I*.

Interest in motor-boat racing was equally strong in the USA, where the American Power Boat Association's (APBA) Gold Challenge Cup was instituted in 1904. The first race was won by C. C. Riotte in *Standard* at a speed of 23.6mph (38kph) and the event was soon established as the principal motor-boat trophy race in America, if not the world. The Gold Cup winners *Dixie II*, piloted to victory by E. J. Schroeder in 1908 and 1909, *Dixie III* (with which F. K. Burnham won the Cup in 1910) and another in the *Dixie* series crossed the Atlantic to win the Harmsworth Cup for the USA in 1908, 1910 and 1911 (there was no race in 1909).

HYDROPLANES

The American dominance of motor-boat racing was broken by Tom Sopwith, who had been introduced to the joys of sailing at an early stage of his upbringing on the Scottish island of Lismore. He travelled to the 1912 Gold Cup at Huntingdon Bay, New York, with his hydroplane, *Maple Leaf IV*. Hydroplanes are faster than conventional motorboats. They use a stepped bottom or hydrofoils to lift the boat so that it rides

Below: In 1904, the mountains of Monaco and the buildings of Monte Carlo provided a spectacular backdrop for 'motorized canoes' – the precursors of the speedboat – to race and be put through their paces before an aristocratic audience.

Above: The hydroplane *Maple Leaf IV* was powered by twin Austin engines, and rode high in the water, giving it the edge in speed over the more conventional designs of the day. The boat won the two most prestigious races of the time, the Harmsworth Trophy and the APBA Gold Challenge Cup.

on or close to the surface of the water, rather than ploughing through it. The extra speed is generated by the reduction of friction.

At Huntingdon Bay, on 4 September, Sopwith powered his way to victory at an average speed of 43.2mph (69.5 kph), proving the *Maple Leaf IV*, powered by a pair of Austin engines and owned by the Canadian Sir Edward Mackay Edgar, the fastest in the world. Later the same month, another hydroplane, Mawdsley Brook's *Baby VI*, won the International Sea Mile record and the *Motor Boat* Challenge Trophy at the Burnham Motor Boat meeting.

Sopwith retained the Harmsworth Trophy for England the following year, managing to raise his speed to 57.5mph (92.5kph), increasing his own unofficial water speed record of 46.5mph (74.9kph).

While it was simply a matter of cost that kept motoring a dream for the most people as the new century approached, powered flight was still an unattainable fantasy. However, in 1899 two American brothers decided that the bicycle-manufacturing business they were running in Dayton, Ohio was prosperous enough for them to diversify. Wilbur Wright, 32, was inspired by stories of the pioneering glider pilot Otto Lilienthal, and encouraged his brother Orville, four years younger, to help him research into the mechanics of flight.

At home the brothers, who were practically inseparable lifelong bachelors, built and tested a biplane kite. In 1900, they moved to Kitty Hawk, North Carolina, where the winds were usually very steady, and experimented first with kites, next with tethered gliders and finally with gliders in free flight. They also carried out wind tunnel tests. Their gliders had not only a rudder to control the direction and an elevator to control the angle of travel, but also a revolutionary system of twisting or 'warping' the wings which allowed a pilot to control the glider's roll.

The lightest form of transport then available was the bicycle,

and the Wright brothers turned to cycle technology to minimize the weight of crucial components, such as the rollers supporting the *Flyer* during its launch, for which they used wheel hubs.

AIRBORNE AT LAST

By 1903, the brothers had gained enough confidence to build a biplane, which was made mainly of linen, wire and wood. They gave it two propellers of their own design, driven by a petrol engine which they had also designed, since there was no existing engine both light and powerful enough for their purpose. On 14 December, they were ready to fly. Wilbur lay prone in the pilot's position, along the centre of the lower wing, and ran the *Flyer* along a 40ft (12m) wooden rail that served as a runway, but in his excitement and inexperience he overcontrolled, and at the end of the rail, the *Flyer* fell to the ground.

Three days later, this time with Orville at the controls, the *Flyer* once again raced down the wooden rail, took off under its own power and flew for a full 12 seconds. This was the world's first powered, sustained and controlled flight. Three more such flights were made that day, the last of them, with Wilbur at the controls, lasting 59 seconds and covering 852ft (259.7m).

Although there were no fewer than five witnesses to these historic events, no one in the outside world believed that the Wrights had succeeded where so many others had failed. Their own attitude to their achievement did nothing to publicize it: their immediate concern was not to spread the news, but to get home to Dayton for the traditional family Christmas. Undeterred by the lack of recognition, they carried on with their experiments; by 5 October 1905, Wilbur was able to keep *Flyer III* aloft for just over 38 minutes, during which he flew some 24 miles (39km).

VINDICATION

In August 1908, Wilbur agreed to demonstrate his *Flyer* in France, near Le Mans. The world was forced to take notice. Then, on 21 September, he set a new world flying record by remaining in the air for one hour, 31 minutes, 25 seconds, covering 41.4 miles (66.6km). When asked to speak at a dinner to celebrate his feat, the taciturn aviator declined, saying, 'I know of only one bird, the parrot, that talks, and he can't fly very high.'

Pioneering aviators who had read about the Wright brothers' experiments had by this time achieved powered flight in Europe; Louis Blériot, a well-known French engineer, had managed a number of flights lasting up to 45 seconds in 1907. Such successes paled into insignificance, though,

Right and above: The two Wright brothers – Orville is on the left – moved from their native Ohio to Kitty Hawk on the North Carolina coast in search of favourable winds for their experiments with gliders, such as the biplane above, photographed in 1902. They added their own engine (inset) to make their first flight in 1903.

beside the superior aircraft and flying skills exhibited by Wilbur Wright, and the brothers were universally hailed as the true originators of powered and sustained flight.

On the last day of 1908, Wilbur took Louis Barthou, France's Minister of Public Works, up in the *Flyer*. After their four-minute flight M. Barthou remarked on the sense of security he had enjoyed. Wilbur, quietly confident and doubtless aware of the recent spate of railway accidents caused by frost, snow and fog, replied, 'Oh, you're much safer in my aeroplane than in your trains.'

Above: The Wright *Flyer,* the first aeroplane to make a powered flight, was a fragile, lightweight construction.

Right and below: Following his successful flight in 1903, Wilbur Wright (in cap and leather jacket) became an accomplished flyer, whose travels and demonstration inspired many others to become aviators.

ACROSS THE ENGLISH CHANNEL

Among those watching Wilbur Wright's flying demonstrations near Le Mans in August 1908 was Louis Blériot's principal designer, Raymond Saulnier. As a result of what he saw, Saulnier devised a completely new design for the Blériot XI, a monoplane remarkable for its compact size, clean lines and small Anzani petrol engine. A successful maiden flight took place in January the following year, but by then Blériot had become desperately short of money.

Fortunately, his wife, Alice, saved the life of the son of a wealthy friend, who in gratitude advanced the flyer FF25,000. This enabled him to compete for the £1000 prize offered by the British *Daily Mail* for the first powered flight across the English Channel.

Blériot later recalled that when he was woken at 2.30 in the morning of Sunday 25 July 1909, the day he was due to make his attempt, 'I took

Left and above: Like many pioneering aviators, Louis Blériot (on right) combined great personal courage with an affecting modesty. The monoplane he designed and built was, if anything, more flimsy than the Wrights' *Flyers*, but his cross-Channel flight fired the popular imagination.

a most gloomy view of my chances of succeeding. I would have been very glad if anybody had come and told me that the wind was too strong.' However, nobody did, and he motored to Barraques, near Calais, where his monoplane was waiting.

At 3.30, he climbed into the aviator's seat, with the hand-operated steering controls between his knees. He made a successful 15-minute trial flight and decided 'to start as soon as it was sunrise'. In this way he would steal a march on his rival, the Englishman Hubert Latham, who was still sleeping, and so improve his chances of taking the £1000 prize.

At 4.35, Blériot's machine soared into the air, circled, then struck across the sand-dunes towards the sea. Taking his bearings from the *Escopette*, a ship which he knew was heading for Dover to provide an escort, he quickly passed her. According to his own account, he travelled at about 45mph (70kph) at a height of about 250ft (75m). 'At times she dipped a little,' he wrote, 'but I then pumped in some more petrol, and worked the apparatus which causes the machine to rise, when the monoplane soared up to 250 feet again.'

The three pistons of Blériot's little engine were connected to a common crank, their cylinders splayed out like a fan so that each was adequately cooled by the draught from the propeller. Together, though, they delivered little more power than a small motorcycle, and Blériot needed to run the engine at full throttle through the whole of the flight just to remain airborne. Despite this, it miraculously kept running steadily throughout the epic flight.

Right: A useful feature of the Blériot XI was that the wings could be folded up so that it could be safely stowed away in a relatively small space. The woman seen here is Madame Blériot, whose action in saving the life of a child allowed Blériot to finance the building of the machine.

Below: Several people had already flown further than the distance across the English Channel; what made Blériot's flight in the Blériot XI so remarkable was that he did it over water with nothing to steer by.

For a short while after passing the *Escopette*, Blériot could still use the ship to steer by, but then he lost sight of her, and an anxious 10 minutes followed during which he kept his motor working at full speed. Then, at last, he sighted the English coast. Realizing that a strong south-westerly had blown him off course, he headed westward, keeping a little way out to sea, but following the coastline to Dover. He flew on until he saw his friend, M. Fontaine, who was displaying a large French tricolor indicating where he was to descend. Despite a difficult landing, in which his monoplane was damaged, the 37-year-old French aviator had crossed the English Channel, covering 26 miles (42km) in under 37 minutes.

When he was asked a little later whether he planned to embark on commercial production of his aeroplane, Blériot's answer was a characteristically modest one: 'Since that simple event, which promised no more than a pleasure trip for me, I am confronted with a great rush of orders, and I must think the whole thing over.' Needless to say, before long his epoch-making monoplane design was being sold all over the world.

Less than three weeks later, Chávez completed the greatest aviation feat yet: flying a Blériot machine, he crossed the Alps from Switzerland into Italy. Tragically, he did not live to savour his feat, as his machine suddenly collapsed as he was coming in to land at Domodossola and he sustained injuries from which he later died.

AIR RACES

In 1911, 52 competitors set out to fly a 'Circuit of Europe' from Paris to Liège, Utrecht, Brussels, Roubaix, Calais, London and Dover before returning to Paris. The first place was taken by a French naval officer, Jean de Vaisseau Conneau, who, in a Blériot monoplane, covered the 1000-mile (1600km) course in 58 hours, 38 minutes of flying.

Conneau, a meticulous man who prepared himself thoroughly for every flight, was the first aviator to use his navigational skills in the air. This meant that he could fly direct from place to place, instead of following routes, such as roads or railways, on the ground. This gave him an advantage over his great rival, Jules Védrines, a mechanic who was also a great racing pilot. Védrines had actually been the first flyer to arrive back in Paris in the Circuit of Europe, but his total flying time of 86 hours, 34 minutes secured him only fourth place overall.

Soon after, both men competed in a race around Britain for the second *Daily Mail* prize of £10,000. Conneau won again, completing the 1000-mile (1600km) course in his Blériot XI in just under 22½ hours, but Védrines had the satisfaction, the next year, of winning the Gordon Bennett Cup at an average speed of more than 105mph (170kph).

Above and below: Jean de Vaisseau Conneau, who raced as 'André Beaumont', was perhaps the greatest of the pioneer air racers. His Blériot won races around Britain and Europe.

HIGHER AND HIGHER

The same year, Armstrong 'Chips' Drexel, a member of a wealthy Philadelphian family, flew his Blériot monoplane at Lanark in Scotland to a record height of 6601ft (2012m). This was promptly bettered, first by a Frenchman, Léon Morane, who reached 8471ft (2582m), and then by the brilliant 23-year-old Peruvian Georges Chávez, who, on 8 September, soared to 8488ft (2587m) above France.

Below: Georges Chávez's epic flight across the Alps is commemorated by this postcard.

Left: The Castrol brand was used by most winning air racers.

Opposite: Pioneer aviators tended to be either racers or record-breakers. Chips Drexel, a wealthy American, pursued the former route to glory, taking his Blériot monoplane to a new record height of 6601ft (2012m) in 1910.

COAST TO COAST

The *Daily Mail* was not the only newspaper to use substantial aviation prizes to build circulation. The immensely wealthy American publisher William Randolph Hearst offered $50,000 to any pilot who could fly from coast to coast across the USA before 10 October 1911. The purse appealed to 33-year-old Calbraith Perry Rodgers, who had been barred from the naval academy at Annapolis because of his partial deafness. In June, he took lessons at a flying school run by the Wright brothers, and proved a natural flyer. By 7 August he had his pilot's licence, and straight away began to win competitions.

Rodgers asked the meat-packing tycoon J Ogden Armour to sponsor his attempt to win the Hearst prize, and Armour pledged to pay him $5 per mile (1.6km) provided he used his Wright EX biplane to advertise a grape soda he wanted to promote. Rodgers agreed, and on 17 September the *Vin Fiz* took off from beside the Atlantic at Sheepshead Bay, New York City and headed westward for Mansfield, Ohio.

ON A WING AND A PRAYER

Rodgers navigated by following railway lines, and was tracked on the ground by a train of three carriages which carried his wife, mother, mechanics, $4000 worth of spare parts and several representatives of the Armour Meat Packing Company.

The mechanics and spare parts were both much in demand. As Rodgers flew from Mansfield to Chicago, then on to Kansas City, Dallas, Fort Worth, San Antonio, El Paso and Tucson, he and his aeroplane survived numerous engine failures and crash-landings. Despite suffering from numerous broken bones and concussion, Rodgers flew on from Tucson to Phoenix and then Pasadena, which he reached on 5 November. He was then only 20 miles (32km) from the Pacific coast,

Below and left: Calbraith Perry Rodgers's *Vin Fiz* crashed no fewer than 19 times during his pioneering flight from Long Island, New York to Long Beach, California, with 82 flying hours spread over 49 days. The aircraft, which was virtually rebuilt during the course of the epic flight, now hangs in the Smithsonian Institute in Washington.

and the reporters covering his flight decided that it was over. Rodgers, though, was determined to see it through to the coast, but flew only another 8 miles (13km) before landing hard at Compton and breaking an ankle. He was hospitalized, and it was not until 10 December that he ended his epic journey to his own satisfaction by landing in the surf at Long Beach. By this time, all that remained of the original aeroplane in which he had set out 84 days earlier were two wing struts and the rudder.

TRAGIC END

Although Rodgers had failed to meet Hearst's deadline, he had made his name as a celebrity, and stayed on in Long Beach, taking part in air shows. Tragically, on 3 April 1912, he flew into a flock of seagulls. One of them caught in his rudder, and his aeroplane plummeted into the sea. The great pioneer, who had survived so many mishaps, was killed instantly, but the machine was recovered and is now in the Smithsonian National Air and Space Museum in Washington, DC.

THE SCHNEIDER TROPHY

Men such as Calbraith Perry Rodgers, pilots of conventional land-based aeroplanes, captured the public imagination by taking on exciting challenges, but very little was heard of pilots of seaplanes before 1911, and the intervention of 33-year-old Jacques Schneider, France's Under-Secretary for Air. Schneider, the heir to a vast industrial empire, was much more interested in sport than in business. His particular love was high-speed boating; he was a notable driver of hydroplanes. In 1908 he met Wilbur Wright and became passionate about flying, but two years later he badly damaged an arm in a hydroplane accident and was never again able to pilot an aircraft.

He resolved instead to use his wealth to encourage others to fly, and was soon busy organizing aviation competitions. In 1911, he watched Jean Conneau land in Italy during a Paris–Turin race, and thought how strange

Above: This Déperdussin monoplane was one of the four competitors in the first Schneider Trophy race, held in Monaco in 1913.

Right: Businessman and politician Jacques Schneider did more to promote flying as a sport than almost any other man.

it was that a naval officer should be flying a landplane rather than a seaplane. Schneider was convinced that the future of commercial flying would be in hybrid craft that combined the attributes of hydroplanes and aeroplanes.

As a result, in 1912 he presented the Aero Club of France with a trophy – La Coupe d'Aviation Maritime Jacques Schneider – to be awarded annually, together with a prize of £1000, to the winner of a new flying contest. He stipulated that the competing aircraft must be capable

Right: Tom Sopwith, who was equally at home racing boats and seaplanes, is seen here taxiing just offshore at Monaco in the Schneider Trophy meeting of 1914.

Below: Roland Garros, a concert pianist, first won fame as an aviator in the Schneider Trophy races, then as a World War I ace who found a way of synchronizing the firing of a machine gun mounted in front of him with the revolutions of his aircraft's propeller.

of operating from the open sea and carrying a good payload: he had no desire to spawn a breed of bizarre racing machines. He also stipulated that any nation that won the race three times within five years would become the outright winners of the cup.

FIRST RACE

The first Schneider Trophy contest was held on 16 April 1913 in Monaco, and proved a popular and immediate success. The four competitors (three Frenchmen and an American) had first to prove the seaworthiness of their craft by taxiing over the water for half the first lap, and then fly a further 173 miles (278km) as rapidly as possible.

The first to set out was Maurice Prévost in a Déperdussin. He was followed by pianist-turned-aviator Roland Garros, flying a Morane-Saulnier; then came Gabriel Espanet and the American Charles Weymann, both in Nieuports. All save Prévost experienced various mechanical difficulties and were forced to drop out of the race. Prévost himself had earlier failed to complete the course according to the regulations, so he took to the skies once again, with Garros as his passenger, flew over the finishing line and was declared the winner, with an average speed of around 45.7mph (73.6kph).

Above: The Avro 504, designed by A. V. Roe, was the mainstay of the British air forces in World War I. It was used as a bomber – with the flyers dropping their payload from the cockpit – for reconnaissance and for training pilots.

DESIGN HERO

In the pioneering days of aviation just before World War I, good pilots such as Maurice Prévost, Roland Garros or Howard Pixton (who won the Schneider Trophy in 1914) were feted as national heroes, but no pilot could do better than his aeroplane allowed. Many of the designers of these early and experimental machines remained unsung heroes. One of the most outstanding and influential of these was an Englishman, Edwin Alliot Verdon Roe, known as A. V. Roe.

Roe, a doctor's son, was born in 1877. He left home at 14 for an adventurous year in Canada, then returned to England to become an apprentice locomotive engineer. He moved on to be a fitter in a boatyard, and, after studying marine engineering at London University, got a job as a ship's engineer at the age of 22. While at sea, he became fascinated by the flight of the birds that soared above his ship, and began to experiment with model aeroplanes when he got back to England after three years away.

In 1907, following a brief period in the USA, where he had helped to build an experimental helicopter, he began to build a full-size biplane. He was able to finance this in part with a £75 prize that he won in a model aeroplane contest organized by the *Daily Mail,* but he lived in extreme poverty for the next few years, while devoting himself full-time to his new aircraft. After testing and modifying his biplane, he made a tentative flight on 8 June 1908, but the official honour of being the first to fly in England went to John Moore-Brabazon later that year.

Despite this, Roe never abandoned his efforts. He built a triplane in 1909, and the following year began to make successful flights and, in partnership with his brother Humphrey, founded A. V. Roe and Company. By September 1913, Roe's quest for perfection led to the first flight tests of a prototype of the Avro 504, a biplane with an 80hp Gnome rotary engine. This was stronger and far more solidly built than the triplane which had preceded it, and ideally suited to training pilots. Not only did it respond well if flown well, but pilot errors became apparent very quickly if it was flown badly, so the instructor could easily correct his trainee's mistakes at no great risk.

Learning to fly was, by this time, as much a science as an art, embracing practical techniques that could be mastered and applied to virtually every type of aeroplane. The 504 was a great commercial success: 9000 were built between 1913 and 1931. In World War I, Britain's Royal Flying Corps and Royal Naval Air Service (RNAS) used the machine first as a bomber and reconnaissance aircraft, and subsequently to train some 26,000 pilots.

WAR IN THE AIR

The outbreak of World War I resulted in a massive injection of money into aviation, as the governments involved realized the advantages to be gained from having a strong air force. At the beginning of the war Germany could mobilize some 250 aeroplanes and 14 Zeppelins, France had no more than 150 aeroplanes and several airships, while Britain had fewer than 100 aircraft ready for military service. Many of these aircraft were flimsy, and powered by engines of uncertain power and endurance. At best they might reach 3000ft (900m) and fly at 70mph (110kph), with a range of 200 miles (320km).

The RNAS had a handful of Avro 504s, three of which made, in November 1914, what has been claimed as the world's first strategic bombing raid by a formation of aircraft. Led by Squadron Commander Featherstone Briggs (who was shot down and captured during the raid), they flew from Belfort in France to Lake Constance, where they dived out of the sky to attack German Zeppelin sheds, dropping 20lb (12 9kg) bombs that destroyed a hydrogen plant and severely damaged one airship. The Avros, which had set off in sub-zero temperatures, had been using Castrol R. This was not only one of the very few oils suitable for rotary-engined aeroplanes, but also the only one that worked at very low temperatures, maintaining its viscosity down to 3.3°C, allowing British planes to go higher and to fly at times when the enemy was earthbound.

By April 1917 the Germans had regained the advantage in the air with their powerful new Halberstadt and Albatros machines, and the Allies suffered massive losses. However, the same year also saw the introduction of the de Havilland Airco DH4, a biplane bomber with a 250hp Rolls-Royce engine so powerful that it could outfly enemy fighters with ease, despite its bomb load of nearly 500lb (225kg).

Right: The Germans' main fighting aircraft in World War I was the Albatros. The DIIIs and DVs seen here were part of the 'Flying Circus' of Baron von Richtofen, the 'Red Baron', Germany's great flying ace.

Below: Bombing was a particularly hazardous business in World War I. The aeroplanes had to fly low – making them vulnerable to ground fire – so that the crew could accurately drop their bombs, by hand, over the side.

Below: Despite the hazards, bombing raids could sometimes be very successful. In November 1914, considerable damage was caused to an airship and equipment in a raid on these Zeppelin sheds at Lake Constance.

The main effect of the war on the development of aeroplanes was the rapid increase it produced in the speed of technological advance. Aircraft manufacture developed into a major industry, with a total of more than 200,000 aeroplanes being produced by Britain, France, Germany, Italy and the USA. As a by-product of this, air passenger travel would become a reality. In fact, the first scheduled aeroplane passenger service was introduced a few months before the war broke out: on 1 January 1914, the St Petersburg–Tampa Airboat Line began to offer a 20-mile (32km) flight across Tampa Bay, Florida, for $5.

By 1918, the fragile machines of the early days of the war, which flew at around 70mph (110kph), had been succeeded by much sturdier aeroplanes that were capable of reaching speeds in excess of 120mph (190kph). Several new designs, developed during the war but built too late to see active service, such as the Vickers Vimy biplane bomber, were destined to play an important role in peacetime.

SPEED AND GLORY

1919–1945

The decades between the wars provided an extraordinary contrast; the 1920s roared and the 1930s slumped, as the long, jazz-fuelled party that followed the end of World War I crashed into the equally long hangover of the worst worldwide economic depression of the century, a depression that only lifted as the great powers of Europe began once again preparing for war. It was the age of the dictators – Hitler, Mussolini, Franco and Stalin – and the Golden Age of Hollywood, when the movies exported American culture to the whole world.

In the industrialized world there were considerable material improvements, especially for the middle classes, despite the depression of the 1930s. In the USA, for example, the first electric refrigerator appeared in 1918, and from small beginnings at The Hague (from 1919) and in Montreal and Pittsburgh (from 1920) radio broadcasts were soon entertaining countless families. Though the first television broadcasts came in the 1930s, the interwar years were very much Radio Days.

Increased car ownership was one of these advances, and motor-racing continued to be popular. Speed was very much a theme of the age, celebrated in the sleek and streamlined styles of Art Deco, and dedicated people fought to become the fastest on land or water in machines that looked less and less like cars and boats. Speed was the theme at sea, too, as huge new liners battled for the Blue Riband and the national prestige that accompanied it.

The most promising area for pioneering achievement was the skies, and the period is notable for a number of firsts sandwiched between the first flight across the Atlantic in 1919 and the first scheduled transatlantic passenger service 20 years later. When war came, so did the jet engine, and the world of aviation would be changed for ever.

Left: The Vicker's Vimy biplane in which Alcock and Brown made their historic flight across the Atlantic in June 1919 was originally built as a heavy bomber for use in World War I. It is constructed mainly of wood, with a fabric covering.

Right: This 350hp Sunbeam took the land speed record no less than three times; first for Kenelm Lee Guinness at Brooklands (where it can be seen today) in 1922 and then, renamed *Bluebird*, for Malcolm Campbell at Pendine Sands in 1924 and 1925.

Below: *Bluebird* is seen here in 1924 undergoing a tyre change between runs at Pendine Sands, with boards beneath the wheels to stop them sinking. The body shows an early hint of streamlining, especially noticeable in the windscreen.

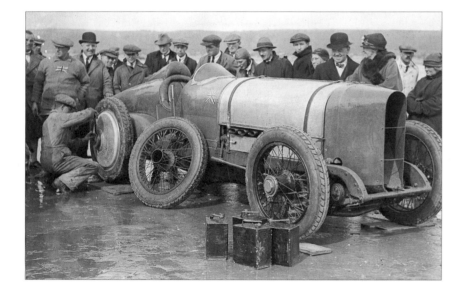

Right: Malcolm Campbell was an accomplished amateur race-driver who raced at Brooklands before World War I.

at Brooklands in a Talbot-Darracq, and two years later he won the French Grand Prix in a Sunbeam – the first-ever all-British Grand Prix victory. These were only the first of a string of racing successes.

Campbell was a millionaire who financed his own record-breaking attempts. He was said to have no nerves on the track, but his changeable personality, veering from caution to daring, from sensitivity to obstinacy and from pessimism to heroic defiance, perhaps betrayed inward fears.

CAMPBELL'S RECORD

In 1924, at Fanöe in Denmark, Campbell was timed at 137.7mph (221.6kph), but this was not recognized. Formal rules governed all new attempts on the record. Since 1909, any officially recognized land speed record had to be the average of two automatically timed runs, one in each direction, over a measured mile or kilometre.

Campbell's first official record came at Pendine Sands in South Wales on 25 September 1924. Driving Lee Guinness's Sunbeam, which he called *Bluebird*, he recorded an average speed of 146.2mph (235.2kph). The following year he raised it again to 150.8mph (242.8kph), but then Henry Segrave entered the fray. He overtook Campbell in 1926, achieving 152mph (245.1kph) in another Sunbeam on the beach at Southport, in north-west England.

THE FASTEST MEN ON EARTH

During the interwar years, the quest for speed increasingly focused on the world land speed record, as a clutch of daredevil drivers, aided by dedicated engineers, vied for the title of Fastest Man on Earth. In 1922, Kenelm Lee Guinness set a new record speed, 133.7mph (215.2kph), in a 12-cylinder, aeroengined Sunbeam at Brooklands, a notoriously bumpy track. In the next 17 years, the record would be broken 24 times.

The two most prominent contenders for the record in these years were Henry Segrave and Malcolm Campbell. Segrave, born in America in 1896 but raised in England, had joined the Sunbeam-Talbot-Darracq racing team in 1921. That same year he won the 200 mile (320km) race

Above: Segrave's Sunbeam had two 22.5 litre, 12-cylinder Matabele aeroengines that generated 1000hp. Its streamlined body, captured in this dynamic Castrol poster (**inset**), was inspired by an upturned boat.

Right: Henry Segrave, born in Baltimore of an Irish family, but brought up in England, first found fame as a Sunbeam racing driver.

FLYING ON THE GROUND

Campbell redoubled his efforts, abandoning the old Sunbeam for a new *Bluebird*, designed by Amherst Villiers and mechanic Leo Villa and powered by a high-performance Napier Lion aeroengine, loaned to Campbell by special permission of the Air Ministry. The engines had a high power-to-weight ratio, and in February 1927, Campbell drove the car at 174.9mph (281.4kph) on Pendine Sands.

In March 1927, Segrave took a new twin-engined Sunbeam to Daytona Beach in Florida, where there was an uninterrupted 15-mile (24km) stretch of packed sands. It was an extraordinary machine, powered by two Matabele aeroengines, only one of which was mounted ahead of the driver in the usual way. The other was placed right behind the driver's

THE POWER OF STEAM

Between the wars, the most useful form of public transport remained the railways. Steam was still the main railway technology, though electric and diesel-powered railway engines were well established in many countries.

While railways were the main – if not the only – way of moving people and goods around the country between the wars, in some countries there was growing pressure from private cars and road haulage. The competition created a pressure to modernize and be up-to-date in what was essentially a 19th-century industry. This was expressed in electrification programmes and the design of increasingly more efficient, more powerful and, where needed, faster locomotives.

PACIFIC CLASS

Important new steam engines were developed in the railway works at Doncaster, England, where Nigel Gresley had been Chief Mechanical Engineer of the Great Northern Railway (GNR) since 1911. In 1922, the first of his famous 4-6-2 Pacific class railway engines was made at Doncaster. *Great Northern* was huge – it weighed around 92 tons (93.5 tonnes) – and very powerful.

In 1928, five years after the GNR had been incorporated into the London and North Eastern Railway (LNER), another Gresley Pacific engine, the *Flying Scotsman*, ran non-stop the 392 miles (631km) in each direction between King's Cross, in London, and Edinburgh, Scotland, creating a new world record for endurance.

GERMAN SUCCESS

Germany had a tradition of innovation in the railway. In the early years of the century, a 12-wheeled electric railcar had set new speed records of over 125mph (200kph) on a military railway between Marienfeld and Berlin. The Germans were also the first to introduce high-speed diesel rail-cars for passengers. The service, first run in the spring of 1932, was timetabled to cover the route from Berlin to Hamburg at speeds of more than 100mph (160kph), making it by far the fastest scheduled rail service in the world. The car was not stretched by this; in tests, it reached speeds of 124mph (198.5kph).

Spurred on by the commercial success of the 'Flying Hamburger', as the diesel rail-car came to be known, the LNER inaugurated a non-stop high-speed service from London to Newcastle in 1934. There was, however, more traffic than the German two-car units

could carry, and the service was given over to steam. Later that year, with extra coaches bringing the total weight of the train to around 210 tons (213.4 tonnes), a Pacific on a downhill stretch of the return run reached around 100mph (160kph).

Gresley's versions of the Pacific were fast but unreliable, requiring a great deal of maintenance to keep them running. William Stanier resolved to do better. In 1934, he became Chief Mechanical Engineer of the London Midland and Scottish (LMS) railway, and began restocking it with a series of locomotives drawing upon the best experience of Churchward's pre-war engines for the GWR and Gresley's for LNER. So successful was Stanier that his Coronation Class engines are widely considered to mark the peak of the British locomotive.

FRENCH DESIGN ACE

Gresley's designs owed much to André Chapelon, born in France in 1892, and the greatest locomotive engineer of the 20th century. In 1926, Chapelon had improved an existing gas and steam exhaust device to create the Kylchap, which produced an adequate draught with minimum back pressure. This was applied to a range of engines with good effect. Chapelon believed he could improve the performance of a Pacific by redesigning and enlarging the steam passages, improving the draughting and increasing the boiler pressure and 'superheat'. He felt he could improve fuel economy and power output by up to 30 per cent, and persuaded the Paris–Orléans Railway to rebuild one of their Pacifics to his specifications. The refashioned No.3566, first run in 1929, performed very well, and Chapelon applied his ideas to several other French locomotives.

Right: The 'Flying Hamburger' diesel railcar which ran in Germany was the fastest scheduled train service in the world in the 1930s.

Left: Comfort was as much a selling point as speed. Britain's Great Western Railway provided footwarmers for first-class passengers.

Gresley himself spent three weeks in France learning from Chapelon about the defects of an engine he had built in 1934, and took on board many of Chapelon's ideas. The result of this cross-fertilization process was Gresley's streamlined A4-class Pacifics, with improved tractive power and a 10-15 per cent increase in the working pressure of the engine.

RECORD BREAKERS

On 27 September 1935, the LNER made a test run of the A4 *Silver Link* from King's Cross to Grantham, Lincolnshire, a distance of 105 miles (169km). The speed twice touched 112mph (179kph), and averaged

Above: The Pacific-class (4-6-2) engines of Gresley (**inset**) and Stanier were the elite locomotives of Britain in the 1930s.

Left and above: The look of the streamlined A4 Pacifics was a gift to poster designers – even though, above, the artist has added extra driving wheels.

107.5mph (173kph) over 25 miles (40km), a world record. After this, LNER used A4 Pacifics for its *Silver Jubilee* express on the daily run between London and Newcastle, covering the distance at a higher scheduled speed than any other train over a similar journey.

Gresley was knighted for these successes in 1936, and on 3 July 1938 another Pacific broke the world steam train speed record, setting a mark that still stands. The streamlined A4 No.4468 *Mallard* reached 126mph (203kph) in a short sprint coming down Stoke Bank in Lincolnshire. Gresley died in 1941, aged 64.

THE GREATEST EVER?

At this time, André Chapelon himself was still alive and at the peak of his career. Between 1942 and 1946 he worked with

Left: The great express trains, such as the *Orient Express*, *Flying Scotsman* and *Nord Express*, represented the last word in futuristic technology between the wars.

Left and above: André Chapelon worked in South America after the French railways decided in favour of an electrified service. There was still a frontier feel to the railway in Argentina (left), where Chapelon did a great deal of work, while lines through the Andes provided a stunning visual backdrop – as well as intriguing technical challenges – for the locomotives that he designed.

Below: Tickets and other memorabilia from between the wars provide an irresistible lure to collectors keen to relive a Golden Age of rail travel.

the French national railway, the SNCF, to produce his three-cylinder compound 4-8-4 No.242 A.1, which is now acclaimed as the greatest steam locomotive ever built, with the highest-ever power-to-weight ratio and very low coal and water consumption.

Chapelon believed that he could now create a fleet of modern steam locomotives capable of competing with either electric or diesel engines, but the SNCF opted, under political pressure, to continue with electrification, introduced in France in 1910. Chapelon's ideas remained influential in South America, especially Argentina – where he was still designing new engines or rebuilds in the late 1950s – and South Africa.

Right: The world-record-holding *Mallard* still runs in Britain, but only in events specially organized by rail enthusiasts; it is 30 years since the last scheduled steam passenger services ended in Britain.

Above: *Mallard*'s top-speed sprint down Stoke Bank, Lincolnshire, lasted just a few seconds, but the record, together with the combination of sleek elegance and extraordinary power that was a feature of all the A4 Pacifics, made the locomotive famous.

The only truly practical way to cross the Atlantic between the wars was on a passenger liner. At the cheaper end of the market, would-be American immigrants travelled steerage from Europe to New York's Ellis Island, while at the other end, the shipping companies competing for the lucrative luxury market aimed to attract passengers by vying for the Blue Riband of the Atlantic, the title claimed by the liner that held the record for the fastest crossing. The great liners were the unofficial flagships of the merchant fleet. Although the Blue Riband was a notional prize, it carried a great deal of prestige, and national pride was as much a spur as commercial advantage in the race across the Atlantic.

CHASING THE RIBAND

In the first years of the century the Riband had gone to various German liners, but it had been held by the British Cunard Line's 32,000-ton liner *Mauretania* since September 1909, when she had made the crossing at an average speed of 26.1 knots (48.3kph). This record still stood in the late 1920s, when companies began to make liners specifically to win the Riband. One of this new generation of liners, built with record-breaking in mind, was the *Bremen* of Norddeutscher Lloyd.

Completed on 24 June 1929, she had room for 2200 passengers and 990 crew on seven decks. She was the first ship to be given a bulbous bow to increase her speed, and also had the plating of her hull overlapped from aft to forward, which increased her speed by about 0.6mph (1kph). She began her maiden voyage to New York from Bremerhaven on 16

Above: Luxury liners such as Norddeutscher Lloyd's *Europa* vied to set the fastest time for the vital Atlantic crossing. Deusol-Castrol (**inset**), a lubricant specially formulated for marine engines, helped speed many of them on their way.

July 1929, and her twelve steam turbines immediately drove her to the Blue Riband, with an average speed of 27.8 knots (51.5kph) between Cherbourg and Ambrose Lighthouse, covering the distance in 4 days, 17 hours and 42 minutes. On the return voyage she did even better, with an average speed between Ambrose Lighthouse and Eddystone of 27.9 knots (51.7kph).

Norddeutscher Lloyd's turbine steamer *Europa* made a westward crossing on her maiden voyage in 1930 at an average speed of 27.9 knots (51.7kph) and held the Blue Riband for three years. Then, in June 1933, after improvements to her engines and the elimination of vibration in her after section, the *Bremen* won it back with an average of 28.5 knots (52.8kph), only to lose it two months later to Italy's *Rex*.

Built in Genoa, the *Rex* had been completed in September 1932. She had 12 steam turbines and room for 2258 passengers and 756 crew. In August 1933, the *Rex* won the Blue Riband by covering the distance from Tarifa Point to Ambrose Lighthouse in 4 days 13 hours 58 minutes, at an average speed of 28.9 knots (53.6kph). She thus also became the first holder of the Hales Trophy, instituted by a British MP who felt that the achievement of being fastest across the Atlantic deserved more than just a notional trophy.

BATTLE OF THE TITANS

The next winner of the Blue Riband was the *Normandie*, launched in 1932 but not completed until 5 May 1935. This French liner was vast, with 10 decks and space for 1972 passengers and 1354 crew. She was driven by four steam turbines. On her maiden voyage from Le Havre to

Left and below: The French liner *Normandie* took the Blue Riband and Hales Trophy on her first trip across the Atlantic to New York, a feat commemorated on a souvenir plate whose design was clearly copied from the photograph below.

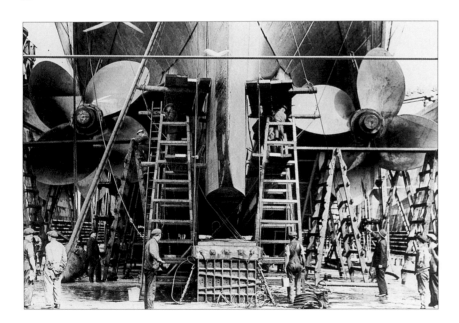

Above and below: Built in Scotland and launched in 1936 – six years after the first plates were laid – the Cunard liner *Queen Mary* vied with the *Normandie* for the Blue Riband. She was deliberately designed on traditional rather than modernist lines, and was one of the largest liners ever built; the ship's three whistles weighed a ton each and could be heard 10 miles (15km) away. In 1940 she was refitted as a troopship, returning to the transatlantic run in July 1947.

Above: After World War I, Germany was virtually stripped of passenger ships. The building of the *Bremen* (and her sister ship *Europa*) in the late 1920s was a source of great national pride, which swelled when the ship captured the Blue Riband in 1929.

New York on 29 May 1935, they took her between Bishop Rock and Ambrose Lighthouse in four days, three hours and 14 minutes, taking the Blue Riband with an average speed of 29.9 knots (55.5kph). She broke the record again on the return journey with 30.3 knots (56.1kph).

The next victor, in August 1936, was Cunard's *Queen Mary*, built by John Brown and Company on the Clyde. Almost as massive as the *Normandie*, she was driven by 16 steam turbines and could carry 2139 passengers and 1101 crew. Her successful voyage from Bishop Rock to Ambrose Lighthouse took 4 days and 27 minutes, at an average speed of 30.1 knots (55.8kph), returning at 30.6 knots (56.7kph).

In 1937, the *Normandie* regained the Blue Riband, and in July became the first craft to make the journey in less than four days, recording three days, 23 hours. Then, in August 1938, the *Queen Mary* broke the record in both directions, travelling first from Bishop Rock to Ambrose Lighthouse in three days, 21 hours and 48 minutes at 31 knots (57.4kph), then coming back in 3 days, 20 hours and 42 minutes at 31 7 knots (58.7kph). This

Right: Among the many souvenirs produced to mark the ascendancy of the great liners of the 1930s was this deck-fanned model of the *Queen Mary*.

record remained unbeaten until July 1952, when a late American entry in the transatlantic race, the *United States,* achieved 35.6 knots (65.9kph) on its way to England and 34.5 knots (63.9kph) on its way home.

THE WORLD WATER SPEED RECORD

The individual water speed record was just as hotly contested as the Blue Riband. Although records had been kept unofficially since the beginning of the century, the first official record holder was an American, Garfield Wood, whose boat *Miss America VII* reached a speed of 92.8mph (149.4kph) in September 1928 at Indian Creek in Florida.

On Friday 13 June 1930, Sir Henry Segrave, fresh from taking the world land speed record the previous year, took the controls of his mammoth Napier-engined *Miss England II* on Lake Windermere, in England's Lake District. Accompanied by two mechanics, he roared up and down the measured mile (1.6km).

Although he did not know it, Segrave had broken the record with a mean speed of 98.8mph (158kph), but he turned for a third run. This time, though, *Miss England II* began bumping slightly over the waves, and then, in the middle of the course, suddenly swerved to the left in clouds of spray – half of the step under the forepart of the hull had been torn off by the turbulence – and a moment later her engines were silenced as she turned right over. One of the mechanics was killed outright while the other escaped with cuts and bruises. Segrave was taken out of the water unconscious, came round for long enough to hear that he had broken the record, but died of his injuries some three hours later.

Above: Lord Wakefield and Kaye Don were committed to retaining the water speed record. They are seen here beside *Miss England III*, the British hopeful that added to the successes of *Miss England II.* Wakefield sponsored and publicized these attempts (**left**) and Castrol motor oil was used in all the British vessels.

Below: *Miss England III* returned the water speed record to Britain from the USA with Kaye Don's new record set in July 1932 on Loch Lomond in Scotland – only to be lost again to Wood on Lake Michigan.

MISS ENGLAND VS MISS AMERICA

Miss England II was salvaged, and the following year, on 2 April 1931, Kaye Don took her along the River Paraná near Buenos Aires at 103.5mph (165.6kph) to take the record from Garfield

Left: After Kaye Don took the water speed record in April 1931, he battled the American Garfield Wood for supremacy for the next 18 months.

Above: In August 1939, Campbell – seen here with his son, Donald – took his new *Bluebird*, codenamed K4, to a new world record on Coniston Water.

Below: In his first *Bluebird*, K3, Campbell sat in front of a huge Rolls-Royce engine that generated 2000hp.

Above and left: Sir Malcolm Campbell's boat – named *Bluebird* like the cars in which he had taken the land speed record – is shown in tests on Loch Lomond. He took the record on Switzerland's Lake Maggiore, then raised it in September 1938 on another Swiss lake, Lake Hallwil.

Wood, who had recently reached 102.2mph (164.4kph). Three months later, on Lake Garda, Italy, Don improved his speed to 110mph (177.4kph). Gar Wood retook the record for the USA in his latest boat, *Miss America IX*, covering 111.7mph (179.8kph) at Indian Creek, so Lord Wakefield, who had sponsored Kaye Don's previous attempts, financed the building of *Miss England III*, fitted with two Schneider Trophy-type Rolls-Royce supercharged engines and two steel propellers. On 18 July 1932, Don took *Miss England III* over a measured mile (1.6km) at Loch Lomond in Scotland and increased the record to 119.8mph (192.8kph) but Wood responded by powering across Lake Michigan, near Detroit, at 124.9mph (201kph) in *Miss America X*.

THE *BLUEBIRD* CHALLENGE

There the record stood until 1937, when Sir Malcolm Campbell was ready, as Segrave had been before him, to move from land to water with his first *Bluebird* boat, powered by a 2000hp Rolls-Royce engine.

He first took her to the Swiss part of Lake Maggiore, where, on 1 September 1937, he raised the world water speed record to 126.3mph (203.3kph), despite the fact that two of the intake pipes burst during the run and *Bluebird* shipped water. The following day he made two more

runs and increased the record to 129.5mph (208.4kph). He beat this in 1938, and in 1939, on Coniston Water in England's Lake District, set a new figure of 141.7mph (226.7kph).

UNDER SAIL

It was not only power boats that made the news in the 1920s and 1930s. Sailing boats featured in several dramatic races and two extraordinary circumnavigations of the world. Much of the best racing came in the America's Cup, as Sir Thomas Lipton, a Scottish merchant, continued his attempts to wrest the trophy from the American yachts that had won it every time since its inception in 1851. His had first made a challenge in 1889, and when *Shamrock IV* won the right to contest the trophy in 1920, it was his fourth attempt. This time, he succeeded in winning the first two races of the series: they were the first won by a challenger since 1871. However, the defending yacht, *Resolute*, won the other three races, and so triumphed.

In 1930, when Lipton was 80 years old, he made his fifth and final challenge with *Shamrock V*, designed by Charles E. Nicholson. Rather than their usual location in outer New York Harbour, the races were run in the sea off Newport, Rhode Island, while the yachts were of the new J class, with a minimum rating of 76ft (23m). Lipton had no more success than he had before. It was no real surprise: the American yacht, *Enterprise,* included many new design features such as a light alloy mast, and was skippered by one of the greatest yachtsmen of all time, Harold S. 'Mike' Vanderbilt.

FAILED *ENDEAVOUR*

In 1934, the aircraft manufacturer Tom Sopwith entered *Endeavour*, a J-class yacht designed by Nicholson. He managed to win the first two races, and lost the last by less than a minute, but was nevertheless beaten by Mike Vanderbilt's *Rainbow*, a yacht that had cost $500,000 to design and build and had a sail area of 7561sq ft (702 sq m). In 1937, two J-class giants, now more than 130 ft (40m) long, clashed for the last time. *Endeavour II* was beaten four times in a row by Vanderbilt's *Ranger*, which achieved the stunning feat of sailing 15 miles (24km) to windward in two hours, three minutes and four seconds.

Two circumnavigations by yachts with crew of two caught the popular imagination. William Robinson and Willoughby Wright set out from New York on 10 June 1928 in their 32½ ft (10m) Bermuda ketch *Svaap*. They sailed via the Panama Canal to Tahiti, where Wright gave up his place to a Tahitian, then on through the South Seas to Singapore and Ceylon, via the Red Sea and Suez to the Mediterranean, thence home to New York via the Canary Islands. A voyage of 32,000 miles (51,000km) took a total of 41½ months.

The second pair, also American, travelled between 1934 and 1937. Professor Strout and his wife – the first woman to make such a voyage – sailed in the *Igdrasil*, a replica of *Spray*, the sloop in which Joshua Slocum had made his historic circumnavigation back in 1895–8.

Top: *Endeavour II*, entered by Tom Sopwith, failed to win a race in the America's Cup of 1937. At this time, challengers for the Cup had to sail to the port where the races were held, which deterred many European challengers.

Left and right: The 1920 races for the America's Cup were among the closest ever. Sir Thomas Lipton's *Shamrock IV* won the first two races, but the American yacht *Resolute*, seen leading in both these shots, came back to win the series.

Although aeroplanes had become both faster and more reliable by the start of the 1920s, forced landings remained commonplace, and regular scheduled passenger services seemed a pipedream. There were, however, some visionaries who saw the conquest of the air as the most important goal of their generation.

They pursued this aim so avidly and so successfully, that by the summer of 1939 flights within the USA or Europe were routine, although the price of tickets ensured that only the wealthy could fly. There was even a regular passenger service across the Atlantic. Little more than 20 years before, the skies had been the province of just a handful of pioneers, spurred on by dreams of glory and some fabulous prizes. These included £10,000 (worth around £1,000,000 today) offered in 1913 by Lord Northcliffe, publisher of the *Daily Mail*, for the first non-stop transatlantic flight.

The main problem faced in flying the Atlantic was to carry enough fuel for the flight without making the aircraft too heavy to get off the ground. On 16 May 1919, three US Navy Curtiss flying boats set out to cross the Atlantic in two stages, with a refuelling stop in the Azores. They met bad weather, and two of them, short of fuel, landed in the sea, but the NC-4, piloted by Lieutenant Commander Albert C. Read with a crew of five, reached the Azores. After waiting a few days, they flew to Lisbon on 27 May, completing the first aerial crossing of the Atlantic.

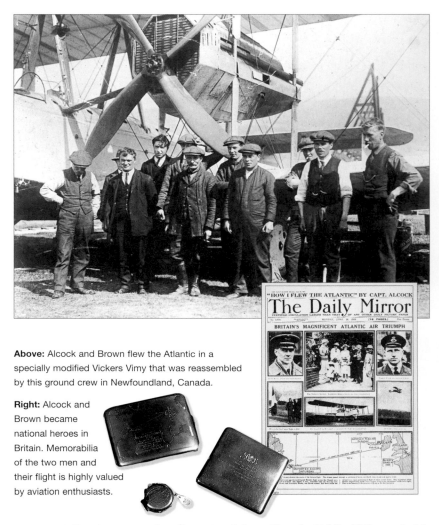

Above: Alcock and Brown flew the Atlantic in a specially modified Vickers Vimy that was reassembled by this ground crew in Newfoundland, Canada.

Right: Alcock and Brown became national heroes in Britain. Memorabilia of the two men and their flight is highly valued by aviation enthusiasts.

Below: Captain John Alcock (left) and his navigator Lieutenant Arthur Whitten Brown (right) are pictured here in uniform before embarking on their remarkable transatlantic flight in 1919.

The following month, Captain John Alcock DSC (26) and his navigator, Lieutenant Arthur Whitten Brown (32), prepared to make an attempt on a a non-stop crossing from Newfoundland. They were flying a modified Vickers Vimy biplane bomber that had been shipped across the Atlantic in crates. Its armament had been removed and some extra fuel tanks had been added instead. It was powered by two Rolls-Royce Eagle engines, lubricated by 50 gallons (225 litres) of Castrol R.

NIGHT CROSSING

At 4.28 p.m. on Saturday 14 June, with the wind gusting strongly across the grassy airstrip at St John's, they took off, climbed to 1000ft (300m) and set out east across the ocean. After the sun went down, they were effectively flying blind, as thick clouds obscured the moon and stars. A brief break in the cloud at 3 a.m. enabled Brown to get 'a cut on Polaris and Vega' before darkness set in again. Two hours later, they were flying through thick fog and, as Alcock later recalled, 'began to have a very rough time.'

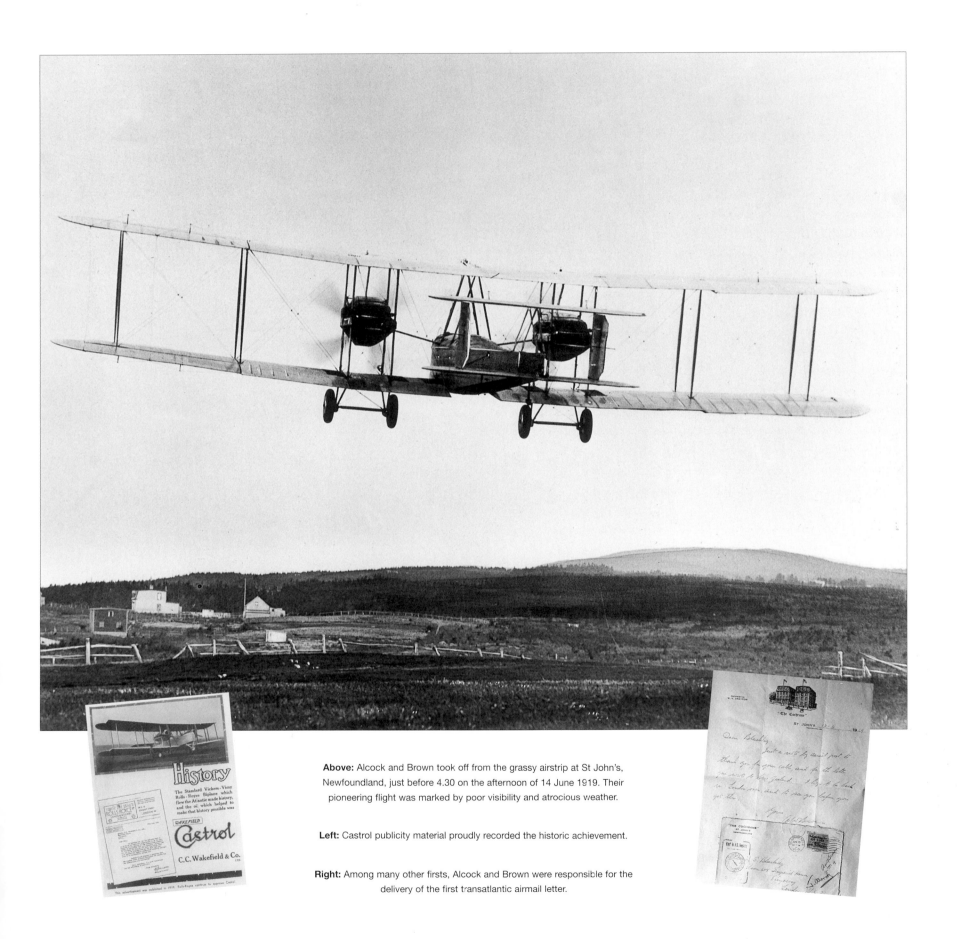

Above: Alcock and Brown took off from the grassy airstrip at St John's, Newfoundland, just before 4.30 on the afternoon of 14 June 1919. Their pioneering flight was marked by poor visibility and atrocious weather.

Left: Castrol publicity material proudly recorded the historic achievement.

Right: Among many other firsts, Alcock and Brown were responsible for the delivery of the first transatlantic airmail letter.

First, the air speed indicator jammed when sleet froze on it, then they apparently went into a steep spiral. 'We had no sense of horizon,' Alcock remembered. 'We came down quickly from 4000 feet [1220m] until we saw the water very near. That gave me my horizon again, and I was all right. That period only lasted a few seconds, but it seemed ages. It came to an end when we were within 50 feet [15m] of the water with the machine practically on its back.'

They climbed from this near-disaster to the relative safety of 11,000ft (3300m), only to run into a hailstorm. Alcock found his aircraft 'covered with ice … and it remained like that until an hour before we landed'. To escape the weather, he flew low over the sea towards Ireland.

Above: Alcock and Brown always acknowledged the importance of Castrol lubricants to the success of their flight.

SAFE LANDING

In the morning, they reached the coast of County Galway, and flew on until they were over Clifden village, where Alcock saw 'what I took to be … a lovely meadow. We came down and made a perfect landing. But it was a bog!' The wheels sank axle-deep in the ooze, and the Vimy toppled over on to its nose. Fortunately, neither man was hurt, although neither had actually enjoyed the experience. Alcock summed up the isolation they had both felt: 'It was a terrible trip. We never saw a boat and we got no wireless messages at all.' They had landed at 8.40 a.m. GMT, after covering 1890 miles (3042km) in 16 hours and 12 minutes. They had won their £10,000, and both were subsequently knighted.

Below: The end of Alcock and Brown's flight was rather ignominious, with the Vimy ending up nose down in a bog.

Right: The Vimy biplane was retrieved from the bog at Clifden and now has pride of place in the Science Museum in London.

Left and below: Following their flight, Alcock (centre) and Brown were presented with a cheque for £10,000 by Winston Churchill, the Secretary for War and the Air. Alcock did not live long enough to spend the money; he was killed in a crash later that year. Brown lived until 1948.

Left: The 1925 Schneider Trophy winner, Lieutenant James H. Doolittle, was something of a daredevil, taking every risk he could think of to get his Curtiss R3C-2 racer round the course at an average speed of 232.6mph (374.3kph).

Left: The aircraft designed by R. J. Mitchell for the Supermarine company were the fastest machines of the early 1930s and dominated the latter years of the Schneider Trophy.

Left: Major Mario De Bernardi won the Schneider Trophy in 1926 and set three new world air speed records in a Macchi M.52 in the next two years.

structure with no external bracing wires or struts – proved insufficiently rigid, and wing flutter caused the aeroplane to crash during trials. The Trophy was won by Lieutenant James H. Doolittle of the US Army, flying a Curtiss R3C-2 racer at an average speed of 232.6mph (374.3kph). He took considerable risks to make his aircraft as light as possible, cornered tightly all the way and completed the course with just 16 pints (9 litres) of fuel left in his tank.

BACK TO EUROPE

Like the Italians before them, the Americans failed to complete the trio of wins that would have given them the Schneider Trophy outright. An Italian, Major Mario De Bernardi, won the 1926 race in a Macchi M.39 monoplane, flying at 246mph (397kph).

The following year's race was held in Venice. Only the Italians and the British took part, as the Americans, lacking government support, had to drop out. The British, by contrast, had made a supreme effort. The Royal Air Force had formed a 'High Speed Flight', with hand-picked pilots and technicians, for an assault on the Trophy, while Mitchell had designed a new Supermarine seaplane, the S.5. The race, which began

at 2.30 p.m. on 26 September, attracted over 250,000 spectators. The superiority of the British machines quickly became evident, and the winner was Flight Lieutenant S. N. Webster in a Supermarine S.5 with a geared Napier engine. He covered the triangular course at an average speed of 282mph (453kph).

HIGHER POWER

After this, it was agreed that the contest should be held every two years, rather than annually. The gap gave Mitchell time to develop the Supermarine S.6, which included the new, extraordinarily powerful, 1900bhp Rolls-Royce R V-12 engine designed by F. H. Royce. This enabled Flying Officer H. R. D. Waghorn to win the 1929 race at an amazing speed of 329mph (526kph).

In 1930, the British government withdrew its support of the Schneider Trophy team because of the growing economic depression. As one more victory would give Britain the Trophy outright, Rolls-Royce and Vickers (which by then owned Supermarine) decided to go it alone. In the event, they did not have to. A private benefaction of £100,000 shamed the government into restoring its support early in 1931.

Shortly before the race, Rolls-Royce built a new version of the R engine, producing a phenomenal 2350bhp. To provide adequate cooling for the much more powerful engine, Supermarine modified the two S.6s they had built and constructed two new aircraft. The S.6Bs were soon dubbed 'flying radiators'; they had radiators built into the wings and float surfaces, while hot Castrol R lubricant from the engine was cooled by pumping it through banks of pipes along and beneath the fuselage to an oil tank in the fin. Orthodox radiators could not be used because of the drag they would generate.

The French and Italians had to drop out of the race as their aircraft could not be made ready in time, but the British went ahead. The 1931 contest was held over seven laps of a triangular course between the south coast of England and the Isle of Wight, a total distance of 218 miles (350km). The leader of the British team, Flight Lieutenant John Nelson Boothman, was an RAF test pilot who specialized in seaplanes. His winning flight was watched by a very large crowd, many of whom were thrilled by the deafening passage of the machine at full speed only 200ft (60m) above their heads. Boothman's average speed for the whole course was 340mph (547kph); the average flying speed in the Trophy races had more than doubled in just nine years.

Below: The magnificent Supermarine Rolls-Royce seaplane S.6B won the Schneider Trophy in 1931. It is now to be found in London's Science Museum.

Above: An American victory in the Schneider Trophy was secured in 1925 by the bold Lieutenant James H. Doolittle, seen here standing proudly on his Curtiss R3C-2.

Above: Souvenir programmes such as this British Royal Aero Club publication for the 1929 Schneider Trophy are now fascinating records of an age of regular competition.

Left: Flight Lieutenant John Boothman being carried ashore after a practice flight for the 1931 Schneider Trophy. This practice aircraft, a Supermarine S.5, had come third in the 1929 competition.

Below: The only real rival to the Supermarines were the Italian Macchi-Castoldi seaplanes. In an MC.72 like this, Francesco Agello pushed the air speed record to 440mph (709.1kph) in 1934, a record that stood for five years.

BUILT FOR SPEED

Seaplanes were, at this time, the fastest aircraft in the world. The air speed record had been set at 318.6mph (512.7kph) by the Italian seaplane ace, Major Mario De Bernardi, in a Macchi M.52, in 1928. Two hours after Boothman's 1931 Schneider Trophy win, Flight Lieutenant George H. Stainforth made four flights along the 1.9 mile (3km) speed course above the Isle of Wight. In his downwind flight, he reached 389mph (732kph) in his S.6B. His average speed of 379.05mph (610.75kph) set a new world air speed record, and three weeks later he improved it to 407mph (655kph). This was one record the Italians were keen to regain. In April 1933, Warrant Officer Francesco Agello, flying

Below: This Curtiss CR.3 took first place in the 1923 competition held in the Isle of Wight. The American Lieutenant David Rittenhouse was the victorious pilot.

a Macchi-Castoldi MC.72 – the new design that had not been ready in time for the 1931 race – set a new air speed record of 423.8mph (682.1kph) flying over Lake Garda, and in October 1934, in the same aircraft, he pushed it up to 440mph (709.1kph), a record that stood until 1939.

NEW YORK TO PARIS

The search for new challenges and the pursuit of great prizes produced great public excitement. In 1926, Raymond Orteig offered $25,000 for the first non-stop flight between New York and Paris. One of the first challengers was the French aviator Captain René Fonck, whose Sikorsky aircraft broke up and burst into flames during take-off. Two more French challengers, Charles Nungesser and François Coli, set off on 9 May 1927 from Le Bourget in a Levavasseur biplane, but disappeared soon after being sighted off the coast of France.

The next man to take up the challenge was Charles Lindbergh, the 25-year-old son of a Minnesota Congressman. Lindbergh had dropped

Right: The need to carry as much fuel as possible meant that the *Spirit of St Louis* presented an unusual profile and looked ungainly in flight. Lindbergh erred on the side of caution and found that he still had large reserves of fuel on his arrival in Paris.

Below: Lindbergh was a reserved, serious-minded man who loved to fly. He made a living as an airmail pilot before persuading local businessmen in St Louis to finance his attempt on the Orteig prize. A highly appropriate means of commemorating his famous achievement was through special airmail stationery (**inset right**).

out of Wisconsin University to enrol in a flying school, and had made stunt-flying tours with a flying circus. Later, he worked as an airmail pilot, and persuaded a group of businessmen from St Louis to back him in a solo attempt upon the Orteig prize.

The aircraft manufacturer Ryan built a specially designed monoplane, the *Spirit of St. Louis,* based on the company's M2 and powered by a 220hp Wright Whirlwind engine. Its chief feature was the huge auxiliary fuel tank mounted in the forward fuselage which, along with the tanks in the wings, gave it a total fuel capacity of 448 gallons (2037 litres). There was one disadvantage, though; the pilot could see what lay ahead only by peering through a periscope or by leaning out of the window.

At 7.50 a.m. on 20 May 1927, Lindbergh took off from Roosevelt Field on Long Island. He only just cleared the trees at the end of the field, owing to the great weight of fuel he was carrying. After that, the aeroplane performed extremely well; Lindbergh's most serious problems were thirst and fatigue. All he had in the way of rations was a couple of sandwiches and two bottles of water; he had rejected the offer of a flask of coffee to take with him as a stimulant. At one point he began dozing off, and nearly crashed into the Atlantic, but at last he saw the Irish coast beneath him. He continued on to Paris, landing at Le Bourget at 10.30 p.m. on 21 May. He had covered around 3500 miles (5600km) in 33½ hours. To his annoyance, he later found he still had enough fuel in his tanks to have flown halfway across Central Europe.

POPULAR TRIUMPH

There was no thought of this on his arrival, though. In his book, *The Spirit of St Louis,* Lindbergh vividly recalled his landing in France, where some 50,000 people were waiting for him. 'I opened the door, and started to put my foot down onto the ground,' he wrote, 'but dozens of hands took hold of me – my legs, my arms, my body. No one heard the sentences I spoke. I found myself lying in a prostrate position, on top of the crowd, in the centre of an ocean of heads that extended as far out into the darkness as I could see. Then I started to sink down into that ocean, and was buoyed up again. Thousands of voices mingled in a roar … It was like drowning in a human sea.'

Lindbergh, who had not only made the first non-stop New York–Paris flight, but also the first solo Atlantic crossing, was suddenly one of the most famous people in the world, and his flight coincided with the beginning of a huge upsurge of interest in commercial aviation in the USA. Within just two years, the number of civilian air passengers in the country had increased sixfold, from 40,000 to around 250,000.

SHIPS OF THE AIR

Although the great pioneering flights such as Lindbergh's were made in aeroplanes, most people assumed at the time that the future of long-distance passenger flight lay with airships. In 1919, the British Navy took delivery of two hydrogen-filled airships, based on the German Zeppelin L.33, and called the R.33 and the R.34. Both made successful trips over Britain, and on 5 July the newspapers reported that the R.34 had left her shed in preparation for a 48-hour crossing to New York.

The first man to arrive in America from Britain by air was, therefore, Major Pritchard, who leapt from the R.34 over Roosevelt Field, Long Island, and descended by parachute to give handling instructions to the ground crew. The trip had, however, been disappointing from the point of view of commercial exploitation. There were several reasons for this: the Atlantic crossing had taken the airship 108 hours, more than the scheduled time of many liners; it had twice, over Newfoundland and Nova Scotia, been badly buffeted and blown off course by thunderstorms that were too high to have affected ocean-going liners; and it had arrived with just enough petrol for one hour's further flight.

General Maitland, her commander, wrote in his log that the dangers of the voyage had been greatly underestimated, and that in his opinion airships could not compete with liners in terms of either speed or safety until weather conditions over the Atlantic were more closely investigated. Nonetheless, the R.34 became the first aircraft of any kind to make a return flight across the Atlantic.

Above: Successful flights by the privately owned R.100 and the government-funded R.101 rekindled British interest in airships late in 1929, but these were doused by the crash of the R.101 a year later.

Below: The R.34 airship, built by the British government to test the potential of airships, made a return trip across the Atlantic in 1919, but the difficulties it encountered cooled British enthusiasm for airships for a while.

THE GOLDEN AGE OF AIRSHIPS

Ten years later the future of airships looked more promising. In August 1929, the *Graf Zeppelin* circled the world in 21 days. Then, on 2 October, journalists were wildly excited by their first view of the R.101, an airship commissioned by the British government. It was capable, thanks to its Beardmore Tornado Diesel engines, of flying at more than 80mph (125kph). Later in the year, the R.100, a privately built counterpart with Rolls-Royce Condor engines, made its first flight. This airship was designed by Barnes Wallis, later famous for designing the Wellington bomber and inventing the bouncing bomb that was used to destroy vital German dams in 1943. In the summer of 1930, the R.100 made a flight to Canada in just 72 hours, faster than any liner.

The British government hoped that the R.101 would prove still more successful, but on Sunday 4 October 1930, having set out the previous

Right: Germany took airship design further than any other country. The two airships named *Graf Zeppelin* brought several records and a great deal of prestige to the country. German airship production continued until the wreck of the *Hindenburg* in New Jersey in 1937 provided a graphic illustration of just how vulnerable these graceful and stately craft are to fire.

day on a flight to India, with the Air Minister Lord Thomson and other senior aviation figures on board, it was buffeted by a heavy rainstorm and crashed near Beauvais, in France. The hydrogen in the gas bags caught fire, and there were only six survivors. After this disaster, Britain stopped building airships, and the R.100 was scrapped.

Production continued for a few years in Germany, but the passenger-carrying potential of airships was dealt a death blow in 1937, when the *Hindenburg* burst into flames while mooring at Lakehurst, New Jersey, killing 33 passengers and crew in a disaster that was captured on newsreel and shown around the world.

EXPLORING BY AEROPLANE

There was no longer any doubt that the commercial future of passenger flight lay with aeroplanes. This threw into sharper focus the exploratory work being done by aviators such as Alan Cobham, who had pioneered several long-distance air routes, often by literally flying off into the unknown. Cobham, who was born in London in 1894, had learned to fly in the Royal Flying Corps in 1918. After the war ended, he spent two years 'barnstorming' at air shows in an Avro 504, and was then signed up as a test pilot by de Havilland.

In November 1924, Cobham turned his attention to the dangerous but exciting task of surveying new aeroplane routes. Together with Air Vice-Marshal Sir Sefton Brancker, he flew from London to India and back in a de Havilland D.H.50 biplane powered by a Siddeley Puma engine. The round trip took a total of 117 days.

A year later, Cobham set out for Cape Town in the same D.H.50, this time fitted with a 385hp air-cooled Armstrong Siddeley Jaguar engine. With him were his engineer, A. B. Elliot, and a cinematographer, B. W. Emmott. They stopped in Athens, where the engine was thoroughly overhauled and adjusted. On 6 December they set off again, and reached Khartoum on 22 December.

INTO THE UNKNOWN

From this point south, Cobham was constantly flying into the unknown. He had to fight his way through all kinds of adverse weather conditions, and navigate his way by compass across unfamiliar territory to find his way to the landing strips that he hoped had been prepared for him. He had had to make complex arrangements for refuelling before setting out: sometimes, cans of aviation spirit had to be carried to the landing strips by bands of porters, as there were no roads for miles around.

AMY JOHNSON

One of the most famous long-distance flyers was Amy Johnson, the daughter of a Hull businessman with Danish ancestry. In 1928, at the age of 25, she took up flying at London's Stag Lane Aerodrome, and on 9 June 1929 made her first solo flight. She then became the first woman to gain an Air Ministry ground engineer's licence, and by the beginning of 1930 had set her mind on breaking Bert Hinkler's record for a solo flight from England to Australia.

Sir Charles Wakefield proved a willing sponsor. He promised to pay for Johnson's petrol and enabled her to complete the purchase of *Jason*, a de Havilland Moth light aeroplane powered by a 100hp Gipsy engine. She took off from Croydon Aerodrome at 7.45 a.m. on 5 May, and landed that evening at Vienna. A stickler for detail, the first thing she did at each halt was to overhaul the Gipsy with her own hands. The time this took left her no more than three hours to sleep each night, yet she seemed to thrive on it, and remained fit and well. By 10 May she had reached Karachi, having knocked two days off Hinkler's record for a solo flight from England to India.

TECHNICAL TROUBLE

On 13 May, however, she ran into trouble. Unable to locate Rangoon, she landed on the Insein playing fields some 10 miles (16km) away. She made a perfect landing, but before the Moth came to a halt it ran into a ditch, smashing the wings, undercarriage and propeller. The necessary repairs delayed her for two days, and ended her hopes of beating

Left: A relaxed and confident Amy Johnson standing beside her aircraft at Croydon Aerodrome in 1930. As the first woman to make a solo flight from England to Australia, she became a celebrity.

Below: In more feminine attire, Amy Johnson was delayed in Rangoon when *Jason* was damaged on landing. This setback ended her hopes of bettering Hinkler's time.

Above: *Jason*, the de Havilland Moth in which Amy Johnson flew to Australia, is now on permanent display in the Science Museum in London.

Left: Amy Johnson's popularity following her flight in 1930 was so great that she received the ultimate accolade of having a song written in her honour.

Right: The professional flyer: above all, 'Johnnie' wanted to be respected as a pilot, not as an extraordinary woman.

Hinkler's time. She set off again on 16 May, and soon discovered that the new propeller allowed the engine to run too fast and guzzle up the fuel; it was only with great difficulty that she was able to cross the mountains between Rangoon and Bangkok to land on 17 May at Singgora in the Malay Peninsula.

There was a further delay when lack of fuel brought her down at Semerang, on Java, and she was forced to stay there while the wings of her machine were mended with sticking plaster. Finally, on 24 May, she

was able to cross the 500 miles (800km) of open sea between Timor and Port Darwin, where she touched down at 3.57 p.m.

MIXED FEELINGS

Although she had failed to beat the record, she was the first woman to make the trip. This was, though, not much of a consolation, according to a radio broadcast she made on her return to England. 'I am afraid,' she said, 'that my flight has received far more than its due in publicity. I admit that I am a woman, and the first one to do it … but in the future I do not want it to be unusual that women should do things; I want it to be recognized that women can do them.'

Now immensely popular, 'Johnnie' (as Johnson preferred to be known) continued to set flying records. For example, in 1931 she flew across Siberia to Tokyo, and the following year broke the record for a solo flight from

12 hours and 30 minutes in a de Havilland Puss Moth. He also flew the northern Atlantic from Ireland to New Brunswick in a light aeroplane, taking just over 30 hours, and flew direct from Croydon to Brazil. Then, in 1936, he set a new record for an Atlantic crossing, flying from Newfoundland to Croydon in 13 hours 16 minutes.

AROUND THE WORLD

Wiley Post was a colourful Texan aviator who broke many flying records. He is mostly remembered as the first man to fly solo around the world, or at least to fly around the northern hemisphere. On 23 June 1931, he set out from New York with a navigator, Harold Gatty, in the Lockheed Vega *Winnie Mae*. They took a route eastwards across the Atlantic, through Europe and the USSR, then over the Pacific to Alaska and Canada. In total, the two men took 8 days, 15 hours and 51 minutes to make the flight, and published an account of the trip called *Around the World in Eight Days*. Two years later, on July 15 1933, Post set out to do the same route again, but this time he flew solo. His journey, which beat his previous time by 21 hours, helped to establish the practical value of various experimental navigational instruments, including the automatic pilot. Post was killed in 1935, along with his passenger, the humorist Will Rogers, when he crashed in Alaska.

Above: Several pioneering flights were made by Jean Batten, a dentist's daughter from New Zealand, whose feats included the first solo flight between England and New Zealand and a north–south trip across the Atlantic from Britain to Brazil in just 13 hours 15 minutes.

Left: This Castrol advertisement of the late 1930s celebrates three women flyers, Jean Batten, Amy Johnson and Beryl Markham. Markham was the first woman to fly the North Atlantic solo from east to west, in September 1936.

Below: Wiley Post was a showman through and through. He did not believe in hiding his light under a bushel, and the aviation feats he performed in his Lockheed Vega, *Winnie Mae*, were emblazoned on the side of the aircraft.

England to Cape Town. During World War II, she joined the Air Transport Auxiliary as a pilot, and in January 1941, at the age of 37, she drowned in the Thames Estuary after baling out of an aeroplane that she was ferrying as part of her military duties.

Amy Johnson was married from 1932 to 1938 to another pioneer flyer, Jim Mollison. Mollison's first major record came in 1931, when he flew from Australia to England in little more than half Hinkler's time. The following year, he set a new London to Cape Town record of four days,

Above: Jim Mollison is pictured above in 1932, when, flying a de Havilland Puss Moth, he set a new record for the journey from London to Cape Town.

Right: Mollison and Amy Johnson married in 1932. In July 1933 they made the first direct flight by aeroplane from Britain to the USA. Here, they are making final plans before leaving Pendine Sands for New York.

Left: The Mollisons successfully crossed the Atlantic, passing over Newfoundland and Nova Scotia before landing, short of fuel, in marshy ground at Bridgeport, only 50 miles (80km) from their final destination. The machine was damaged but they were soon able to continue to New York and an enthusiastic welcome.

Above: Sir Charles Wakefield, an enthusiastic supporter of aviation achievements, sent this congratulatory telegram on hearing of Mollison's successful flight from Australia to England.

Above: The DC-3 was developed for American Airlines by the Douglas Aircraft Company following the success experienced by TWA with the DC-2.

Left: A luggage label for first-class flight, c.1937. Ten years after Lindbergh's transatlantic first, the name was still one to conjure with.

COMMERCIAL PROMISE

The successes of the aviation pioneers inspired both a great expansion in passenger flights and new designs of purpose-built passenger aircraft. One of the most famous passenger aeroplanes was the Ford Trimotor of 1925, which could carry up to 15 passengers. There was no need for anything much bigger. The Douglas DC-3, introduced in 1936, had room for 21 seated or 14 sleeper passengers.

By this time, Juan Trippe had launched Pan American Airways. It took him some time to come to an agreement about transatlantic routes, but on 5 July 1937 a Pan Am Sikorsky S-42 flew to Southampton, while a Short C Class Empire flying boat flew the other way to New York. Both aeroplanes were at the extreme limit of their capability, and the first proper scheduled transatlantic service was begun, by Pan Am's Boeing 314 Clipper fleet, only in the summer of 1939. The service was suspended within three months on the outbreak of World War II.

Above: Passengers on a Short C Class flying boat enjoy a civilized in-flight meal in spacious surroundings.

Below: In 1945, the Short Sandringham was the last flying boat in service. Its two-level interior was divided into cabins to preserve the luxurious feeling of sea travel.

Left: In July 1938, a Short S.21 Maia flying boat took off from Foynes in Ireland carrying a Short S.20 Mercury seaplane. The two then separated and the smaller plane flew on to Montreal, Canada, carrying mail.

THE JET ENGINE

As in the war of 1914–18, World War II gave a great impetus to technological development. In Britain, there was particular encouragement for a new means of propulsion for aeroplanes that had first been mooted by Frank Whittle in the 1920s.

Whittle had joined the RAF in 1923 at the age of 16, and was still a cadet at Cranwell, Lincolnshire, when he began thinking about gas-turbine propulsion. He felt that if an aeroplane were to fly very far and very fast, it would need to go very high, and conventional piston engines could not work efficiently in the thin air at great altitude. Besides, propellers were not suitable for speeds of more than 500mph (800kph).

His idea to get round this problem was to create an engine that pulled in air at the front and compressed it into combustion chambers. There, the injection and burning of fuel would heat and expand the air, giving it enough energy to drive a turbine. Whittle patented his 'jet engine' in 1930, but making a practical reality of his drawings and dreams was much

more difficult. Not only did he face the technical difficulties of designing a new kind of engine, but also enormous hostility to his work from the engineering and aeronautical establishment.

BUILDING AN ENGINE

Two years later, Whittle was granted leave of absence from his work as a test pilot, and in 1935 some private investors formed Power Jets Ltd, which enabled him to assemble a team to begin serious work.

As he was too poor to test components individually, Whittle and his team built a complete non-flying jet engine, which they finished in 1937. When Whittle switched on the new engine, the speed shot up so fast that it was soon out of control. Terrified members of his team ran for cover, but Whittle himself bravely remained behind to screw down the control valve. For a few more seconds the engine continued to accelerate, but at last it slowed down and stopped.

Despite this demonstration of the enormous potential power within a jet engine, the British Air Ministry remained largely unimpressed, but Whittle persevered. With the Germans developing a jet-powered aircraft – the prototype flew in 1939 – the Air Ministry relented. By May 1941, the jet-engined Gloster-Whittle E. 28/39 was undergoing trial flights. By the summer of 1944, the twin-engined Gloster Meteor jet fighter was in squadron service. At the same time, Whittle was being sidelined. Power Jets Ltd was nationalized in 1944, and he returned to the RAF. The following year, a Gloster Meteor powered by a pair of Rolls-Royce Derwent jet engines set a new world air speed record of 606.3mph (975.7kph), and in 1948, when Whittle left the Service, he was knighted.

FAST FIGHTERS

In the absence of the jet fighters that Whittle might have been able to produce had his ideas been encouraged earlier, the decisive British victory in the aerial battles of 1940 depended mainly on two traditionally powered fighters, the Hawker Hurricane and the Supermarine Spitfire. The Hurricane was a single-seat, low-wing monoplane that had made its maiden flight in 1937. Its main military asset was its great speed; it was the first British fighter to fly at more than 300mph (480kph).

Below: Frank Whittle pictured in 1948 in the room where he planned the RAF's first jet engine. In the foreground is a model of a Gloster Meteor I, the first British jet fighter in squadron service, which set a new air speed record in 1945.

Right: The rocket-powered fighter, the Messerschmitt 163B, was the fastest aircraft in World War II, though it was unstable at top speed and had other drawbacks. Its revolutionary swept-back wings and lack of a tail-plane influenced the design of a whole generation of fighter aircraft.

Below: Whittle is seen here explaining the principles behind his jet-engine design.

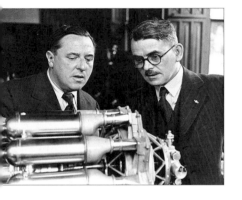

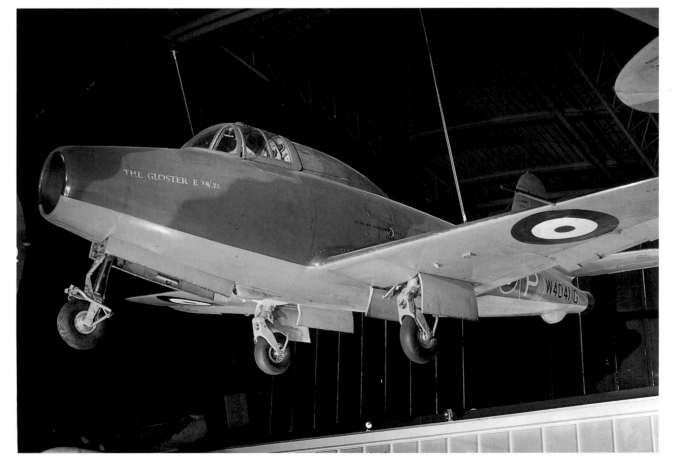

Left: The first British fighter to be fitted with a jet engine was the Gloster-Whittle E.28/39 (seen here in the Science Museum in London). Trial flights began in May 1941.

Above: The mainstays of the British war effort, particularly in the Battle of Britain of 1940, were the Hurricane (above) and the Spitfire, a direct descendant of the Supermarine seaplanes that had won the Schneider Trophy.

THE SPITFIRE

In the winter of 1934–5, a meeting with some German pilots had convinced designer R. J. Mitchell that war with Germany was inevitable. He had already begun to design a fighter aeroplane, the Supermarine Spitfire, and determined to complete it as quickly as possible. His Spitfire prototype flew on 6 March 1936, but the sustained effort involved took its toll on Mitchell's health, and he died of cancer the following year, aged 42.

The Spitfire was an all-metal cantilever low-wing monoplane, highly elegant, highly manoeuvrable and extremely fast, with a top speed of 349mph (562kph); one of its later versions, the Spitfire XIV, which had a Griffon engine, could attain 450mph (724kph). The Spitfire's original engine – a Rolls-Royce Merlin II or Merlin III – was an improved version of the Rolls-Royce R, built for Mitchell's Schneider Trophy racing aeroplanes. In the original model, it drove a two-blade, fixed-pitch wooden propeller; later Spitfires had a de Havilland three-blade, two-position, controllable-pitch metal propeller. The aeroplane's landing gear was retractable. The pilot, who sat in an enclosed cockpit, was always in touch with other pilots and with his base by radio, and had supplies of oxygen for flying at high altitude.

THE MESSERSCHMITTS

The fastest aeroplanes of World War II, though, were German; the Messerschmitt Me.163 Komet interceptor and the Messerschmitt Me.262. The first of these was rocket-powered and, on occasion, had an inadvertent brush with the sound barrier in level flight. However, the production models were limited to a maximum speed of 560mph (900kph) because of the problems experienced by the pilots when the Komet approached the speed of sound. With their swept-back wings and lack of a tail-plane, the Me.163s looked like nothing seen before. They

Above: The Me.262 was the first operational jet aircraft, taking to the skies in 1942, but, like the Gloster Meteor, it did not see service until two years later. The Me.262 was probably the first aircraft to achieve 500mph (800kph) in level flight.

Right: The Messerschmitt Me.163 Komet's swept-back wings inspired the de Havilland Comet 1, the jet airliner of the 1950s, and are still used today. The launching method of the rocket-powered interceptor also makes it an ancestor of the Space Shuttle.

first went into action in the summer of 1944, intercepting American bombers. Their rocket motors, which used a highly volatile mixture of hydrogen peroxide and a hydrazine hydrate solution in methanol, had a thrust of 6000hp, and they could climb at a staggering 14,000ft (4250m) per minute. Speed made the Me.163s alarming opponents, but their flight endurance under rocket power was only eight (later 12) minutes. They also had difficulty in closing with conventional aircraft, and were designed to take off from a jettisoned trolley and land on a skid. This meant that the aeroplane, although superb to fly, was highly dangerous to land.

The jet-engined Messerschmitt Me.262 was mass-produced from late 1944. Powered by two Jumo 004 engines, it was 100mph (160kph) faster than any other fighter of the time and was impossible to catch unless it was taken by surprise on take-off or landing. In July 1944, a high-speed version of the Me.262 achieved an unofficial world record when it flew at 624mph (1004kph), making it the fastest aeroplane in the world.

SOUND AND GLORY

1946–1959

For many countries, the late 1940s and 1950s were a time of rebuilding after the cataclysm of World War II. Austerity and rationing persisted in Europe long after the war ended. In Europe and the USA, the 1950s were politically and culturally conservative, although the middle of the decade saw in the emergence of rock 'n' roll the first stirrings of the youth culture that would stamp itself on the 1960s.

World politics in the late 1940s and 1950s was dominated by the Cold War between the USSR (at times backed by the new Communist regime in China) and the USA (plus its European partners in NATO). The Cold War was basically a heavily armed stand-off between two great powers with widely divergent philosophies. The fact that both possessed nuclear weapons – used by the USA to devastating effect in 1945 to bring World War II to an end – kept the whole world embroiled in their squabbles. Sometimes the squabbles intensified, notably in the Korean War of the early 1950s.

Just as the interwar years were a Golden Age for film and radio, so the 1950s saw the triumph of television. Many television programmes still came, like the majority of films, from the USA, which extended its cultural influence. Materialism was a keynote of the decade. The use of private cars increased steadily, while rail travel was boosted by electrification and the numbers of air passengers rose enormously as jet airliners took over many services.

Although air records came to be the exclusive province of military pilots in jet fighters, there was still scope for a handful of dedicated, wealthy or well-connected individuals to challenge the land and water speed records; both were taken to new heights in the 1950s. The main achievement of the period, though, was the opening up of a new frontier, outer space. Perhaps inevitably, the development of space travel in the USA and the USSR was fuelled by intense national rivalry as the empty reaches of space became a battleground in the Cold War.

Left: Frank Whittle's jet engine for the Gloster-Whittle E28/39, 1941. He had earlier conceived the idea of jet propulsion while writing a thesis on 'Future Developments in Aircraft Design'.

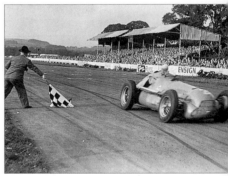

Left and above: When his head won over his heart, Giuseppe 'Nino' Farina was unbeatable. His greatest year was 1950, when he formed part of Alfa's famous 'Three Fs' team with Fangio and Fagioli. In his Tipo 158 he took the chequered flag in both his heat and the final of the International Trophy at Silverstone and went on to win the World Drivers' Championship.

LAND

SOUND AND GLORY 1946–1959

In much of the world, and particularly Europe, the immediate postwar period was one of reconstruction and austerity. Germany and Japan, helped by substantial American aid, were able to rebuild their industrial base from scratch, taking advantage of new technologies to become major players in the world economy by the 1960s. By contrast, in Britain the late 1940s and early 1950s were years of relative economic decline, and ones in which the Empire was broken up.

These years saw the start of the Cold War between the countries of NATO, dominated by the USA, and the communist bloc, dominated by the USSR and China. Although the Cold War tensions, particularly the fear that it would heat up into a nuclear holocaust, were real enough, in practice the world was a much safer, more secure place than it had been in the 1930s. Medical advances, notably the use of antibiotics and the development of effective vaccines against smallpox, polio and other serious diseases, had a profound effect, and almost everywhere in the West the 1950s were a decade of social stability, focused on the idea of the traditional family, and steadily increasing wealth.

RETURN TO RACING

Although private motorists had a lean time in the immediate postwar years, with fuel hard to come by in many countries, motor sport was relatively quick to recover from the devastation and disruption of World War II. In fact, the first 'postwar' motor-racing meeting in France, the Coupe de Paris, took place on 9 September 1945, three days before the surrender of Japan. Although all the cars and motorcycles entered were of pre-war vintage, the competition was fierce.

The Indianapolis 500 and European Grand Prix racing both resumed in 1946. The Indy 500 had been in decline in the 1930s, and the track had been unused in the war. A local businessman bought and renovated the weed-covered track, and the race was won by George Robson in the Thorne Sparks Special. After this, the sport grew again, as other tracks updated their surfaces and modernized in response to the increased amounts of leisure time and money in the booming American economy.

The first Grand Prix at St Cloud went to Raymond Sommer, driving a Maserati 4CL. Sommer was fortunate to win: the Alfa-Romeo 158s of Giuseppe Farina and Jean-Pierre Wimille were faster, but the cars developed clutch problems. For the next five years, though, the pre-war Alfa-Romeos would dominate Europe's racetracks.

FORMULA ONE

The nature of motor racing was changed with the creation in 1950 of a world championship for racing cars. The entry formula, Formula A – which became known as Formula One – called for single-seater cars powered either by 1.5-litre supercharged engines, such as Maseratis and Alfa-Romeos, or by 4.5-litre atmospheric-induction engines, such as Ferraris and French Talbots. The supercharged engines produced more power than their more conventional rivals, but consumed more fuel, requiring at least one more stop for refuelling.

UNBEATABLE ALFA

Alfa-Romeo's regular team in 1950 included three outstanding drivers; the Argentinian Juan Manuel Fangio and the Italians Giuseppe Farina and Luigi Fagioli. In their hands the Alfa-Romeos proved unbeatable. They were seriously challenged only twice; once by Raymond Sommer in his Talbot in the Belgian Grand Prix, and once by Alberto Ascari in his V-12 Ferrari Tipo 375 in the Italian Grand Prix.

In that final World Championship race at Monza, Farina – who had accumulated 22 points to Fangio's 26 and Fagioli's 24 – took the lead, but was soon being hard pressed by Ascari. For a while, Ascari went into the lead, but Farina re-passed him and the Ferrari's engine failed. Since drivers forced to retire were allowed to take over a team-mate's car, Ascari was soon back in the race, and the places; but it was Farina who won both the Italian Grand Prix and the 1950 World Championship. Alfa-Romeo repeated their victory a year later, when Fangio won the Drivers' Championship.

Right and below: Italy was the epicentre of racing in the 1940s and 1950s. At first, Alfa seemed invincible, but in 1951 Fangio (seen here in his Tipo 159 Alfetta in the German Grand Prix) started to come second to Ferrari.

Above and right: In the postwar period motorcycle racing was still an affordable sport for working people who competed as amateurs against works-supported riders such as Norton's Geoff Duke, seen here getting close to his public at the Junior TT on the Isle of Man in 1950s.

MOTORCYCLE CHAMPIONSHIPS

Motorcycle racing introduced its own World Championships in 1949, with classes for 125cc, 250cc, 350cc, 500cc solo and 500cc with sidecar. Early contests were dominated by the rivalry of the Italian Gilera and British Norton teams. In 1950, when the 500cc title went to Umberto Masetti on a Gilera, he was hard pressed all the way by an enormously talented young Norton rider, Geoffrey Duke.

Duke's machine, nicknamed the 'Featherbed' because it was so comfortable to ride, was designed by Rex McCandless and incorporated a revolutionary frame that set new standards in road-holding. Before the 1951 season began, McCandless improved the frame, while a few more

horsepower were coaxed from the Norton engine. The Gilera still had the edge in speed over the Norton on a straight run, but Duke's riding ability, combined with the superior road-holding of the Norton, more than made up for this advantage, and he won both the 500cc and the 350cc World Championships.

Next year, Duke retained his 350cc title, but Masetti regained the 500cc World Championship. This convinced Duke that to have a chance at the 500cc title he would have to switch to Gilera . In 1953 his decision was vindicated when he regained the 500cc title on an Italian machine. Nortons now reigned supreme only on the tortuous Isle of Man course, where in 1953 they scored their tenth Junior and Senior 'double'. Ray Amm was in the saddle, and in 1954 he won the Senior TT again.

BLAZE OF GLORY

Duke rode his Gilera to the 500cc world title in both 1954 and 1955, when he also gained his third victory in the Senior TT. In 1956, his hopes of winning a fourth world title in a row were shattered when he was suspended from racing after acting as a spokesman for private riders in a dispute over starting money in the Dutch TT. The following year, a crash in a pre-season race put Duke out of action for three months, and at the end of 1957 Gilera decided to quit racing. Despite Duke's incapacity, the Gileras finished their racing years in a blaze of

glory; Libero Liberati won their sixth 500cc world title, while Bob McIntyre took both the Senior and Junior TTs and became the first to lap the Isle of Man Mountain Circuit at more than 100mph (160kph.

The World 500cc Moto-cross Championship began in 1957. Moto-cross, the most physically demanding form of motorcycle racing, is an exciting spectator sport that continues to grow in popularity. Competitors race around courses that run 1-3 miles (1.5-5km) over open ground that includes steep rises and falls, tight turns and even boggy patches. The winner of the first championship was Sweden's Bill Nilsson, riding an AJS 7R racing machine.

Above right: Umo Masetti was the top Gilera driver in the early 1950s, before Geoff Duke switched from Norton. He is seen here riding in the Spanish Grand Prix of 1952, the year he took the 500cc title from Duke.

Right: Although the Norton was seldom a match for the faster Italian Gileras on the racetrack in the 1950s, it still reigned supreme on the winding switchback course of the TT races on the Isle of Man, where Ray Amm took his Norton to consecutive wins in the Senior event in 1953 and 1954, coupled with a Junior TT title in 1953.

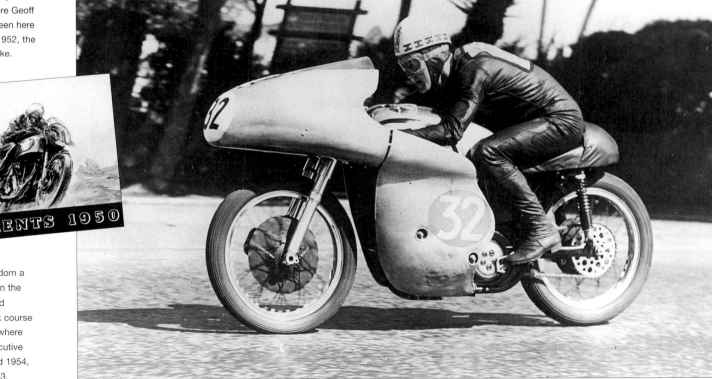

Opposite: Alberto Ascari, of the Ferrari team, races to victory in the 1953 Belgian Grand Prix at Francorchamp.

Left: Giuseppe Farina, Alberto Ascari and Piero Taruffi – three of Italy's finest racing drivers of the 1950s.

The Drivers' Championship also went from strength to strength in the 1950s, though Formula One racing was occasionally in the doldrums. This followed an announcement that the formula was to be altered from 1.5-litre to 750cc supercharged, and 4.5-litre to 2.5-litre atmospheric-induction. This was meant to encourage the development of engines without superchargers, making Grand Prix racing more relevant to production-car engineering.

Alfa-Romeo had abandoned Formula One at the end of their highly successful 1951 racing season; the Alfettas had been improved to the limits of their performance. The Ferraris were left with no real competition, and when the BRM team withdrew before the start of a non-championship race at Turin early in 1952, Ferrari had a walkover.

FORMULA TWO

The Fédération Internationale de l'Automobile had, however, announced a Formula B – soon known as Formula Two – in 1948 for 2-litre (500cc supercharged) engines. The supercharged option was never taken up, but Formula Two races with cars powered by 2-litre engines rapidly became popular. In the absence of any credible challenger to Ferrari at Formula One level, promoters switched their focus to Formula Two racing, and the FIA agreed that, for the next two years, winners of Formula Two races would gain points towards the world championship.

Although Ferrari remained dominant, with Alberto Ascari winning the Drivers' Championship in 1952 and 1953, there were some exciting races, as they faced fierce opposition from Maserati. In the meantime, the old Formula One was effectively put into cold storage, while motor manufacturers began working on cars that would be able to compete when the new Formula One came into operation in 1954.

NEW MERCEDES

Mercedes-Benz were one of these manufacturers. They had reopened their racing department in 1950, and by 1952 were busily designing their new Grand Prix car, the W196. It was a magnificent piece of engineering: its engine, with eight cylinders in line, developed 280bhp and was the first Grand Prix racing car to have fuel-injection. The engine was fitted into the space-frame chassis on its side, at 37° to the

Above: The Mercedes team of Fangio and Kling carried all before it in the mid-1950s. Fangio is seen here at the 1955 Monaco Grand Prix in a specially modified W196; the wheelbase was shortened and the car made lighter to suit the course's tight turns.

Left: Fangio, Kling and Moss are reunited with one another and their cars of yesteryear at the Mercedes-Benz test track at Unterturkheim, near Stuttgart, Germany, in 1990.

horizontal. This allowed the body to be constructed with a low frontal area, to reduce wind resistance.

The car was not ready in time for the first Grand Prix races of 1954, but Fangio, who had joined three German drivers – Karl Kling, Hans Herrmann and Hermann Lang – in the Mercedes racing team, built up a number of championship points by winning the Buenos Aires and Belgian Grands Prix in Maseratis.

On 4 July 1954, over 100,000 spectators lined the extremely fast French Grand Prix circuit at Reims – made up of normal public roads in the country round the city – to see the W196 make its racing debut. The Mercedes cars, with their full-width streamlined silver bodies covering their wheels, looked sensational and performed brilliantly. Fangio took pole position on the starting grid – and won 50 bottles of champagne – by ushering his Mercedes round the circuit at approximately 125mph (200kph).

When the race began, Fangio and Kling shot in front, and in the eleventh lap Hans Herrmann, in the third W196, passed the Ferrari of the Argentinian Froilan González ('The Pampas Bull') to put the

Above: Fangio described the Mercedes W196 as 'The perfect car, a sensational machine that drivers dream about all their lives.' In 1955, Fangio drove this one to the World Championship.

German cars into first, second and third places. A lap later, González was back in third place, but then his engine caught fire and he had to retire. He was followed shortly afterwards by Herrmann, who had over-revved his engine. Herrmann had the consolation of having clocked the fastest lap at 121.5mph (195.5kph), while Fangio and Kling fought out the race; Fangio beat his team-mate by just 0.2 seconds.

FERRARI STRIKES BACK

Two weeks later, at Silverstone in England, the Mercedes were beaten by Ferrari. The all-enveloping bodies of the 'Silver Arrows' prevented the drivers from seeing exactly where they were placing their front wheels, and Fangio and Kling came in fourth and seventh. However, in the German Grand Prix at Nürburgring, with new, conventional bodywork that was finished the day before the race, Mercedes were unbeatable. Fangio won convincingly before a crowd of 350,000, and won again in Switzerland and Italy to become World Champion.

At the Monza Grand Prix, Fangio had been given a fright by a young British driver in a Maserati 250F. Stirling Moss had led the field by as much as 22 seconds until an oil pipe burst. This demonstration of his skill led to his being asked to join Mercedes-Benz for 1955, when the team won the Grands Prix in Argentina, Belgium, the Netherlands,

Right: Fangio first came to the notice of Mercedes in 1951, when he drove this 1939 W154/163 to victories in Argentina. The car is currently displayed in the Daimler-Benz Museum in Stuttgart, Germany.

Below: Fangio did not confine himself to Formula One. He is seen here in a Maserati 300S, probably the best-handling sports racer of the 1950s.

Britain and Italy. Fangio was again the individual World Champion. At the end of the season, however, Mercedes-Benz decided to withdraw from motor racing. Fangio went to Ferrari, to drive a modified Lancia D-50, and Moss found a new home with Maserati.

FIRST SIGHTING OF THE BRM

The competition between the two men kept interest in motor-racing at a high pitch in 1956, which also saw the debut of the British BRM P25, driven mainly by 27-year-old Mike Hawthorn. Although Hawthorn displayed genius as a driver, the car was not so dependable, and Fangio won his fourth World Championship with 30 points, three ahead of Moss.

NEW ALLIANCES

In 1957, Fangio moved to Maserati and Hawthorn became one of the Ferrari team. Moss joined Anthony Vandervell, an industrialist and former racing driver who had begun funding racing cars under the 'Vanwall' name in 1954. Hawthorn had a relatively undistinguished season, though he managed one second place and a third. Moss took over team-mate Tony Brooks's Vanwall, after his own engine began to fail, to win the British Grand Prix at Aintree in 1957. Later in the year, he also won at Pescara and Monza, but once again it was Fangio who dominated the World Championship, with victories in Buenos Aires, Monte Carlo and Rouen before the decisive race at the Nürburgring.

SPEED AND TACTICS

Fangio knew that his Maserati 250F could not complete the 312-mile (500km) race at Nürburgring without refuelling, while the Ferrari 801s of Hawthorn and Peter Collins – the only serious contenders on a track too rough for the Vanwalls – could carry enough for the entire distance. He therefore began with enough for just four laps, so he could get a substantial lead while his car was far lighter than those of his opponents. Fangio was well ahead when he went into the pits, but

the wheel change accompanying the refuelling was slowed down by the loss of a hub nut. When he rejoined the race, his 30-second lead had turned into a 45-second deficit. It was not until the 16th lap that Fangio began closing the gap to Hawthorn and Collins, narrowing it to 33 seconds. Two laps later it was down to 13 seconds, and by lap 20 Fangio was only two seconds behind Collins. On the very last lap the Argentinian got past both drivers to win by just over 3½ seconds.

FANGIO'S FIFTH

This victory clinched Fangio's fifth World Championship – a record that still stands – at the age of 46. In a remarkable career, he amassed 24 Grand Prix wins – in just 51 races – a total that was not surpassed until the late 1960s, by the Scot Jim Clark. Alfred Neubauer, the legendary team boss of Mercedes-Benz's racing department, summed up the Argentinian's skill and courage. 'Even when it was raining Fangio didn't care,' he said. 'He was like a bull on the racetrack, a bull with troubles in his head, and with enormous strength. You could throw bottles at him and he'd still drive cheerfully through.'

The 1958 motor-racing season was chiefly notable for a surprising victory by Stirling Moss. Since the Vanwall team was not ready in

Top left: Stirling Moss is universally regarded as the best driver of the 1950s never to have won the World Championship.

Top right: Fangio did not race in Europe until he was 37 years old. Even when he retired ten years later he still had remarkable stamina to add to his uncanny skill. He is seen here at the 1955 Belgian Grand Prix.

Left: Fangio won the 1957 German Grand Prix, and so clinched the championship, after an epic tussle at the Nürburgring with Mike Hawthorn and Peter Collins. 'I'll never drive like that again,' he acknowledged after the race, 'not for any trophy or title.'

Above: At the Nürburgring in 1990, Fangio is reunited with the Maserati 250F in which he won his famous victory in 1957.

Left: Stirling Moss sits on the grid in his Vanwall at the British Grand Prix at Aintree in 1957, the year he joined Anthony Vandervell's team.

time for the Argentine Grand Prix, Moss won the race for a private owner, Rob Walker, driving a mid-engined Cooper T43 with a 1.9-litre Climax engine. Many racing journalists regarded this victory as a flash in the pan, but in fact the Cooper Climax proved, in design terms, to be the precursor of the modern racing car.

Moss went on to win two more Grands Prix that year, but was beaten to the World Championship by Hawthorn, who was driving for Ferrari. Hawthorn was helped to the Championship by Moss, who sportingly gave evidence on his behalf when Hawthorn was in danger of losing points and being wrongly disqualified on a technicality at the end of the Moroccan Grand Prix. Moss did, though, help Vanwall to win the Manufacturers' Championship.

LAST OF THE GREAT ROAD RACES

Road races were also popular in the postwar years. One of the greatest was Mexico's Carrera Panamericana, first run in 1950 to celebrate the official opening of the 2180-mile (3500km) Mexican section of the Pan-American highway, which runs from Alaska to Cape Horn. The saloon car class was dominated by Lincoln, who won it in 1952 and 1953 with sprint car ace Chuck Stevenson, and in 1954 with Ray Crawford. The sports car class was won in 1952 by Karl Kling in a Mercedes 300SL, in 1953 by Fangio in a Lancia D24 and in 1954 by Umberto Maglioli in a 4.9-litre Ferrari 375 Plus. After this race, in which the total number of lives lost – spectators and drivers – since the contest began reached 20, the Mexican government ended the series.

ITALIAN FAVOURITES

Two old favourite events, the Mille Miglia and the Targa Florio, were revived. The first postwar Mille Miglia, run on the Italian mainland in

June 1947, was won by Clemente Biondetti in an Alfa-Romeo. In April 1948, Biondetti also won the first postwar Targa Florio, this time driving for Ferrari, and less than a month later he won his second Mille Miglia, driving a V-12 Tipo 166 sports car for Ferrari.

A succession of drivers, including Giannino Marzotto, Luigi Villoresi and Giovanni Bracco, gave Ferrari victory in the Mille Miglia each year until 1954, when Alberto Ascari won in a Lancia. In 1955, Mercedes-Benz launched a major challenge, with a strong team that included Moss and the more experienced Fangio, each at the wheel of a 310-bhp Mercedes 300SLR. Fangio drove alone, but Moss had beside him his navigator, Denis Jenkinson, a British journalist with whom he had made the most meticulous preparations.

Above and right: The 1955 Mille Miglia was won by Stirling Moss, with Denis Jenkinson navigating. This shot of the winning car, taken early in the race, shows debris already beginning to collect in its radiator air inlet.

Left: In 1954 the pre-war land speed record-holder George Eyston, a Castrol director, made an attempt on the Mille Miglia with a team sponsored by the company.

Together they had prepared, on a roll of paper, detailed notes about every twist and turn of the course. As they came up to each bend or rise in the road, Jenkinson was able to signal to Moss, telling him whether, for example, he could go straight on at top speed over a rise, or use a lower gear and prepare for a turn. The strategy was successful: Moss raced to victory in a record time of ten hours, seven minutes and 48 seconds.

Mercedes-Benz withdrew from racing at the end of the season, and in 1956 and 1957 the Mille Miglia went once more to Ferraris, driven by Eugenio Castellotti and Piero Taruffi respectively. Taruffi's victory was, though, overshadowed by a terrible crash during the race. Alfonso de Portago was travelling at around 120mph (190kph) when one of his tyres burst, causing his Ferrari to career into the crowd. Both he and his co-driver were killed, as were 11 spectators, five of them children. The outcry that followed was so great that the Mille Miglia was never run again. One by one the great road races were being abandoned for safety reasons. Only the Targa Florio remained; it lingered on until 1973, when the final race was watched by some 750,000 people.

STOCK CAR RACING

Two comparatively new forms of motor racing, stock car and drag, spread across the USA after World War II, then throughout the world. Stock-car racing is said to have originated in the 'souped-up' cars used by gangsters to smuggle whiskey across state borders in the Prohibition era of the 1920s. At first, the races involved hard-living amateurs who hobby-raced ordinary cars (taken from 'stock') at weekends.

These hazardous and sometimes sensational contests were informal. They took place in a number of locations, some more official than others, but found a home in Daytona, Florida. The last land speed record attempt on the Daytona sands was made in 1936, and the local businessmen, looking for a fresh attraction to pull in tourists, built a stock-car racing course that included the sands and a parallel road. In 1947, a governing body was established for the sport: the National Association for Stock Auto Racing (NASCAR) was founded by 'Big' Bill France and established the Winston Cup as its major trophy.

THE DAYTONA SPEEDWAY

In 1959 a permanent speedway with steep 31° banking was opened at Daytona. The season-opening Daytona 500 has been NASCAR's most

Above: The driver sits behind the rear wheels in this dragster, which has a supercharged V8 engine and a Fiat Topolino body shell.

Below: This early 'Lakester' dragster combined a Ford chassis and a tuned Ford V8 engine with a simple, lightweight body.

Above: After World War II, auxiliary fuel tanks originally destined for use on aircraft became available as war surplus, and proved to have the perfect streamlined shape for the body of a hot rod.

prestigious event ever since. The first race there, for the Winston Cup, was particularly exciting. John Beauchamp, in a Ford Thunderbird, was declared the winner in a close finish, but three days later, after studying the photos, the judges changed their mind. Lee Petty, driving an Oldsmobile, was awarded the cup for the third time since 1954.

ON THE DRAG STRIP

Drag racing began on the streets and in the deserts of postwar Southern California, where teenagers raced each other illegally at night in 'hot-rods', ordinary cars whose engines had been tuned for maximum acceleration. The police lobbied for formal race meetings to be held, and the National Hot Rod Association (NHRA) was established in 1951. Drag racing, the principal form of hot-rod racing, was formalized as a rapid-acceleration contest in which two cars at a time raced against each other (from a standing start) over a straight, flat, 440-yard (400m) track.

Above: Built in 1955, the prototype Deltic proved so efficient in trials that British Rail ordered another 22 of them to replace 55 steam locomotives on the East Coast line between London and Edinburgh.

NEW-LOOK RAILWAYS

Such fabulous speeds were very remote from the experience of the great mass of people, even the minority who could afford to run private motor cars. The electrification of major railway lines was a far more significant development to most of them. Electric trains were more efficient than steam, but electrification meant substantial capital investments followed by high maintenance costs. Electrified railways depended on extremely heavy passenger traffic, as found in, say, Japan or England.

As electric locomotives do not have to actually generate motive power, but draw it instead from a third rail or overhead cable, they can call on central resources when extra power is most needed, as in starting a heavy train or pulling it up a steep gradient. The efficiency of the electric system was proved on 28 March 1955, when French electric locomotive CC7107, pulling a three-coach train of 98.4 tons (100 tonnes), travelled for 1.2 miles (1.9km) at a world record speed of 205.6mph (330.9kph) on the Bordeaux–Hendaye line. The very next day, another French electric locomotive, BB9004, equalled this record.

DIESEL-ELECTRIC LOCOMOTIVES

Electrification was not the only alternative to steam. Where it was impractical or uncommercial to electrify a route, steam locomotives were gradually replaced as the standard type of railway engine by diesel-electric locomotives, or diesels. These locomotives have diesel-fuelled compression-ignition engines, which run a generator to produce the electricity that in turn powers the traction motors. They are basically a form of electric locomotive that carries its own power source with it.

Diesels were widely used first in North America and then found a home in Europe, where they were widely welcomed as much more economic than steam engines. For example, they required less fuel to produce the same amount of power, since their thermal efficiency was approximately four times as great; this meant that the average shunting engine could run for days without refuelling. Diesels also needed far less servicing than steam engines, and in certain circumstances could run faster while causing less damage to the track, although their top speeds were generally below those of the top steam express trains.

This meant that diesel-electric locomotives were mainly used for hauling freight trains or shunting rolling stock, although diesel-electric units were used for local rail traffic. Following the withdrawal from service of Gresley's streamlined A4-class Pacific steam locomotives in Britain, the important East Coast line between London and Edinburgh was usually served by diesel-electric 'Deltic' engines. The locomotives of this series were fitted with two engines and generators giving 3300hp, and Deltics could maintain speeds of 100mph (160kph).

Below: On 29 March 1955, BB9004, a French Boyer 30697 double electric locomotive, equalled the record of 205.6mph (330.9kph) set the previous day by CC7107.

Right: In North America, private cars and commercial aircraft began to depress passenger numbers on the railways, which turned increasingly to freight, hauled by huge, efficient but visually unexciting electric and diesel locomotives.

Many large passenger liners were refitted and converted into troop transports or merchant ships during World War II. Several of them had been lost, including the *Rex*, the *Bremen*, the *Conte di Savoia* and, largest of them all, the French *Normandie*, which capsized in New York harbour in 1942 under the weight of water that had been pumped aboard to put out a fire.

As soon as the war was over, those vessels that had survived their period of service were quickly reconverted to liners. Cunard's *Queen Mary* and *Queen Elizabeth* were operating a weekly service between New York and Southampton – successfully promoted under the slogan 'Come to Britain' – in 1946. Before long they were reckoned to be earning over $50 million per year in foreign exchange for Britain, and the administration of US President Harry S. Truman decided to act.

THE *UNITED STATES*

Truman commissioned William Francis Gibbs to design a passenger liner to be known as the *United States*. Her keel was laid in February 1950. Although she was designed to be much the same size as the Cunard transatlantic liners, she was around 35 per cent lighter in the water. This was because her entire superstructure – and even the lifeboats and their oars – was made of light aluminium alloy, the first time this had been done. Apart from the weight advantages, aluminium suited Gibbs's almost obsessional determination that the ship should have no flammable wooden fittings; the *Normandie* disaster was still fresh in everyone's mind. Gibbs could not persuade Steinway to make him an aluminium grand piano, but in due course he would be able to boast that the only other wooden items on board the ship were the butcher's blocks.

The *United States* had two vast funnels and was powered by four sets of Westinghouse turbines which, at maximum revolutions, could deliver 240,000 shaft horsepower. On her trials, the *United States* reached as much as 40 knots (74kph), a speed which compared very favourably with the maximum of around 31 knots (57kph) achieved by the *Queen Mary* and *Queen Elizabeth*.

WINNING THE BLUE RIBAND

Despite appalling weather, the *United States* set out to win the Blue Riband for the fastest crossing of the Atlantic on her maiden voyage in July 1952. The record had been held by the

Left: The transatlantic crossing was the main prestige route in world passenger shipping, and attracted state-of-the-art liners. The Cunard line's *Queens* held sway until 1952, when the *United States* – seen here coming into dock in New York – was launched and immediately beat the record for the fastest crossing.

Above: This cutaway illustration shows the extraordinary complexity of a luxury ocean-going liner – in this case the *Queen Mary* – from the engines and boiler rooms below the water-line through steerage and various public rooms to the rarefied atmosphere of the upper decks and the first-class staterooms.

Queen Mary since August 1938, when she had crossed from west to east in three days, 21 hours and 48 minutes at an average speed of 31 knots (57.4kph), and from east to west in 3 days, 20 hours and 42 minutes at an average 31.7 knots (58.7kph).

From the first, the *United States* went at such a rate that it was clear she would take the Blue Riband. Many of her passengers, including President Truman's daughter Margaret, stayed up for an all-night party on the last day of the voyage. They were still dancing when, at 6.15 am, Margaret Truman sounded the ship's whistle to announce that the record had been broken. The *United States* had raced across the Atlantic in 3 days, 10 hours and 40 minutes, averaging 35.6 knots (65.9kph). She made the return journey in three days, ten hours and 40 minutes: not quite so fast, but still the quickest east-west crossing.

The resultant publicity ensured she was solidly booked months in advance. The total number of people crossing the Atlantic by ship climbed steadily year by year, from 500,000 in 1948 to around 800,000 in 1952, and continued to grow until 1958, when it was well over a million. The heyday of the great passenger liners was, though, coming to an end as it peaked; the number of people making the transatlantic crossing by air was also increasing steadily, from around 250,000 in 1948 to 500,000 in 1952. By 1958, close to a million people were flying, and the next year, for the first time, more travelled by air than by sea.

SCIENTIFIC EXPLORATION

Some extraordinary feats were performed in smaller craft in the 1940s and 1950s. The best publicized, and perhaps most important, was that of the Norwegian anthropologist Thor Heyerdahl, who had developed a theory that South American Indians might have used prevailing winds and currents to settle Polynesia. In 1947, he proved his theory was practicable by building a balsa-wood raft, the *Kon-Tiki,* and sailing it – accompanied by five men and a parrot – from Peru to Tahiti.

Another man with an inquiring scientific mind and adventurous experimental spirit, Dr Alain Bombard, set out in 1952 to prove that it was possible to live on and off the sea. He spent 12 days drifting across the eastern Atlantic from Casablanca to Las Palmas in a 15ft (4.5m) rubber raft with no food or water supplies on board, and a further 65 days from there across the Atlantic to Barbados. In this time – apart from one occasion when he was tempted to eat a modest meal on a passing ship – he lived entirely on plankton, fish and rainwater.

UNDER SAIL

In August 1953, Anne Davison became the first woman to sail single-handed across the Atlantic. She made the trip in the *Felicity Ann,* a 23ft (7m) wooden sloop that carried only 237sq ft (22sq m) of sail.

Although yacht racing remained popular, no fresh challenger for the America's Cup could be found until 1958. Suitable boats were getting far too expensive to build. One British yacht, David Boyd's *Sceptre,* was built for the competition and sailed by Graham Mann, but it was not good enough to match the defender, Olin Stephens's *Columbia,* which was sailed by Briggs Cunningham.

Above: Anne Davidson was the first woman to sail single-handed across the Atlantic, She is seen here in her little sloop *Felicity Ann* after her journey, which began on 18 May 1952 and ended on 13 August the following year.

WATER SPEED RECORD

The world water speed record had been set in August 1939 by Sir Malcolm Campbell, and currently stood at 141.7mph (225.6kph). Sir Malcolm died in December 1948. The following spring, Henry J. Kaiser announced that he was building a boat, *Aluminium First,* in which he intended to regain the record for the United States. When he heard about this, Sir Malcolm's son, Donald, went to Coniston Water in the English Lake District with an improved *Bluebird,* to undertake a fresh attempt of his own.

Donald Campbell attached a St Christopher medallion to the instrument panel of *Bluebird.* His father had been given it by a well-wisher, and it accompanied him in all his record attempts. In August 1949, Donald Campbell came within 2mph (3.2kph) of his father's record established ten years earlier. Kaiser's attempt on the record ended in failure, and Campbell was back at Coniston Water in June 1950 with a new propeller and propeller shaft on *Bluebird.*

While he was there, the news broke that another American, Stanley Sayres, had smashed the world water speed record. Sayres, a car dealer from Seattle, built *Slo Mo Shun IV* purely for speed. Powered by an Allison engine, the 28ft (8.3m) *Slo Mo Shun IV* had an idling speed of

Right: The world's first nuclear-powered vessel, the submarine *Nautilus*, was launched in 1955. Three years later it made the first voyage under the ice-cap of the North Pole.

50mph (80kph). The main reason the boat could move so fast was that it was a 'prop-rider'. Boats normally ride on their two forward planes and the transom, but at speeds of around 140mph (225kph) the transom lifts, and the third point of support becomes the propeller – hence 'prop-riding'. The boat runs with the propeller shaft and one blade of the propeller clear of the water, and runs faster because there is less water resistance.

PROP-RIDERS

Convinced that *Slo Mo Shun IV*'s time could never be bettered by a conventional speedboat, Campbell and co-designer Leo Villa remade *Bluebird* as a prop-rider. This involved, among other things, moving the engine forward 6ft (2m), forging a new rudder and altering the angle of the two forward planes. When they were ready, they tried out *Bluebird* and found her 'steady as a rock' at over 150mph (240kph). On the second run, she reached 170mph (275kph), then hit a submerged log and sank. Campbell was uninjured, but his craft had to be stripped of her machinery before she could be refloated; and there seemed to be no point in rebuilding her when John Cobb was close to making his own attempt on the record in his jet-powered boat *Crusader*.

In the event, it was Sayres who raised the record. As his rivals followed his prop-rider design, Sayres found it expensive keeping ahead of the pack. 'What started out as a hobby,' he complained, 'is beginning to

Left and right: The futuristic lines of John Cobb's jet-powered *Crusader* spoke of its enormous speed but did not help its stability. Cobb was going at around 30 per cent faster than the previous record when *Crusader* broke up around him.

Below: Donald Campbell at Coniston Water on 2 July 1950 in the conventional *Bluebird* that preceded the jet-propelled *K7*. Below is the co-designer, Leo Villa.

turn me into a slave.' A public fund, the Greater Seattle Incorporated, was set up to support him. Some of the money went on giving *Slo Mo Shun IV* a new G-16 Allison engine, and on 7 July 1952, with 2000 people watching from the shore, Sayres and chief mechanic Elmer Leinschmidt increased the record to 178.5mph (287.3kph).

TRAGEDY ON THE LOCH

John Cobb chose Scotland's Loch Ness for his first attempt on the world water speed record. The futuristic *Crusader* had enormous potential power in her jet engines. On its first official run across the lake, on 29 September 1952, she was travelling at around 240mph (385kph) when she suddenly disintegrated, killing Cobb.

News of this tragedy spurred Campbell to fresh efforts. He had already decided to build a new *Bluebird* to pursue the Harmsworth Cup, which had been in American hands ever since 1920, and was now even more determined to go after the world record. With the help of the engineers Lewis and Kenneth Norris, Campbell and Villa planned a new, jet-propelled craft. First, they studied and analyzed the films and photographs of Cobb's runs on Loch Ness to help them design a new shape. They decided that the boat should be entirely built of alloy, making it light but strong, and Campbell secured the help of Saunders-Roe, who had built the first *Bluebird* for his father back in 1937.

A NEW *BLUEBIRD*

In 1953, a rocket-powered, radio-controlled model was built and tested, first in the Saunders-Roe experimental tank and then on a lake, but Saunders-Roe were unhappy about building a full-scale boat around the Beryl jet that Campbell favoured. Campbell and his team decided to design the new boat themselves – with the co-operation of the Beryl's designers, Metropolitan-Vickers – and somehow raise the capital to have it built. On 26 November 1954, the new *Bluebird* was shown publicly for

Above: The Norris brothers, Lewis and Kenneth, seen here flanking Donald Campbell, were involved in the design of *Bluebirds* for Campbell's attempts on both land and water speed records.

Left: At Coniston Water in autumn 1956, mechanics (Villa is in the centre) prepare the jet-powered *Bluebird K7* for Campbell's new assault on the world water speed record.

Below: Campbell's attempts to emulate and perhaps surpass his father's achievements on land and water made him a celebrity in the 1950s and 1960s, when his various *Bluebirds* were the last word in streamlined power and dash.

Above: Campbell finally took the water speed record he had sought so long in July 1955, when *Bluebird K7* performed perfectly in its two runs on Ullswater to register an average speed in excess of 200mph (320kph).

the first time at an official ceremony. She was far from ready to make a record attempt, but a further appeal for cash brought promises of help from C.C. Wakefield and Co Ltd and others, and Campbell was ready for his first trial run in England's Lake District in February 1955.

Five more months of trials and modifications gave Campbell the confidence that *Bluebird* had sufficient stability and thrust to establish a new record. On 23 July, he made an official attempt on Ullswater. The sky was heavy with grey clouds, and the lake looked forbidding, but Campbell, wearing a blue silk suit with a built-in lifejacket, and carrying a helmet and mask given to him by the test pilot Neville Duke, stepped

into the cockpit of *Bluebird K7* at around midday. Soon he was speeding towards the beginning of the measured run.

'Accelerating fast,' he recalled, 'we hit the measured course. Going very fast indeed – fairly rocketing into space. Now pay attention. Keep on track. Must keep into the middle. Wind comes down and catches the boat. Sliding away slightly. Bring her back, not too fast. Gently, gently, gently, gently. Back again, back again. Not too much, you'll over-correct.

'We're in the middle. Have a look at the air speed indicator. My godfathers – the needle's off the clock!'

Campbell completed his first run in 10.4 seconds and his second in 11.8 seconds, giving an average speed of 325.6kph (202.3mph) and a new world water speed record. After six years of 'bitter disappointment, frustration and hard work' it was a substantial triumph.

AIR

After the end of World War II, the advances that had been made in military technology began to be applied to more peaceful pursuits. New aeroplanes quickened the pace of air travel and brought down its cost, leading to a dramatic increase in passenger traffic. Pan Am soon resumed its transatlantic passenger flights. By the late summer of 1946 it had been joined by American Overseas Airlines, TWA and three European airlines: KLM of the Netherlands, Air France and BOAC from Britain. Growing confidence in the commercial future of air travel led to the opening in 1946 of London Airport (later Heathrow), which handled over 63,000 passengers in its first year.

In the postwar years, most of the the world's passenger traffic was accounted for by flights within the USA, with 12 million individual journeys out of a worldwide total of around 19 million. In 1948, Idlewild airport opened near New York City, and cheaper 'coach-class' fares attracted even

Below: The prototype de Havilland DH106 Comet first flew in 1949. It was the first jet airliner, setting the standard for those to come. Although it took relatively few passengers its other advantages assured the future of jet travel.

more passengers. Travelling by aeroplane became commonplace in the USA, and grew in popularity worldwide throughout the 1950s. By the end of the decade, the number of individual journeys taken each years was close to 100 million. Air travel, once the exclusive province of the rich and the adventurous, was becoming available to all.

COMMERCIAL JETS

In 1945, no one was sure whether the future of civil aviation lay with conventional piston engines driving propellers, or with jets. The question was soon resolved. On 4 September 1949, the gigantic Bristol Brabazon, equipped with eight Bristol Centaurus piston engines, made its maiden flight. This impressive aircraft could carry 100 passengers in luxurious conditions, but it was already outdated as, just six weeks earlier, on 27 July, the de Havilland DH106 Comet had made its maiden flight.

The Comet, the world's first jet airliner, was an elegant aircraft with a pressurized cabin that could accommodate 36 passengers. On 2 May 1952, a BOAC Comet took off from London for Johannesburg, inaugurating the world's first scheduled passenger service by jet airliners. At first, the Comet had no rivals. Then, on 15 July 1954, the

CASTROL
was chosen to lubricate the
Centaurus Engines of the Bristol
BRABAZON
Castrol
THE MASTERPIECE IN OILS

Above: The Bristol Brabazon was a huge aircraft. It made its maiden flight just a few weeks after the Comet, and could carry nearly three times as many people, but proved both too large and too slow for the developing passenger market.

Boeing 367-80 took off for the first time in Seattle. This was the prototype of the four-engined Boeing 707 jet airliner, which made its first scheduled flight on Pan Am's North Atlantic route on 26 November 1958, just three weeks after the Comet 4 was introduced. Another jet airliner, the McDonnell Douglas DC-8, was first used by United Air Lines and Delta Air Lines in 1959. In just a decade of use, the speed of jet airliners, their comparative safety – although the Comets were grounded temporarily for checks after crashes caused by metal fatigue – and the much greater comfort they offered passengers compared with their piston-engined rivals showed where the future of aviation lay.

Jet technology was applied to propeller-driven aircraft to produce 'turboprop' aircraft, with gas turbine engines driving propellers. On its first scheduled flight, on 29 July 1950, the Vickers Viscount 630, powered by Rolls-Royce Dart 502 turboprop engines, cut 20 minutes from the normal London–Paris flight time of 90 minutes. Sir Frank Whittle, inventor of the jet engine, was guest of honour in the cabin.

DEVELOPMENT OF THE HELICOPTER

Another 20th-century invention, the helicopter, saw great advances after World War I. The first helicopter to fly had been built by Frenchman Paul Cornu. He became airborne in it on 13 November 1907, but could only do so for a few seconds at a time, and rise no more than 1ft (30cm), since his machine became unmanageable on leaving the ground.

A Russian, Igor Ivanovitch Sikorsky, built two helicopters in 1909 and 1910 that could lift their own weight, but realized that it was impossible to produce a practical helicopter, given the existing state of scientific knowledge. He turned to designing aeroplanes, first in Russia and then in the USA, where in 1922 he founded a manufacturing company. Other helicopter pioneers included Louis Brennan, who achieved partially successful free flights in the early 1920s; Etienne Oemichen, whose machine established in 1924 the first 0.6-mile (1km) distance record; Louis Beguet and René Dorand, whose *Gyroplane Laboratoire* flew successfully in 1935; and Professor Heinrich Focke, whose twin-rotor Focke-Wulf Fw 61 made its first free flight on 26 June 1936.

In the 1920s, Spaniard Juan de la Cierva developed autogiros, aircraft with windmilling rotors that helped to keep them airborne. He solved the problem of control brilliantly, by using independently articulated rotor blades. This inspired Sikorsky to design and build his VS-300 helicopter. On 14 September 1939, he made a tentative, tethered initial flight in what would become the world's first successful single-rotor helicopter; on 6 May 1941, he kept the much-modified machine airborne for a world record time of one hour, 32 minutes and 46 seconds.

INTO BATTLE

Sikorsky's R-4 helicopter went into production in 1940, and was bought by both the USAAF and the British Army. It was used for both military and humanitarian purposes. On 10 January 1946, its successor, the R-5, was introduced, while the Sikorsky S-51 went into production as a purely civilian machine.

Below: Autogiros, economic on fuel and safe to fly and land, were marketed in the USA in the 1930s as personal runabouts. In this photograph Australian pioneer aviator Bert Hinkler poses in one of the craft.

Helicopters came into their own as military aircraft in the Korean War of 1950–1953. S-51s were introduced for reconnaissance purposes, and were then adapted to carry stretchers in order to transport wounded soldiers to Mobile Army Surgical Hospital (MASH) units. They proved so efficient at this that the death rate among wounded soldiers was the lowest recorded in modern military history.

Helicopters were used for tactical purposes, such as airlifting infantry battalions to inaccessible areas, and became invaluable for sea and mountain rescue. The first recorded helicopter rescue took place in January 1944, when Commander Frank Erickson, a pioneer helicopter pilot, negotiated a snowstorm in a US Coast Guard Sikorsky R-4 to take blood plasma to 100 sailors who had been burned when an American destroyer blew up off New York.

The introduction of smaller gas-turbine engines, which could be mounted on top of the aircraft, increased the cabin space in helicopters and made for steadier flight. On 13 June 1958, Jean Boulet flew an Alouette II with a gas-turbine engine to a world altitude record for helicopters of 35,150ft (10,714m).

THE SPEED OF SOUND

Other aviation records were tumbling as aircraft engineering improved by leaps and bounds. In 1945, a twin-jet-engined Gloster Meteor set a world air speed record of 606mph (976kph), and taking an aircraft to or beyond the speed of sound – around 762mph (1226kph) at sea level, falling to 660mph (1062kph) at 36,000ft (11,000m) – seemed for the first time to be an achievable target.

Passing through the 'sound barrier', though, creates an aerodynamic problem. An aircraft flying at less than the speed of sound pushes air away in front of it in the form of sound waves, which disperse easily, like ripples on a pond. At the speed of sound, known as Mach 1, these sound waves do not have time to disperse, and manifest themselves as shock waves that buffet the aircraft's fuselage and wings, sometimes causing loss of control. An expanding 'Mach cone' of pressure is left in the wake of the aircraft. When this reaches the ground it produces a 'sonic boom' capable of shattering windows.

THE BELL X-1

In the USA, research into supersonic flight centred on the US Army Air Force Flight Test Center at Edwards Air Force Base in California, where the Bell Aircraft Company's experimental X-1, a rocket-powered aircraft, was flight-tested. The short, somewhat stubby Bell X-1 was launched from the bomb bay of a Boeing B-29 Superfortress, which carried it to a height of about 25,000ft (7500m).

Above: Helicopter pioneer Igor Sikorsky tests his VS-300 – tethered to the ground by weights and ropes – in the winter of 1939–40. He always acted as test-pilot on his creations. The VS-300 had a 75hp engine and a rotor with three blades that described a circle 28ft (8.5m) in diameter.

The volunteer test pilot in 1946 was former fighter pilot Charles 'Chuck' Yeager, a 23-year-old USAAF captain who built up his speed over a number of flights. Several times he approached Mach 1, experienced the buffeting that had already cost several pilots their lives, then slowed down. Then, on 14 October 1947, Yeager felt the customary loss of control as he approached Mach 1, but at Mach 0.96 regained it.

Suddenly, the speed jumped to Mach 1.05, the buffeting stopped and the X-1 was easier to handle. The shaking stopped once he was flying faster than sound, and Yeager pushed the aircraft to Mach 1.15 before returning safely to base.

A great rivalry developed between the US Navy and Air Force in the postwar years for the overall world speed record. In August 1951, the Navy's Douglas D-558-II Skyrocket, which was air-launched like Yeager's X-1, reached Mach 1.88. Two years later, on 20 November 1953, Scott Crosfield, a civilian test pilot, flew the same aeroplane beyond Mach 2, becoming the first man to travel at twice the speed of sound.

Above: The V-2 rockets launched at England from northern Europe in 1944 and 1945 were the models not only for all future ballistic missiles but also for the rockets used in the exploration of space.

JOURNEY INTO SPACE

The most momentous technical achievement of the 1950s was, though, the development of rocket technology as the first step towards space travel. The idea of rocket-powered travel between worlds had been explored in two 19th-century novels, Jules Verne's *From the Earth to the Moon* (1865) and H.G. Wells's *The War of the Worlds* (1898). These books not only entranced the reading public – both were best-sellers – but also inspired serious scientific consideration of space travel. Verne's novel was an important influence on Konstantin Tsiolkovski (1857–1935), a

schoolteacher from provincial Russia who researched in both aeronautics and astronautics. He believed that 'not only the earth, but the whole universe is the heritage of mankind'. *Investigation of Cosmic Space by Reactive Machines,* published in a Russian technical journal in 1903, dealt with the problems of using rocket engines in space.

Hermann Oberth (1894–1990), a Transylvanian German who also admired Verne, was a follower of Tsiolkovski, of whom he wrote 'You have lighted the flame and we will not permit it to go out'. Oberth's *By Rocket into Interplanetary Space* (1923), contained all the formulae that were needed to work out the speed needed for a rocket to escape earth's gravity. The science was done; from now on, rockets were the province of engineers.

In 1919, unknown to Oberth, Robert Goddard, Professor of Physics at Clark University in Worcester, Massachusetts, published a paper, *A Method of Reaching Extreme Altitudes.* Goddard, another whose interest in space travel had been awakened by Wells's novel, worked secretly on constructing liquid-fuelled rockets, and on 16 March 1926 succeeded in launching one, the world's first. It reached a height of 41ft (12.5m) and travelled a total distance of 184ft (56m).

ROCKET TECHNOLOGY

In 1930, the Guggenheim Foundation provided Goddard with enough funds to pay for a permanent research and test centre at Roswell, New Mexico. There, in 1935, he launched the first liquid-fuelled rocket to travel at or close to the speed of sound.

Meanwhile, Oberth and a group of amateur rocket enthusiasts from the German Rocket Society, including a young Wernher von Braun, had been experimenting with liquid-fuelled rockets. In 1932, von Braun joined an army-controlled rocket development group near Berlin. He was soon appointed Technical Director, and in 1937 this group began to transfer operations to Peenemünde on the Baltic coast.

The US military saw little potential in rocket development in World War II, and Goddard's technical lead was eroded by von Braun's team, which developed the first long-range ballistic missile. The V-2, which could carry a tonne of explosives 200 miles (325km), was the forerunner of all today's space rockets. Von Braun and many of his fellow engineers surrendered to advancing American troops at the end of the war, while the Soviet troops advancing from the east found blueprints and a few rockets. Several Germans from the rockets project also went to the USSR.

THE COLD WAR IN SPACE

Both the great powers used the V-2 as the basis for rocket research, concentrating at first on missile development. The US army established

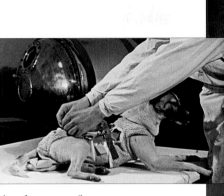

a test range at White Sands, New Mexico. Von Braun, who settled in the USA in September 1945, along with six colleagues – many more would join him in the next few years – was technical director of the Army's Rocket Section. Four years later, the V-2, with an added second-stage rocket, reached the staggering height of 244 miles (390km).

Sergei Korolyov (1907–1966), who had launched the USSR's first liquid-fuelled rocket in 1933, led the Soviet rocket programme. His work increased the V-2's effective range to over 400 miles (650km), fostering the development of the intercontinental ballistic missile (ICBM).

THE SOVIET UNION TAKES THE LEAD

A modified two-stage ICBM inaugurated the Space Age on 4 October 1957, when it lifted the world's first artificial satellite into orbit. *Sputnik 1* was an aluminium alloy sphere, 22in (56cm) in diameter. It contained electronic instruments and a chemical battery to power them. Four antennae relayed information to stations on the ground. The satellite orbited the earth every 96 minutes 10 seconds at a height varying between (142 miles) 229km and 585 miles (941km).

News of the Russian achievement came as a tremendous shock in the West. For three weeks, *Sputnik 1* transmitted an eerie 'beep-beep' that filled the general public with what Dr Allen Hynek of the Smithsonian Astrophysical Observatory described as 'a strange mixture of awe, admiration and fear'. *Sputnik 2*, launched on 3 November 1957, had a passenger. A Russian husky dog, Laika, was installed in a closed cylindrical capsule. The dog was fed from a device that dispensed a nutritious gelatine and expelled waste products into a rubber container. Sensors attached to Laika beamed back data proving that mammalian physiology could survive space travel, a necessary precursor to the first manned space flight. No attempt was made to recover the dog.

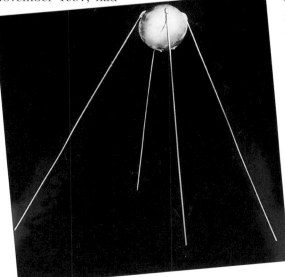

THE AMERICANS REPLY

Just five days after *Sputnik 2* was launched, von Braun received clearance to go ahead with his own project to launch a satellite. He was ready in less than three months. *Explorer 1*, which was carried by a modified Jupiter-C rocket, was launched from Cape Canaveral, Florida, on 31 January 1958. *Explorer* was smaller than the *Sputniks*, and contained a device to detect and measure radiation. The data it sent back allowed the American physicist James Van Allen to discover the innermost of the two radiation belts in the atmosphere that are named after him.

Later that year, the National Aeronautics and Space Administration (NASA) was formed as an independent US government agency with a mission to explore and conquer space. Wernher von Braun and his team were transferred to this new organization, and in 1960 he was made the Director of the NASA George C. Marshall Space Flight Center in Huntsville, Alabama. The Space Race was on.

FRESH CHALLENGES

1960–1979

The 1960s are remembered as the decade when youth culture – a heady mix of popular music, fashion, liberal ideas, revolt and protest – was in the ascendant; when American certainties were challenged by the assassination of its reforming leaders and the grinding, destructive war in Vietnam. In the same way as the hedonistic 1920s gave way to the grim 1930s, the 'Swinging Sixties' led to a decade of economic recession and conflict as oil-producing countries banded together to force up the price of fuel and the oil-consuming economies struggled to cope.

New achievements in transport generally came from the quest for speed rather than exploration, as rocket- and jet-propelled vehicles made assaults on the world land speed record. Japan made an impressive entry into international motorcycle sport, and competition was sharpened on the motor-racing circuit by the introduction of rear-engined cars, the Lotus 'ground-effects' design and Renault's turbo-charged engine. New generations of locomotives cut railway journey times dramatically, while new speed records were also set on water, notably when a boat was driven at just over 300mph (480kph) in 1978.

The first supersonic transport aircraft flew in 1968, and passenger airliners followed in the 1970s, but it was the subsonic Boeing 747 'jumbo jet' that revolutionized air travel; passenger air-miles more than doubled between 1971 and 1979. Something of the spirit of the old aviators could still be seen when, for example, a lone flyer circled the earth by passing over both poles in 1971.

The true pioneering spirit was, though, to be seen in abundance in the exploration of outer space. In 1961, the first man left the Earth's atmosphere. Eight years later, men walked on the Moon, and by the end of the 1970s cosmonauts were living and working in orbit, while unmanned craft explored the solar system.

Left: Supersonic scheduled air travel became a reality in January 1976 when a British Concorde took off from London for Bahrain and a French Concorde left Paris for Rio de Janeiro.

LAND

Although the Cold War continued to threaten world peace, the conflict remained largely symbolic, and the continuing peace, coupled with a manufacturing boom as world economies finally recovered from the ravages of war, made the late 1950s and 1960s a time of growing stability and material prosperity in the developed world. The market for consumer durables, such as televisions, washing machines, refrigerators and various labour-saving devices grew as more and more people decided they could afford them.

BUILDING ROADS

In the more prosperous countries, private cars were increasingly seen as a necessity rather than a luxury, and networks of new, high-speed roads were built to take the new burden of traffic. The first motorways had been built in Germany in the 1930s, and the country had 1310 miles (2108km) of *autobahn* by 1942. Much of this fell into disrepair in the immediate postwar years, but it provided a framework for a new road system when the German economy recovered its strength.

Above: In 1960 Germans Walter Schock (left) and Rolf Moll (right) won the Monte Carlo Rally and the European Rally Championship driving a production car, the Mercedes-Benz 200SE. This photograph, taken on 27 January that year, shows them with 1950s racing legend Karl Kling, Sports Director of the Mercedes team.

Above: Although never envisaged as a competition car, the Mini proved itself on the road and even more so on rallies, with 1964 a golden year.

Left: The greatest motoring achievement in a Mini in 1964 was probably the overall victory of Paddy Hopkirk and Henry Liddon in the Monte Carlo Rally.

Right: The team of Pat Moss and Ann Wisdom dominated women's rallying in the late 1950s and early 1960s. They were several times European champions and winners of the Coupes des Dames in the Monte Carlo Rally. They are seen on the right in the 1959 rally in an Austin A40.

CASTROL WINS IN 1962 RALLYE MONTE-CARLO

LADIES CUP
won on Castrol for the 7th time in succession

1ST PAT MOSS & ANN WISDOM
(MORRIS MINI-COOPER)

2ND ANNE HALL & VALERIE DOMLEO
(FORD ANGLIA)

also 5 class wins

(below is official confirmation)

For carefree winter motoring–you need Castrol to for a start

Below: Like her brother Stirling, Pat Moss liked to race. Here she is seen in her Austin Healey 3000 during the 1961 Tulip Rally, in which, as well as taking the Ladies' Award, she also won in her class. Pat later married the Swedish rally driver Eric Carlson, who drove to victory many times for Saab.

THE INTERSTATE

The USA launched its own motorway network, the Interstate Highway System, in 1956. Between 1920 and 1960, the total road mileage in the USA went up by just 21 per cent. In the same period, the population grew 70 per cent and the number of car registrations by 700 per cent. The quality of the roads, though, improved dramatically. Just 13 per cent were paved in 1921; by 1960, 72 per cent were surfaced, and the USA had more than 34,000 miles (55,000km) of multi-lane carriageway.

The Italian government also made roadbuilding a priority. The system reached its peak in 1964 with the creation of the 500-mile

(800km) 'Autostrada del Sole' motorway, linking Milan, Genoa, Rome and Naples. Britain moved into the motorway era with the opening in 1959 of the M1, linking London with the north of England, while Japan started relatively late; the first freeway to open there was the Meishin Expressway between Osaka and Kobe in 1965.

PRODUCTION CARS IN SPORT

Although legal limits were soon imposed on many of these new roads, the promise of speed that they held out to ordinary motorists was an enticing one. Production cars were getting quicker all the time, and manufacturers soon realized that they could effectively promote their wares by competing in rallies and touring-car races in modified versions of production cars. A sporting image was very desirable now that mere reliability – the main selling point of cars up to the 1940s – could be pretty much taken for granted.

For example, in 1960 Walter Schock and Rolf Moll became European Rally Champions after winning in the Monte Carlo, Acropolis and Polish Rallies in the factory Mercedes-Benz 220SE. That same year, Pat Moss – Stirling's sister – and Ann Wisdom won the Coupe des Dames in the Monte Carlo Rally in an Austin A40, and also took the Liège–Rome–Liège rally in an Austin Healey 3000, the first-ever outright win by a female crew in a European Championship. It led to Moss and Wisdom winning the Ladies European Rally Championship a second time.

In 1961, the BMC Mini-Cooper, developed by Alec Issigonis, was launched. For five years, from 1962 to 1967, it won a series of major rally

Above and left: The 1970 World Cup Rally pitted production cars against some of the world's most challenging terrain. Seven works Ford Escort twin-cams were entered, and they won the manufacturers' prize with five finishes in the first eight. Hannu Mikkola and Gunnar Palm (above) were outright winners; car 103 (Timo Makinen and Gilbert Staeplacre) was fifth.

victories. The successes that made the Mini world-famous included back-to back overall wins in the Monte Carlo Rally 1964 and 1965, the first by Paddy Hopkirk with Henry Liddon, and the second, in weather conditions that made any sort of driving virtually impossible, by Timo Makinen and Paul Easter.

The Mini was, though, not merely a good rally car. In 1963, Paddy Hopkirk's drive in the ten-day Tour de France de l'Automobile confirmed its potential as a racing touring car; and the following year Warwick Banks, driving a Mini entered by the Cooper Car company, won the European Touring Car Championship.

THE WORLD CUP RALLY

The 1970s began with what proved to be the most exciting motor-sport event of the decade, the 1970 World Cup Rally, which covered a 16,500-mile (26,500km) route from London, venue of the 1966 football World Cup finals, to Mexico City, where the final stages of the 1970 competition were to be held.

It was one of the most ambitious rallies ever staged. The competitors first had to negotiate a 4000-mile (6400km) 'tour' of Europe, which took in much of the continent's most demanding rally country. The first part of the rally ended at Lisbon, where the cars, drivers, navigators and crews were shipped *en masse* to Brazil, where the most demanding part of the rally began in Rio de Janeiro.

From there, the course headed south along jungle tracks into Uruguay, led across the flat plains of the pampas in Argentina and over the Andes into Chile. Here, the rally cars headed north, following the spine of the Andes. They reached altitudes of over 14,000ft (4250m) on

their way through the mountains of Bolivia, Peru and Ecuador to Colombia. From there they were shipped to Panama for the final part of the rally, a trek through Central America.

LOGISTICAL NIGHTMARES

From Rio de Janeiro onwards, the rally teams faced major logistical problems. No fewer than 50 fuel and oil dumps had to be created to provide fuel and lubrication for the competitors. Since most service points were remote, the fuel had to be put into drums and trucked to its destination. The poor quality of the fuel that was available also posed problems. In Argentina, special racing fuel was used, but in Bolivia, Brazil, Costa Rica and Ecuador the British Leyland and Ford teams, running on 92-octane fuel, had to make do with domestic petrol mixed with high-octane aviation fuel.

The race winners were Hannu Mikkola and Gunnar Palm driving a works Ford Escort. Brian Culcheth and Johnstone Syer were second in a factory Triumph 2.5 PI, and Rauno Aaltonen and Henry Liddon in another works Escort came third. Ford took the manufacturers' team prize. Of the 96 cars that started the rally, 23 reached Mexico City.

Right: Nineteen seventy-eight was a good year for Sweden and Ford. Swedes Björn Waldegaard and Hans Thorszelius are seen here in the Ford Escort in which they won that year's Swedish Rally. Second, also in an Escort, were Hannu Mikkola and Arnie Hertz. For Ford, it was the first event following their switch to Castrol lubricants.

Below: GTX is a high-performance multigrade engine oil containing high-quality mineral oils which offer protection and improve efficiency. Since its introduction in 1968, the brand has undergone continuous improvement so as to meet the changing needs of developing engine technology.

Left: Donald Campbell's *Bluebird-Proteus CN7*, pictured here at the National Motor Museum at Beaulieu, Hampshire, was powered by a Bristol-Siddeley gas-turbine engine. It was built specifically to win back the land speed record for Britain and the Campbell family. Campbell's success led to a flurry of other attempts on the record.

Below: Campbell – watched by his wife, Tonia Bern, with fingers crossed – made his successful attempt on Cobb's 17-year-old land speed record on a dried-up lake bed in Australia. His average speed of 403.1mph (648.8kph) over two runs surpassed Cobb's record by just 8.9mph (14.4kph).

FASTEST MAN ON WHEELS

Although victory in a prestigious rally or a race could be a wonderful advertisement for an individual manufacturer, national pride and prestige still tended to be vested in world record attempts. John Cobb's 1947 land speed record still stood at the beginning of the 1960s. In total, it lasted for 17 years, before Donald Campbell took it in his *Bluebird-Proteus CN7*, which was powered by a Bristol-Siddeley Proteus gas-turbine engine capable of delivering 4100 shaft hp. He made his two runs on the dried-up bed of Lake Eyre in South Australia on 17 July 1964, reaching an average speed of 403.1mph (648.8kph).

Campbell's success prompted an American, Bob Summers, to make his own attempt on the record. On 12 November 1965, he drove *Goldenrod,* a long, low, narrow vehicle powered by four 608bhp Chrysler Hemi engines in a row, across the Bonneville Salt Flats in Utah at a speed of 409.27mph (658.7kph). This speed stands to this day as the

fastest ever achieved by a wheel-driven vehicle. This is mainly because later would-be record-breakers focussed their attention on free-wheeling vehicles propelled by rockets or jet engines.

SPIRIT OF AMERICA

The first jet-engined supercar to set a record was Craig Breedlove's *Spirit of America,* which first ran in August 1962. After some steering problems had been ironed out, Breedlove and his crew went to Bonneville in July 1963 and made a record attempt on 5 August. On the first run, using just 90 per cent power, Breedlove reached 388.5mph (625.2kph). On the second run, he used 95 per cent, and was timed at 428.4mph (689.4kph), but the record was unofficial as the car was a three-wheeler.

In the autumn of 1964, there was a flurry of activity at Bonneville. On 2 October, Breedlove lost his overall record to Tom Green, who reached 413.2mph (665kph) in *The Wingfoot Express*, with its Westinghouse J46 triple-jet engine. Three days later, a General Electric J79 jet drove Art Arfons at 434mph (698.5kph) in his *Green Monster*. Breedlove fought back, regaining the title on 13 October. Two days later, he was the first

Below: The aptly named *Goldenrod* had an astonishingly low build – little of it projects above the level of Bob Summers's knees – and was powered by four Chrysler 6.9-litre V8 engines arranged in a row.

through 500mph (800kph), smashing the old record and setting a new one at 526.3mph (847kph). But he was lucky to survive this attempt. His braking parachutes tore away on the second run, and *Spirit of America* went into a 6-mile (10km) skid, snapping a telegraph pole like a matchstick, then flew 150ft (45m) over an embankment, skipped across a pond and ended up submerged in a lake of brine. Breedlove opened the cockpit, and swam to shore uninjured.

This was not the last action at Bonneville during that dramatic month. On 27 October, Arfons set yet another new mark, achieving 536.7mph (863.8kph) before the weather broke.

The following October, both Breedlove and Arfons were back at Bonneville. While Breedlove was preparing for his attempt, he handed control of his improved *Spirit of America – Sonic 1* to his wife, Lee. Lee Breedlove emerged after four runs as the world's fastest woman driver,

clocking up 308.6mph (496.6kph). Breedlove himself was ready to go on 2 November, when he set a record of 555.1mph (893.4kph). Five days later, Arfons raised the stakes again, pushing *Green Monster* to 576.6mph (927.9kph). This record stood until 15 November, when Breedlove set a record of 600.6mph (966.6kph).

RECORD-BREAKING ROCKET CAR

This speed was not bettered until 23 October 1970, when Gary Gabelich, a 30-year-old drag racer, piloted *The Blue Flame*, a rocket car fuelled by hydrogen peroxide and liquefied natural gas, across the salt flats at an average speed of 622.4mph (1001.7kph).

Below: In his first *Spirit of America*, Craig Breedlove set a new world land speed record of 408.5mph (657.3kph) on 5 August 1963.

Left and above: Craig Breedlove pushed the land speed record to new heights in jet-propelled vehicles called *Spirit of America*. The main colour picture shows him setting a record of 526.3mph (847kph) in October 1964 in the first *Spirit of America*. This was succeeded in 1965 by *Spirit of America – Sonic 1* (top), which Breedlove took to 600.6mph (966kph), setting a record that would stand for five years.

While the USA was dominating the land speed record and several other areas of motor sport in the 1960s and 1970s, a revolution in motorcycle racing centred around a remarkable challenge from Japan. It began in 1954, when Soichiro Honda, founder of the Honda Motor Company, announced he would send a team to compete in the 125cc class of the 1959 Isle of Man TT races. The aim was to take the manufacturers' team prize, and Honda succeeded by finishing sixth, seventh and eighth.

JAPANESE RACERS

Honda became involved in Grand Prix motorcycle racing in 1959, and introduced several technical innovations in the next few years. The 1960 250cc machine had a four-cylinder, 16-valve engine and six-speed

Above and left: Mike Hailwood was associated with Honda right from the start, and won the first and last of his world titles with them. Honda quit racing at the end of the 1967 season – when Hailwood was pictured (far left) at the front of the grid at Brand's Hatch – and Hailwood attempted to emulate John Surtees by exchanging 500cc bikes for a Formula One racing car, although he had much less success. The inset shows Hailwood in 1968 with a caricature of himself on his helmet.

gearbox, for example, while other 250cc machines had single cylinders, or at most two. The calibrations on the rev counter began at 6000rpm, close to the bursting point of most rival engines. Suzuki also came to Europe to race in 1960 and were joined the next year by Yamaha. Both had their successes, but Honda led the way. Between 1959 and 1967, when they withdrew from racing for 12 years, they won 18 manufacturers' world titles and their drivers took 17 individual world championships.

Among Honda's riders was the Briton Mike Hailwood, a millionaire's son who won his first world title on a 250cc Honda at the age of 21 in 1961, the year when he also won three classes in the Tourist Trophy. He switched to the Italian make MV Augusta, and won the 500cc world championship four years running, but returned to Honda in 1966, when he won the 250cc and 350cc titles, a feat which he repeated in 1967

Above: The supreme motorcyclist of his generation, eclipsing even Hailwood, was the Italian Giacomo Agostini, who put together a winning record that has not been, and may never be, equalled. He is seen here at Silverstone in 1975.

when he once again won three Tourist Trophy classes. When Honda pulled out of racing in 1967, he switched to four wheels; he had already raced in Grands Prix in the 1964 season.

THE GREAT AGOSTINI

The greatest racing motorcyclist of this – perhaps any – era was, though, the Italian Giacomo Agostini. His total of 15 world titles and 122 Grands Prix victories far outstrips his nearest rivals, and his record of ten Isle of Man TT wins is bettered only by Hailwood and Joey Dunlop. In 1970, he equalled Hailwood's record of 19 wins in a Grand Prix season.

When Hailwood rejoined Honda in 1966, Agostini became MV's lead rider and took the world 500cc title for the next seven years before losing it to team-mate Phil Read in 1973. At the end of that year, Agostini, unhappy at MV, moved to Yamaha, where he retained his 350cc world title but again lost out to Phil Read for the 500cc crown.

On 24 August 1975, though, Agostini won a record eighth title at 500cc by edging out Phil Read in the Czechoslovakian Grand Prix at Brno, the first rider to win the championship on a two-stroke machine. At the end of the season, Yamaha pulled out of racing, citing a depressed world motorcycle market and the need to invest in research and development for anti-pollution and noise-restriction measures. Agostini went back to MV in 1976, when he won his 122nd and last Grand Prix, and retired after the 1977 season to be a team manager.

Above: Austrian driver Niki Lauda – in the main picture he is driving a Ferrari 312T in 1975's US Grand Prix; the inset shows him in May 1976 – was the world champion in 1975 and 1977. In the intervening year he was narrowly beaten for the title after a horrific, near-fatal accident kept him out of racing for months.

Right: Graham Hill became the main Lotus Ford driver following the death of Jim Clark in 1968, and went on to become world champion that same year. His Lotus 49B is shown cornering at the Monaco Grand Prix.

Left and below: The 1976 world champion, James Hunt (seen below after that year's victory in the British Grand Prix at Brand's Hatch), was in many ways a throwback to the devil-may-care racers of the inter-war years. Early mishaps in his racing career earned him the nickname Hunt the Shunt, but he had the last laugh on his detractors, taking the title with a courageous drive in the rain at the year's final Grand Prix, in Japan.

Right: The extremely high boiling point of SRF brake fluid makes it ideal for highly demanding braking conditions such as those of racing. Launched in 1985, it benefits from patent silicon ester technology and can be filled into any non-mineral oil braking system.

DOMINANT V8S

The Lotus 49 made its debut at the Dutch Grand Prix at Zandvoort on 4 June 1967. Hill had to withdraw with a mechanical problem, but Clark swept through to win, establishing the Cosworth V-8 as the dominant racing engine. In the next decade it would power 154 Grand Prix winners.

After Clark was killed in a crash in 1968, Hill took the Championship in a V-8 Lotus 49B. Jackie Stewart was champion in a V-8 Matra MS80 in 1969, and the same engine powered the cars of world champions Jochen Rindt (1970), Jackie Stewart (1971 and 1973), Emerson Fittipaldi (1972 and 1974), and James Hunt (1976). The only break in the pattern came in 1975, when Niki Lauda won in a 312T Ferrari.

Aerodynamic devices introduced in the 1970s improved road-holding and cornering in Formula One cars. In 1977, when Lauda won the championship for the second time, Colin Chapman produced a brilliant innovation, the Lotus 78 'ground-effect' car, designed to behave like an upside-down wing. Mario Andretti took it to four Grand Prix wins that year, and won the championship in the improved Lotus 79 the next.

The first turbo-charged engine in Grand Prix racing, the Renault RS01, was also introduced in 1977. In July 1979, after many teething troubles, a Renault RE10, driven by Jean-Pierre Jabouille, won the French Grand Prix, marking the beginning of a new era in Formula One racing.

Below: Jackie Stewart emulated his fellow-Scot Jim Clark in becoming Formula One world champion. The two men had very different personalities, and Stewart's extrovert nature often showed in his driving.

ELECTRICITY AND THE RAILWAYS

The switch away from steam power on the railways, which began in a small way at the beginning of the century, had gathered pace since the end of World War II. By the end of the 1960s steam locomotives were a thing of the past in the developed world, although they were still widely used in countries, such as India and China, with good supplies of cheap lower-grade fuel but no capital to fund an electrification programme.

Although many countries opted for the powerful diesel-electric engines built in the USA, where electrification was a non-event, electricity was firmly established as the main motive power for high-speed passenger railways. The first railway service scheduled at over 100mph (160kph) began in Japan on 1 November 1965 on the Tokaido line between Osaka and Tokyo. On this ultra-fast line, high-speed trains took their power from overhead wires supplying a 25,000-volt alternating current. By 1974 some 340,000 passengers per day were using the 'Bullet Train', as it came to be known, and over the following years Japan National Railways introduced more high-speed lines to its networks.

Above: The Japanese 'Bullet Train', seen here passing Mount Fuji, is named as much for the distinctively rounded ballistic profile of its nose as for its speed.

CAPITAL INVESTMENT

The successful modernization of the railways depended largely on the amount of money available for investment. In China, for example, the government increased its commitment to railways, and the total length of new lines built there in the 1960s and 1970s was greater than that of all the lines that were closed in the rest of the world.

Many other countries moved investment away from the railways in favour of roads, which were increasingly being used for private travel and freight transport. In Britain, for example, the rail network was cut drastically between 1963 and 1965, in favour of developing high -speed electric passenger trains and freight transport. Britain also used diesel locomotives, and in 1973 the British HST (High Speed Train) set a world speed record for diesel-electric traction at 143mph (230kph). This was later raised to 148.5mph (239kph), a record that still stands.

SEA

FRESH CHALLENGES 1959–1979

In the 1960s and 1970s, there were dramatic changes in the face of seaborne transport. Economies of scale led to bigger and bigger oil tankers being built, while a new generation of liners – smaller, luxury ships intended for cruising – were built to meet the demands of those who believed that it was just as pleasurable to travel in style as to arrive.

During the same period a number of speed records were broken, and yachtsmen competed in extraordinary races, or even made solo voyages around the world. The most exciting technical development of the time, though, was the introduction of the air-cushion vehicle (ACV).

EARLY HISTORY OF THE ACV

Sir John Thornycroft, a British naval architect, took out a patent in 1877 on the concept of a ship with a plenum chamber – an empty box, open at the bottom – instead of a hull. By pumping air into this chamber at high pressure, he believed, he could lift the ship out of the water, thus reducing 'drag' and allowing it to travel more rapidly over the water.

The problem was in keeping the air cushion in place. Thornycroft's idea was only realized when another Englishman, Christopher Cockerell, replaced the plenum chamber with a 'peripheral jet'. Air was jetted at a slight inward angle from a slot which ran around the entire base, causing it to mass beneath the craft and raise it up.

THE HOVERCRAFT

Cockerell filed his own patent in 1956, and approached the government authority responsible for buying military equipment. In November that year the ACV was classified 'secret', and aircraft manufacturer Saunders Roe was contracted to build the craft. The power of the peripheral jet

Below and right: The prototype hovercraft, SR.N1 (below), was built by Saunders Roe. The inset shows Cockerell's 1955 original, based on a model aircraft engine.

Above: Crowds of onlookers surround the SR.N1 before its test trip across the Channel from Calais to Dover on 25 July 1959. Piloted by Peter Lamb, the hovercraft took just over 115 minutes to make the crossing.

proved insufficient to keep the air cushion in place, so a rubberized skirt was placed around the outside of the craft. In 1959, on the 50th anniversary of Blériot's historic flight across the English Channel, the first ACV, the SR.N1, was launched.

Within four years hovercraft, as ACVs came to be known, were operating a regular cross-Channel service, and ACVs became relatively commonplace as car and passenger ferries. There were problems, though, both with the design of the skirt – which had to withstand constant friction with the sea at high speeds – and with the maintenance of the gas turbines, which hated salt water. This meant that commercial success did not come easily, although in the 1960s and 1970s Westland developed a range of hovercraft for a variety of purposes, including military transport, and from 1968 the SR.N4 regularly crossed the English Channel carrying up to 254 passengers and 30 cars.

WISHING YOU A VERY MERRY CHRISTMAS
MAY 1958 BRING YOU EVERY HAPPINESS AND SUCCESS
From
DONALD CAMPBELL

In the mid-1960s there was a flurry of activity around the world water speed record, as an American dragboat pilot and water-skier, Lee A. Taylor, set out to wrest it from Donald Campbell. Campbell's record, set on Coniston Water, in England's Lake District on 14 May 1959, stood at 260.35mph (419kph). When he heard of Taylor's interest, Campbell once again climbed into his *Bluebird K7*, powered by a Metropolitan-Vickers Beryl engine, and on 31 December 1964 raised the record to 276.3mph (444.7kph).

EXTRAORDINARY COMEBACK

Taylor did not make an attempt on the record that year. While he was putting his 33ft (10m) boat, *Hustler*, through a speed trial on Lake Havasu, Arizona, USA, a bent throttle spring prevented him from slowing down after he reached 250mph (400kph). He managed to roll himself out of the boat before it shot out of the lake and up a hill, but the impact with the water fractured his skull and crushed his left eye, among other injuries, and left him in a coma for 18 days.

In 1965, Taylor learned to walk and talk again. Then he showed great courage in again setting out to challenge the record, but found he had lost confidence at very high speeds. His money then ran out, but he found a backer in a tyre dealer from his home town of Compton, California.

DEATH OF DONALD CAMPBELL

By the end of 1966, Taylor was ready for a new attempt, and Donald Campbell responded to the threat, as he always did, by trying to push the target higher. In January 1967, his jet-powered *Bluebird* hit something in the water at more than 300mph (480kph) on Coniston Water. It flipped over and was wrecked, killing Campbell instantly.

Above: This image of *Bluebird K7* appeared on the Campbell family's Christmas card in 1964, just after it took the world water speed record.

Below: *Hustler* was capable of great speeds, but its driver, Lee Taylor, became reluctant to use full power after an accident at 280mph (450kph) almost killed him. He eventually took Campbell's record when his crew tricked him into going all out.

Right and below: Francis Chichester made it into the record books in the 1920s as a pioneer flyer, but he is best remembered today for his extraordinary feats as a single-handed yachtsman in the 1960s. In *Gypsy Moth III* (below) he won the first single-handed transatlantic yacht race in 1960, and in 1967 (right) completed the first-ever solo circumnavigation – with a stopover in Australia – in the larger *Gypsy Moth IV*.

This did nothing for Taylor's shaky confidence. Though he could get close to the record in practice on Lake Guntersville he could not keep the throttle full on without panicking. His sponsor's patience began to run out. Taylor's team decided desperate measures were called for. They altered the throttle so that when Taylor applied it at 70 per cent he got 100 per cent power, and moved back the balloon markers on the lake so that Taylor would get on the power earlier and apply it for longer. It worked. On 30 June, *Hustler*'s Westinghouse J46 turbo jet engines took Taylor across the lake at 285.2mph (459kph).

HOME-MADE RECORD BREAKER

This record stood for more than ten years. It was taken by Ken Warby, whose *Spirit of Australia*, with a Westinghouse J34 turbo jet engine, set a new record of 288.6mph (464.5kph) on Blowering Dam Lake in New South Wales on 20 November 1977. On 8 October 1978, he became the first man to break through the 300mph (483kph) and 500kph (311mph) barriers on water. In the same boat, and on the same stretch of water, he set a record of 317.2mph (510.5kph) that still stands.

Warby was the first man to design, build and drive a boat to capture a world water speed record. It had taken him two years to build the wooden *Spirit of Australia* in suburban Sydney. Wind-tunnel work to improve the hull's shape was directed by Professor Tom Fink of the University of New South Wales, who had helped in the same way with the design of Donald Campbell's boat *Bluebird* 20 years earlier.

LONG-DISTANCE YACHTING

A series of single-handed transatlantic yacht races began in 1960, sponsored by the British Sunday newspaper, the *Observer*. The first race was won by Francis Chichester, a map publisher whose 39ft (12m) yacht *Gipsy Moth III* made the journey in 40 days. Chichester had already shown his great determination and intrepid nature three decades earlier; in 1929, in his aircraft *Gipsy Moth*, he had become only the second man to fly from England to Australia.

Chichester now planned a more ambitious feat. On 27 August 1966 – just before his 65th birthday – he set out in the 53ft (16m) *Gipsy Moth IV* to sail single-handed around the world. He reached Sydney, Australia in December after a voyage of 107 days and 14,100 miles (22,700km), and on 29 January 1967 began the journey home across the South Pacific and around Cape Horn. He reached Plymouth on 28 May 1967, after a further 119 days and 15,517 miles (24,970km) at sea. Chichester's great achievement was repeated a year later by Alec Rose, who sailed from Portsmouth on 16 July 1967 in his 36ft (11m) *Lively Lady* and, after two stops on the way, was home again by 4 July 1968.

In 1968, Chichester organized the first *Sunday Times* Golden Globe round-the-world yacht race, won on 22 April 1969 by 30-year-old Robin Knox-Johnston in his 32ft (9.8m) Bermuda ketch *Suhaili*. Having sailed 30,000 miles (48,250km) in 312 days at an average speed of just over 92 knots (170.4km) a day, Knox-Johnston had become the first man to sail round the world alone without once touching land.

The postwar trend towards using jet propulsion for commercial passenger aircraft intensified in the 1960s and 1970s, and the number of people who chose to fly rose accordingly. Between 1971 and 1979, the number of passengers through New York and London airports alone rose from 36.8 million to 57.7 million, while the overall passenger miles travelled worldwide more than doubled.

In October 1958, a Pan Am Boeing 707 began a daily jet service between New York and Paris, with a stop in Newfoundland, and a year later Pan Am launched a round-the-world service, also using 707s. The only serious rival to the Boeing 707 for the jet passenger trade was the new, larger-capacity de Havilland Comet 4B, which made a successful maiden flight on 27 June 1959. By 3 December 'proving flights' had begun from Copenhagen, and in 1960 BEA inaugurated the first direct commercial jet service from London to Moscow. The Comet 4B, which cruised at around 525mph (840kph), did the journey in 3½ hours, almost halving the previous journey time.

ENTER THE JUMBOS

As the demand for flights increased, Boeing became convinced that there was a need for a jet airliner that could carry as many as 400 people, more than double the number that would fill one of its successful 707s.

By 1966 they had a firm order from Pan Am for 25 of the proposed new

Left and below: The de Havilland Comet 4B was more reliable than early models of the Comet. Large jet airliners, with their much greater passenger capacity, radically changed the experience of flying.

Above: Boeings await delivery, around 1970; from bottom: a 737 for TAAG Angola; three American Airlines 727s and one for Western Airlines; one 737 for Frontier Airlines and one for Air Europe; and a Northwest Orient 747-200B.

aircraft, and 9 February 1969 marked the maiden flight, with Jack Waddell at the controls, of the Boeing 747. The massive scale of the airliner soon earned it the nickname 'jumbo jet'.

Jumbo jets entered scheduled service in January 1970, when a Pan Am 747 flew from New York to London. 'High-capacity' passenger jets from other makers soon appeared; the Douglas DC-10 first flew on 29 August 1970, and the Lockheed TriStar took to the air on 16 November 1970.

A HALF-CENTURY OF PROGRESS

On 16 June 1959, to celebrate the 50th anniversary of Blériot's flight across the Channel, a USAF Lockheed F-104 Starfighter took off from Le Bourget – watched by Blériot's widow – flew to the skies above London

and returned in about 31 minutes. It was an impressive demonstration of the massive technical advances of the previous half-century, advances that were further highlighted during the next six months.

First, on 17 September 1959, at Edwards Air Force Base in California, the North American X-15 – the latest in a long line that had begun with Chuck Yeager's X-1 – made its first rocket-powered flight. It was specially designed to go higher and faster (up to seven times the speed of sound) than any other aircraft in existence. On 12 August 1960, a new world altitude record was set when an X-15 piloted by Major Robert White was launched from under the wing of a B-52 bomber at over 6.5 miles (10km) and climbed to 25.75 miles (41.6km).

Three years later, on 22 August 1963, an X-15 piloted by NASA test pilot Joe Walker smashed this record, reaching 67 miles (108km), while on 3 October 1967, Major W. J. Knight, piloting an improved X-15A-2 with additional fuel tanks, reached a world record speed for an air-launched craft of 4534mph (7297kph), or Mach 6.72.

Other Edwards pilots set new records in more conventional ground-launched aircraft. In 1961, Lieutenant Colonel R. B. Robinson set a new air speed record of 1607mph (2585kph) in a McDonnell F4H-1F. In July 1962, the USSR took the record when Colonel G. Mosolov flew a Mikoyan E-166 at 1666mph (2681kph). Colonel R. L. Stephens, in a

Above: The Lockheed F-104 Starfighter was, for obvious reasons, nicknamed the 'missile with a man in it'. Versions of the jet fighter aircraft established world speed and altitude records at the beginning of the 1960s.

Above: Castrol was chosen for the TSR-2, in 1965 one of the world's most advanced aircraft.

Right: The world air speed record set by the Lockheed YF-12A in 1965 stood for 11 years before Captain Eldon Joersz and Major George Morgan of Edwards Air Force Base, California, took this Lockheed SR-71 Blackbird reconnaissance aircraft to 2193mph (3530kph) on 18 July 1976.

Lockheed YF-12A, returned the record to Edwards and the USA in 1965, reaching 2070mph (3332kph) on 1 May. This record stood for 11 years, until Captain Eldon Joersz and Major George Morgan flew a Lockheed SR-71 Blackbird reconnaissance aircraft from Edwards at 2193mph (3530kph) on 28 July 1976. The same aircraft set a new record for a transatlantic crossing in September 1974, when Major James Sullivan hopped across to Europe in just over 115 minutes.

PIONEERING SPIRIT

At the other end of the scale, a few aviators kept the pioneering spirit alive by making adventurous journeys without the benefit of modern flight technology. One of these was Sheila Scott, an English actress who learned to fly in 1959 when she was 32. She was soon winning races in a modified Tiger Moth biplane, *Myth*, and in 1964 turned her attention to breaking flight records in a single-engined Piper Comanche 400.

On 18 May 1966, she took off from Heathrow Airport in the larger Piper Comanche 260 *Myth Too* to fly solo around the world. It was a flight full of incident, including the near-catastrophic bursting of a cabin fuel tank over the Atlantic, but 33 days later she returned to London, having set a new world record for the longest solo flight in a single-engined aircraft of 28,656 miles (46,117km).

The following year she broke the London to Cape Town record, and by the end of 1970 had broken no fewer than 94 world-class records. Her

Above: Ihe Bell X-14, powered by two Armstrong Siddeley Viper turbojets, was, in 1957, the first jet aircraft to take off vertically from a level position. Here an X-14B is in use by the US Army.

most notable flight was her 1971 attempt to travel round the world on its north-south axis, going from equator to equator, making a dangerous crossing of the North Pole on the way. She flew a modified twin-engined Piper Aztec named *Mythre,* fitted with extra fuel tanks to increase its range from 1100 miles (1770km) to 3000 miles (4830km). *Mythre* also carried a number of scientific experiments, including several arranged by NASA, whose 'balloon interrogation package' meant that her position would be continually transmitted first to the polar orbiting satellite *Nimbus,* and thence to the Goddard Space Center.

She set out from Nairobi on 11 June 1971, flying first to London and then on to the military airfield of Bate in Norway. From there, despite a broken autopilot, she took off to begin her journey across the North Pole. Excessive drag caused by faulty landing gear meant she was using too much fuel and travelling too slowly, so she diverted to a landing strip at the Nord research station in Greenland. From there, a 17-hour flight took her over what she would later describe as 'a desolate but magnificent' landscape. Most of the time there was no sun by which she could reckon her position, while the radio compass had 'given up the struggle'. It was only when she reached Barrow in Alaska that it was confirmed that she had indeed flown over the North Pole.

Adventurers such as Scott were, however, very much in the minority. Most aviation experts felt their achievements – although undoubtedly heroic and sometimes spectacular – were much less important than the solid technical progress that was being made. A prime example of this was the constant research that had been taking place in both Britain and

Below: Actress Sheila Scott, shown here in 1969, found far greater fame when she switched to flying, setting a number of new records for single-engine records and making a notable solo flight across the North Pole.

Above: The forerunner of all British delta-winged vertical take-off and landing aircraft, following on from the 'Flying Bedstead', was the Short S.C.1, which made its maiden flight, piloted by Tom Brooke-Smith, in April 1957.

the USA since the British 'Flying Bedstead' trials of 1954 into designing a military aircraft that could take off and land vertically, obviating the need to provide landing strips.

STRAIGHT UP

A USAF Ryan X-13 Vertijet had taken off vertically, made the transition to horizontal flight, then returned to the hover to land, in November 1956, but for both take-off and landing it needed a special trailer that pointed its nose at the sky. The first jet aircraft to take off vertically from a level position was Bell Aircraft's X-14, on 17 February 1957. The X-14 was powered by two Armstrong Siddeley Viper turbojets, which could be used either for vertical thrust or to provide forward flight.

On 2 April 1957, the chief test pilot for Short and Harland, Tom Brooke-Smith, made the first flight of the Short S.C.1 delta-winged vertical take-off and landing (VTOL) research aircraft. It was not until 6 April 1960, though, that the S.C.1, with four Rolls-Royce turbojet engines to give vertical lift and one for horizontal flight, made the full transition from one mode of flight to the other, flying conventionally before hovering, then returning to wing-borne flight again.

JUMPING JETS

The following year, in September, the experimental Hawker Siddeley P.1127 vertical/short take-off and landing (V/STOL) aircraft – the technical name for what came to be called a 'jump-jet' – made the first complete transitions from vertical to horizontal flight using a single engine incorporating the ideas of Frenchman Michel Wibault. The thrust from the four nozzles of the Bristol Siddeley Pegasus could be directed down for lift and to the rear for normal flight.

Above: The British RAF team in the 1969 transatlantic race used Harrier jump-jets to take off and land in the heart of London and New York. Refuelling in flight, the Harriers made the flight from London to New York in under six hours.

In 1963, the P.1127 became the first VTOL aircraft to fly from an aircraft carrier, the *Ark Royal*, while March 1964 saw the maiden flight of the Hawker Siddeley P.1127 Kestrel, which, in 1965, became the world's first operational VTOL fighter. From this was eventually developed the Harrier, the first fixed-wing 'flat riser' to go into production for squadron use. Then, in 1969, a two-seat trainer version of the jump-jet, the Hawker Siddeley Harrier T.2 prototype, made its first flight.

RACE ACROSS THE ATLANTIC

Vertical take-off aircraft figured prominently in 1969 in a transatlantic air race that was organized by the *Daily Mail* to commemorate the 50th anniversary of Alcock and Brown's historic flight across the Atlantic. The race started at the top of London's Post Office Tower and finished at the top of New York's Empire State Building. Around 400 competitors entered, chasing £60,000 in prize money. Appropriately enough, the first to set out from London was Anne Alcock, Sir John Alcock's niece.

It was a colourful and sometimes bizarre contest. One competitor used a stagecoach for part of his journey, while another, sponsored by the Italian national airline, dressed as a tribune and travelled to London Heathrow in a chariot; Tina, a chimpanzee famous for her appearances in TV commercials, made the same journey in a Rolls-Royce. One of several celebrity entrants, Stirling Moss, began his attempt by racing on a motorcycle to a speedboat on the Thames. This took him to a barge waiting midstream with a helicopter on board.

RECORD-BREAKING CROSSINGS

The main excitement, though, was seeing who would win the £6000 prizes for the fastest times from east to west, and west to east. The main contenders were an RAF team using jump-jet Harriers, and Britain's Royal Navy, using supersonic Phantoms. Both types of aircraft could make the journey non-stop, refuelling in flight.

Using the Harrier's VTOL capacity to reduce the distance between start and take-off, and between landing and finish, the RAF team managed a shortest time overall of six hours, 11 minutes and 57 seconds, with the Harrier recording five hours and 58 minutes for the westbound flight. The Royal Navy set a new record for the east-west transatlantic crossing at five hours, three minutes and 19 seconds and an overall time of five hours, 30 minutes and 24 seconds, then broke their own record twice more during the race. The prize for the shortest overall time – five hours, 11 minutes and 23 seconds – went to Lieutenant Commander Peter M. Goddard. On the last day of the race, in a Phantom piloted by Lieutenant Commander Brian Davies, he crossed the Atlantic in four hours, 46 minutes and 58 seconds at an average speed of 723.8mph (1164.9kph), having travelled at up to 1200mph (1900kph).

Right and below: The 1969 Alcock and Brown 50th anniversary transatlantic race attracted a wide range of forms of transport. There were examples ancient and modern, from chariots, horses, balloons (below) and bicycles to speedboats, VTOL jets and helicopters (right), the latter seen starting from the Thames in London.

Above: In 1976, a French Concorde operated the first scheduled supersonic airline service in the world, between London and Rio de Janeiro. Soon afterwards a regular passenger service between London and New York was introduced.

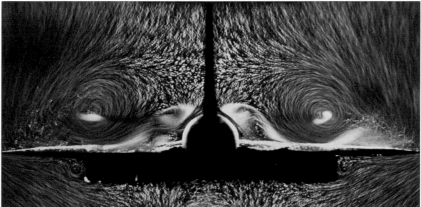

Left: This rear view of the Concorde shows the airflow pattern created by the aircraft.

THE SUPERSONIC DREAM

Soon after the sound barrier had first been breached, designers began to take the idea of a supersonic airliner seriously. Some set about trying to build one. In 1956, the British government set up the Supersonic Transport Aircraft Committee (STAC) to see whether such aircraft were feasible. In the next three years the STAC came up with three designs.

The projected development cost of any of these was huge, so the British and French governments went into partnership in November 1962 to build a supersonic airliner that soon came to be known as Concorde. By 1969, the French and British prototypes were ready to make their maiden flights. Yet neither took the honour of being the first supersonic airliner to fly, as on 31 December 1968 the Tupolev Tu-144 made its maiden flight in the Soviet Union.

MAIDEN FLIGHTS

Andrei Tupolev's aircraft had a wing outline and drooping nose – for better visibility on take-off and landing – similar to those on Concorde. This resemblance earned the Tu-144 the nickname 'Konkordski' in the West. The aircraft, designed to take 121 passengers, had four powerful NK-144 after-burning turbojets grouped together under the centre of the fuselage that would enable it to cruise at speeds higher than Mach 2 for a range of just over 4000 miles (6500km), but it could be difficult to handle at lower speeds.

The French Concorde prototype, assembled by Aérospatiale, flew on 2 March, and its British counterpart, built by BAC, took to the air on 9 April 1969. Both flights were successful, and attracted large crowds. The new aircraft, which was designed to carry 118 passengers at a cruising speed of Mach 2.2, was driven by four noisy, but hugely powerful Rolls-Royce/Snecma Olympus 593 turbojet engines.

Late in 1974, a French Concorde demonstrated its speed advantage over other airliners by travelling from Boston to Paris, spending over an hour on the ground, then returning to Boston in 11 minutes less than a Boeing 747 travelling one way from Paris to Boston.

SUPERSONIC SCHEDULES

It was not, however, until 21 January 1976 that a French Concorde carried 100 passengers to Rio de Janeiro on the world's first scheduled supersonic flight for fare-paying passengers. It covered the 6000 miles (9600km) in seven hours and 26 minutes (including a 78-minute refuelling stop at Dakar). The London-New York service soon followed, and Concorde proved an attractive option for anyone who felt it was worth paying a good deal extra to fly from London to New York, as Concorde did on 16 December 1979, in less than three hours.

Below: The Tupelov Tu-144 was the first supersonic airliner to fly, but it suffered many development problems. There is a visual similarity between 'Konkordski' and Concorde because similar solutions were found for the same problems.

Above and left: Yuri Gagarin became the first man in space when *Vostok I* launched him into orbit in April 1961. The USSR's President Krushchev proclaimed him a hero, but the unassuming cosmonaut lost favour when Krushchev fell. Gagarin died in a crash on a routine military flight in 1968.

LEAVING THE PLANET

Although such developments as supersonic and high-altitude flight were exciting enough in themselves, they were thoroughly overshadowed in the 1960s, at least in terms of historical significance, by the progress being made towards the conquest of outer space.

The launching into orbit of the dog Laika in *Sputnik 2* in 1957 had proved that living creatures could survive space travel. The next step came in August 1960 when, after a day's orbit, a capsule separated from *Sputnik 5* and parachuted to Earth. A container including two dogs (Strelka and Belka), some mice, rats and fruit flies, was ejected at an altitude of 4.5 miles (7km) and landed by parachute. It was the first time living creatures had travelled into space and returned safely.

MAN IN SPACE

The Soviet Union and the USA were both striving to put a man into space. Seven potential astronauts had

began their long training in the USA in April 1959. Soon after, the USSR called for trainee cosmonauts, and a group of military pilots were selected around February 1960.

In January 1961, NASA successfully launched a chimpanzee, Ham, into space and recovered him. They were planning the first manned sub-orbital flight when the Soviets announced, on 12 April 1961, that they had not only put a man into space, but into orbit around the Earth. Major Yuriy Alekseyevich Gagarin, the 'pilot space navigator' of *Vostok I*, became, virtually overnight, the most famous man in the world.

Gagarin, a quiet, unassuming man, was the son of a carpenter. He was born in 1934, in a village near Smolensk, west of Moscow, and had trained as a foundryman. He was, though, determined to be a flyer, and graduated from pilot training school in 1957. He joined the Soviet Air Force, and in March 1960 was chosen for the 20-strong Soviet cosmonaut team, 12 of whom would eventually fly in space.

TEETHING TROUBLES

The pioneering days of manned space flight had not gone at all smoothly. There were five unmanned test flights of Vostok system rockets before Gagarin climbed into *Vostok I*; two of them failed on the launch-pad, one burnt up on re-entry and another was sent in error into a higher, rather than a re-entry, orbit, and was lost.

Having four failures in five flights taxed Soviet confidence, but the launch of *Vostok I* from Tyuratam in Kazakhstan – at 9.07 a.m. local time, 6.07 GMT on 12 April 1961 – went smoothly, and the capsule containing Gagarin went into free flight on a round-the-world orbit. He completed his orbit in just over 89 minutes in a total flight time of 108 minutes. The furthest he got from the Earth's surface was 203 miles (327km).

While over South America, Gagarin radioed that 'The flight is normal. I feel well.' Half an hour later he was over Africa. His second message was equally matter-of-fact: 'I am withstanding the state of weightlessness well.'

After the orbit, the capsule began to drop to Earth. At 4 miles (6.5km) up, the drogue parachute in the capsule deployed, slowing its descent. Soon after, the parachute hatch in the Vostok capsule was released and the ejector seat operated, flinging Gagarin from the capsule. At 2.5 miles (4km) the ejector seat fell away, leaving the cosmonaut to parachute safely to

Left: The first woman in space, Valentina Tereshkova, followed Gagarin into orbit in *Vostok VI* on 16 June 1963. Tereshkova was the only woman astronaut of the 1960s, and the USSR made great use of her for propaganda purposes.

land near the town of Engels in the Saratov region of the USSR at 10.55 a.m. local time.

Professor Sir Bernard Lovell, of Britain's Jodrell Bank experimental radio astronomy station, summed up Gagarin's flight as 'The greatest scientific achievement in the history of Man.' After being debriefed, Gagarin was sent on a goodwill tour of the world.

AMERICAN RESPONSE

His triumph came as a bombshell to the USA, where NASA went ahead with their first planned space flight on 5 May 1961. Former fighter-pilot Alan B. Shepard Jr climbed into *Freedom 7*, a Mercury capsule that weighed around 3000lb (1400kg) and was launched into space by a Redstone rocket. His 15-minute sub-orbital flight ended, as planned, in the Atlantic Ocean 40 miles (65km) from Bermuda. The Americans could now also claim to have put a man into space.

Three months later, on 6 August 1961, the Soviet Union reaffirmed its technical lead when *Vostok II* made 17 orbits of the Earth carrying the cosmonaut Gherman Titov, who, at 25, was two years younger than Gagarin had been at the time of his epic flight.

It was not until 20 February 1962 that an American first made an orbital flight. John Glenn was launched into space by an Atlas rocket in the Mercury capsule *Friendship 7*. Travelling from west to east, he completed three orbits before firing retro-rockets from 98 miles (157km) above California. This were designed to slow down the capsule so that it could re-enter the atmosphere.

There was a problem during the flight when monitors indicated that the heat shield had been dislodged, but NASA got round this by using the retro-rocket pack in position to hold the heat shield on, and Glenn landed safely in the Atlantic near the Bahamas. When the capsule was examined later, it was found that the shield was perfect; it was the monitors that had been faulty. Glenn at once became a national hero: he was given an emotional ticker-tape reception in New York, with people openly crying in the streets as he was driven by.

WALKING IN SPACE

The Mercury and Vostok flights continued. The Soviets scored another first on 16 June 1963, when Valentina Tereshkova, in *Vostok VI*, became the first woman in space. Like other cosmonauts and astronauts, Tereshkova was little more than an observant passenger, rather than a pilot, since she could not vary the flight path of her craft in its 48 orbits.

The purpose of the Voskhod (a modification of the Vostock) and Gemini programmes that followed was to extend the capabilities of both the spacecraft and the pilot. They also involved heavier craft. On 12

Above: The Atlas rocket carries John Glenn into space in February 1962.

October 1964, *Voskhod 1* carried three cosmonauts into space and returned them to a 'hard' landing which was achieved with the use of retro-rockets and parachutes.

Then, on 18 March 1965, the USSR scored another first. *Voskhod 2* was launched with a two-man crew, one of whom, Alexei Leonov, went out through an airlock to perform the first Extra Vehicular Activity (EVA), or 'space walk'. Afterwards, Leonov had difficulty re-entering *Voskhod 2*, as his inflated spacesuit had ballooned in the vacuum of space. After eight minutes of struggling he reduced the pressure in the suit enough to squeeze back into the spacecraft.

The American astronaut Edward H. White made a 20-minute space walk from *Gemini 4* two and a half months later, but the main purpose of

Left: Astronaut David R. Scott carries out a maintenance procedure just outside the command module of *Apollo 9* on 6 March 1969, the fourth day of the US spacecraft's Earth-orbital mission. The Earth can be seen in the background.

Below: Edward H. White was the first American to leave a spacecraft in flight in 1965, when he left *Gemini 4* for a 20-minute 'walk' in space.

the two-man Gemini flights was to develop enough manoeuvrability in space so that a future series of spacecraft would be able to meet and dock with other spacecraft in orbit. It was the *Gemini 8* mission in March 1966 that produced the first docking of two spacecraft in orbit – a vital preparation for the Apollo Moon-landing programme.

THE APOLLO PROGRAMME

President Kennedy, in a speech made on 25 May 1961, had committed the USA to landing a manned spacecraft on the Moon 'before this decade is out', although NASA had had no settled plans to do this at the time. The method finally chosen was to launch a three-manned Apollo spacecraft on its way to the Moon using the massive Saturn V rocket.

The spacecraft itself would be in three parts; a service module, lunar module, and re-entry capsule. The service module's engine would put the spacecraft into lunar orbit. Two of the crew would then descend to the surface of the Moon in the lunar module. At the end of the stay, a rocket in the upper section of the module would lift it back into lunar orbit to dock with the rest of the spacecraft. The men would then be transferred and the module jettisoned as the service module's engine put the spacecraft back on course for Earth.

The Apollo programme received a setback in January 1967. Three astronauts were killed in the spacecraft's cabin when a fire broke out during a ground test. There were no more flights until 11 October 1968, when *Apollo 7*, launched by a Saturn 1B rocket, orbited the Earth 163 times. The flight of *Apollo 8*, which was launched on 21 December 1968, was a triumph. Just three months after the Russian *Zond 5* had made the first circumlunar flight and return to Earth with a live cargo of turtles, flies, seeds and plants, *Apollo 8*, with astronauts Borman, Lovell and Anders aboard, headed for the Moon, orbited it ten times, then returned to Earth.

LUNAR LANDING

The next two Apollo spacecraft tested out the Lunar Module – first in terrestrial orbit and then in lunar orbit. Finally, on 16 July 1969, came the launch of *Apollo 11*. This carried Neil Armstrong (38), Edwin 'Buzz' Aldrin (39) and Michael Collins (38). They achieved lunar orbit without a hitch, then the Lunar Module, *Eagle,* with Armstrong and Aldrin aboard, separated from the main craft, *Columbia.*

Armstrong and Aldrin were given permission by Mission Control at Houston to place Eagle into the correct orbit for descent. As *Eagle* neared

Above and left: The only astronaut to feature in the photographs that were taking during the first Moon landing is Buzz Aldrin (right in inset), as Neil Armstrong (left) had the camera attached to his own space suit and Michael Collins (centre) was orbiting the Moon in *Columbia.*

the surface, Armstrong realized that the auto-targeting was taking *Eagle* right into a crater. He took back control from the computer, hovered at 200ft (60m) and piloted the landing craft manually over the rock field at around 7mph (10kph) to find a better place for landing. At 8.17 p.m. GMT on 20 July 1969, mankind first landed on the Moon.

Six hours and 39 minutes later, Neil Armstrong left the *Eagle* to become the first person to set foot on the lunar surface, saying as he did so, 'That's one small step for man, one giant leap for mankind.'

It was a true global event. About a million people had gathered in Florida to watch the launch; as many as a billion (one-fifth of the world's population) watched both the launch and Moon landing on television.

Above: In the 1970s, the emphasis of space exploration switched away from manned flights to the sending of probes to photograph and broadcast back data to Earth. *Viking 1* was the first to land on and survey Mars.

Armstrong was ever the pilot rather than the explorer. After the *Apollo 11* mission he told a press conference that the Moon walk had not been the highlight of the mission. 'The most exciting and rewarding part,' he insisted, 'was the descent to the lunar surface.'

THE SOYUZ PROGRAMME

The Soviet Union had lost the race to the Moon, but the outcome of this particular space race had been in doubt for some time. In April 1967, the Soviets had successfully launched what was then the world's most advanced spacecraft, *Soyuz 1*, into orbit. However, the cosmonaut, Vladimir Komarov, was killed when the recovery parachute became entangled on re-entry and the spacecraft crashed. This accident led to the suspension of the Soviet space programme for 18 months, by which time the Americans had forged ahead in the space race.

However, the Soviets used further *Soyuz* craft to perfect docking techniques of the kind that had been so vital to the American success. On 19 April 1971, they established a 'first' that was not, perhaps, so dramatic as the American Moon landing, but was equally as important, when they put *Salyut 1*, the world's first space station, into orbit.

Three or four days later *Soyuz 10*, with a crew of three led by Vladimir Shatalov, was launched to rendezvous with *Salyut 1*, and succeeded the following day in approaching, docking with and separating from the space station. Then, on 7 June, three cosmonauts from *Soyuz 11* entered

Salyut 1, and remained aboard for 23 days. Tragically, a valve on *Soyuz 11* failed during re-entry, and air from the pressurized capsule rushed out into the void. Though their capsule landed safely, all the cosmonauts – none of whom were wearing spacesuits – were dead when it was opened.

LIVING IN SPACE

The next Russian space station, *Salyut 2*, disintegrated soon after its launch. *Salyut 3* and *4* went up in 1974, and *Salyut 5* in 1976. In September 1977, the first of a new generation, *Salyut 6*, was launched. It was on this space station and the following *Salyut 7* that the long-stay missions began. In 1978, Vladimir Kovalenok and Alexander Ivanchenkov spent 140 days aboard *Salyut 6*. The Americans, lacking a foothold in space, were unable to compete, and it was not until the launch of their first Space Shuttle in 1981 that they regained some of their former prestige.

After the success of *Apollo 11*, NASA devoted most of its energies to further landings on the Moon. A Lunar Module from *Apollo 12* set down in the Ocean of Storms on 18 November 1969, and a successful run of *Apollo* flights continued up to and including the December 1972 voyage of *Apollo 17*. The only problem came with *Apollo 13*, which was nearly lost after an explosion in the Service Module, but returned safely to Earth.

Even before *Apollo 11* was launched, there was a debate about the relative merits of manned and unmanned space flights. This intensified after the Moon landings. The scientific community, in particular, felt that more could be achieved at less expense if man-rated technology was not required. For example, the Soviet Union used the *Luna 16* spacecraft to bring back Moon samples to Earth in September 1970 at far less expense than the *Apollo* landings. The more cautious approach now holds sway, and no one has walked on the Moon since 1972.

EXPLORING THE SOLAR SYSTEM

Because of the human element and danger involved, the *Apollo* Moon landings have tended to eclipse the unmanned exploration of other planets that followed, even though the scientific benefits of the latter probably outweighed those of the Moon landings. Venus proved a particularly productive destination for Soviet probes. *Venera 7* made the first successful descent to the surface in 1970. Five years later *Venera 9* and *Venera 10* returned pictures and data from the planet's surface. Mars was the subject of successful American probes, culminating in *Viking 1* and *Viking 2*, which landed in 1976. *Viking 1* sent back data for six years.

The USA launched the first probe to the outer planets, *Pioneer 10*, in 1972. *Pioneer 11* followed in 1973. Both flew past Jupiter, taking photographs as they went, and *Pioneer 11* then went on to take a close look at Saturn. In 1977, two more American spacecraft, *Voyager 1* and

Above: This photograph of Skylab floating serenely above the weather systems far below was taken by a crew member on arrival or departure in 1974. Skylab's orbit above the atmosphere made it an ideal base for astronomical observations.

Voyager 2, began flights that would take them to Jupiter, Saturn and beyond. *Voyager 2* continued to Uranus and Neptune, reaching the latter some 12 years after its launch and radioing back extraordinary close-up pictures of the planet and its satellites.

EXPLORING THE SOLAR SYSTEM

After *Apollo 17,* the Americans switched the focus of their manned flight programme on to making up the lead the Soviet Union had achieved in developing space stations. Five months after the last Moon landing, on 14 May 1973, the Skylab space station was launched into orbit. Skylab was essentially an astronomical research station. It carried several pieces of equipment designed to observe and monitor the sun, and a major scientific instrument, the Apollo telescope mount. The station also included an Orbital Workshop that had been made from a converted fourth stage of a Saturn V rocket. This included the living and working areas for the crew. Attached to it was an Airlock Module, through which the astronauts could leave Skylab to work in space.

Skylab also had a Multiple Docking Adaptor. This allowed *Apollo* spacecraft to dock with the space station, so that crews could be brought and returned to Earth. Three teams of three astronauts successively conducted experiments in Skylab between 25 May 1973 and 8 February 1974, and the station remained in orbit until July 1979, when it fell back into the Earth's atmosphere and broke up.

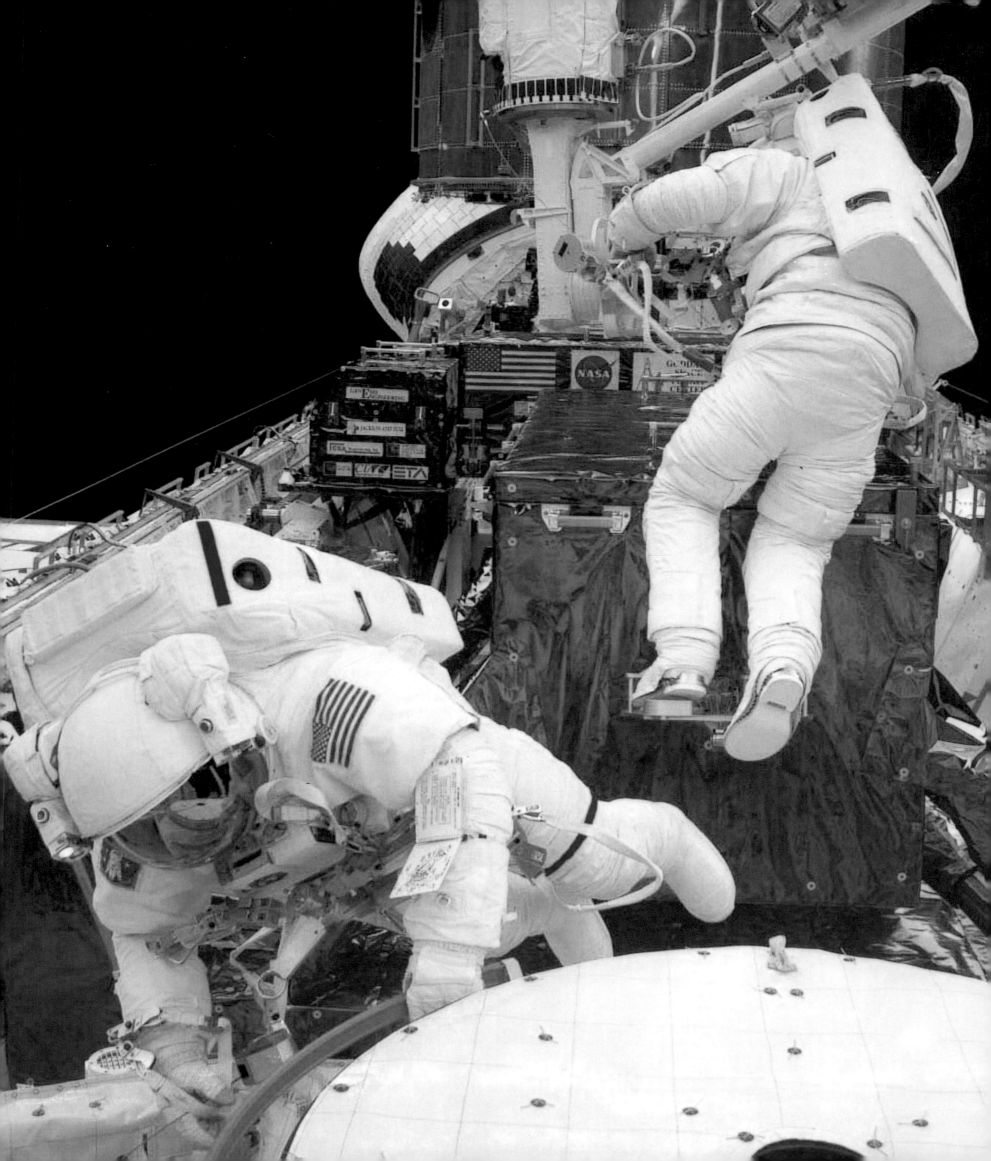

INTO THE UNKNOWN

1980–1999

World history in the last two decades of the 20th century has been dominated by the end of the Cold War. Mikhail Gorbachev's commitment to *perestroika* ('restructuring') and *glasnost* ('openness') in the 1980s paved the way for the Soviet Union to dismantle itself. At the end of the decade, its constituent republics and the satellite countries of Eastern Europe became more or less independent republics and took on elements of the free-market economy as the Iron Curtain was lifted and the major symbol of global tension, the Berlin Wall, was demolished. The thaw in international relations was marked by increasing co-operation in space exploration.

In the 1980s, the politics of much of the developed world moved to the right, as the belief that controlling the money supply would deliver economic stability took hold. This led to a continuing decline in manufacturing and a growth in financial and service industries, bringing widespread unemployment and economic insecurity as well as new forms of work. At the same time, the exponential growth of microchip technology revolutionized life at home and in the workplace.

The number of road vehicles continued to rise, despite growing concerns about the depletion of global energy resources, while the development of new, high-speed trains and national investment in new routes brought a resurgence in the fortunes of rail transport. Passenger ships were by now largely confined to pleasure cruises, and giant oil tankers, not liners, ruled the seas. Passenger jets got bigger and bigger: Boeing's 747-400 'superjumbo' first flew in 1988.

Increasingly, transport achievement came through sport rather than record-breaking or exploration. Again, the exception was space, where global co-operation has become the norm, and the American Space Shuttle and the Soviet (later Russian) space stations have combined to pursue the scientific exploration of the solar system and what lies beyond.

Left: Two astronauts from the USA's STS-82 Shuttle carry out maintenance work on the Hubble Space Telescope in February 1997.

In the field of transport as well as so many others, the main theme of the 1980s and 1990s has been the extraordinary development and exponential growth of information technology. Competition between record-breakers on land, at sea and in the air has been sharpened still further by the use of computer controls, but there is still a place for old-fashioned skill and courage.

LAUNCHING THE *ROCKET*

In 1979, for example, Stan Barrett, a 36-year-old Hollywood stunt man, attempted to become the fastest man on earth. Barrett, the protégé of movie director Hal Needham, was a devout Christian who was not attracted by the trappings of stardom. He was more interested in the challenge and the thrill of speed itself than official recognition. Because of this, he was not prepared to make the two timed runs over a one-mile (1.6km) course necessary to take Gary Gabelich's official record of 622.4mph (1001.7kph) for rocket or jet-propelled wheeled vehicles.

Barrett's *Budweiser Rocket,* a long, slim, three-wheeler, was the creation of rocket-propulsion expert Bill Fredrick, who also designed its Romatec V4 rocket motor and had it built by one of his companies. The car was designed to provide a burst of physically punishing acceleration to a top speed around Mach 1, then almost immediately decelerate. On 9 September 1979, Barrett touched 638.7mph (1027.8kph) in a single run over the Bonneville Salt Flats, but found the surface too rough. On 17 December he made a fresh attempt at Rogers Dry Lake in California's Mojave Desert. This

Left and below: Stan Barrett, in true pioneering spirit, was more interested in testing the limits of human achievement than in fame. As a result, the astonishing speeds he achieved in his *Rocket* went unratified.

Above and right: The new world record speed of 633.5mph (1019.5kph) set by Richard Noble in *Thrust 2* was the latest in a long sequence of record-setting performances using Castrol lubricants.

time, the *Budweiser Rocket* had the rocket motor from a Sidewinder missile attached, to allow Barrett to call on a further brief burst of power.

In the chill dawn, Barrett ignited the engine of the *Budweiser Rocket,* and it roared away in a cloud of smoke. Within three seconds he was travelling at over 400mph (650kph). After 12 seconds he had reached 640mph (1030kph) and was subjected to a force of 4g. Then he fired the Sidewinder motor, and achieved another g of acceleration. Seconds later the main rocket engine cut out, and Barrett deployed braking chutes to bring the vehicle to a halt.

THROUGH THE BARRIER

From start to finish, the run took 70 seconds, but it took seven hours to calculate Barrett's top speed over a time trap of just 52ft (15.8m). There was a moment of panic when the first reading showed 30mph (48kph): the radar had picked up a passing water truck. Eventually, though, it was confirmed that Barrett had reached 739.67mph (1190.37kph). This speed represented Mach 1.01, making Barrett the first man to go through the sound barrier on land.

There was no official challenge to Gabelich's unlimited world land speed record until Richard Noble in 1983. Noble, an Englishman who was inspired as a boy by seeing John Cobb's boat *Crusader* on Loch Ness, took the record on 4 October, in Nevada's Black Rock Desert. He drove *Thrust 2,* a jet-powered vehicle with an Avon 302 series engine, to an average speed over two timed runs of 633.5mph (1019.5kph).

Above: Two huge Rolls-Royce engines powered *Thrust SSC* through the sound barrier in October 1997, giving Andy Green a world land speed record that is unlikely to be challenged for years to come.

Below: Richard Noble (right) came close to his dream of going through the sound barrier in *Thrust 2*, taking Gary Gabelich's record on the way, but eventually achieved it by proxy through Andy Green (left) in *Thrust SSC*.

Noble's dream, though, was to take the official record past the speed of sound. In 1993, he began assembling a team to construct a supersonic rocket car, and took on RAF pilot Andy Green as driver. In 1996, the *Thrust SSC* (Super Sonic Car) was ready, and that November Green drove the 54ft (16.5m) projectile to 325mph (522.9kph) in Jordan's Al Jafr Desert. The following autumn, in Nevada, a fresh pair of 100,000hp Rolls-Royce engines with just 10 hours of life but providing 20 per cent extra thrust, took him to a new world record of 714.1mph (1149.2kph).

FASTER THAN SOUND – OFFICIAL

More was to come. On 15 October, Green smashed his own record with an average speed of 763.035mph (1227.983kph) that took him through the sound barrier. He was officially credited with reaching Mach 1.015 on his outward run and 1.02 on his return. This feat grabbed the headlines around the world, and made Green one of the great achievers of the 20th century. As Richard Noble said, 'Most of us on the *Thrust SSC* team will fade into the background, but Andy is a worldwide hero.'

Green's record is likely to stand for some time; becoming the second man through the sound barrier is unlikely to inspire the necessary level of financial backing and interest that Noble's project was able to secure.

WORLD SERIES SPORTS CARS

Back in the world of more conventional cars, there was a notable resurgence of interest in World Series sports-car racing, in which, from 1982, engine power was restricted only by a limit on the fuel consumption each vehicle was allowed. In the early 1980s, the German manufacturers Porsche were so dominant in this Group C class of racing that it was unusual for their 956/962 prototype models to lose.

Then, in 1985, Jaguar decided to re-enter sports-car racing at world championship level after an absence of nearly 30 years. Although the normally aspirated Jaguar V-12 engine, even after it was specially modified for

Above: Jaguar-Castrol's Lammers, Dumfries and Wallace won the Le Mans 24-Hour event in 1988. That same year, Nielson, Brundle, Lammers and Boesel's XJR-9 were victorious at Daytona, after Castrol began the season with a three-year, $3-million-per-annum sponsorship of Jaguar in the USA, with extra funds for the World Sportscar Championship.

racing, could not provide the same amount of power as the turbocharged Porsches, the new restrictions meant the Porsches could not use their extra power for anything like the full race distance.

Jaguar's twin objectives were the World Sports Prototype and the Le Mans 24 Hours race. In 1985, Jaguar took part in a limited number of races using the brand-new Jaguar XJR-6 built by Tom Walkinshaw Racing, carrying only Castrol sponsorship. The following year, the first year of a partnership with Silk Cut and Castrol that was to last until the

end of the 1992 season, they attempted the full programme. Mechanical problems which had little to do with the car's basic design meant Jaguar won only one of the world championship races. However, had one more second place been secured in the final round at Fuji, Derek Warwick would have taken the Drivers' title and the team would have won the Team title. In 1987, the Silk Cut-Castrol Jaguar team won eight of the ten races to take that title, while Raul Boesel won the Drivers' overall championship.

In 1988, Jaguar extended their programme to include America's premier sports-car series, the International Motor Sports Association (IMSA) Camel GT Championship. Although they did not win the overall championship, the Castrol-Jaguar IMSA Team scored a spectacular victory in their first race, the SunBank 24-Hours at Daytona. The winning XJR-9, driven by John Nielson, Martin Brundle, Jan Lammers and Boesel, crossed the line a lap and a half ahead of the second-placed Porsche, and another Jaguar finished third.

VICTORY AT LE MANS

In 1988, Jaguar achieved the second of its goals with a victory in the 24-hour race at Le Mans. The Le Mans Grand Prix d'Endurance, first run in 1923, had become the most prestigious single event in motor racing, and this year produced a thrilling, race-long engagement between Jaguar and Porsche. Jan Lammers, Johnny Dumfries and Andy Wallace gave Jaguar its first Le Mans win since 1957. This was one of six victories which brought Jaguar the world team championship again, with Martin Brundle taking the drivers' title.

Interestingly, Jaguar's closest competitor in 1988 was no longer Porsche, but Mercedes, who had returned to motor sport after an absence of 33 years. Their turbocharged V8 Sauber Mercedes cars won the other five world championship events.

The cost of sports-car racing escalated in the next few years with the introduction of 3-5-litre engines. These were used mainly in the Sprint races, although Jaguar continued to use the trusted V12 at the established endurance classics, Le Mans and Daytona, achieving race victories again at both venues in 1990.

Following a seriously under-supported season in 1992, the world championship was abandoned. However, in 1997 the sport's governing body sanctioned a new official sports-car series that was immediately supported by high-tech cars from Mercedes, Porsche and BMW. Mercedes won the title to pave the way for a new era of long-distance racing.

In Formula One, the early 1980s were notable for a fierce battle fought not so much between individual teams as styles of car; large

Above: The Jaguar team also reigned supreme in the World Sportscar Championship in the late 1980s, with drivers such as Raul Boesel and Martin Brundle (inset) taking the drivers' title.

Right: Introduced in the UK in 1995, SLX was the first commercially available zero-viscosity engine oil. It provides excellent high-temperature durability and lasts up to five times

turbocharged machines vied with smaller 'ground-effect' cars with normally aspirated engines. At first the smaller cars took the main prizes. Jody Scheckter of South Africa became world champion in 1979 in his Ferrari 312T4, and in 1980 Australia's Alan Jones won in his Williams FW07-Ford; his closest rival, the Brazilian Nelson Piquet, drove a Brabham BT49 with a Ford-Cosworth engine. The Williams team continued their domination of the racetrack for much of the following season, although the eventual winner was Piquet in a Brabham-Ford, and in 1982 Keke Rosberg of Finland took the championship in a Williams-Ford.

TRIUMPH OF THE TURBOCHARGERS

By this time, though, turbocharged cars had begun to come into their own. In 1981, a turbocharged Renault driven by France's Alain Prost – in his second Formula One season – won the French, Dutch and Italian Grands Prix, and might have won others but for mechanical problems. At the same time, flaws in the design of ground effect cars were becoming apparent. The very stiff springs that were needed to ensure the road-holding of the cars put a great deal of physical strain on the driver, and this, combined with cornering forces of up to 4g, was producing a crop of chronic neck and back injuries.

This led FISA to order that from 1983 the undersides of Formula One cars must be flat, and that was the end of the 'wing-car'. Although normally aspirated cars managed a few victories in 1983, turbocharged cars had effectively won the day; and the 1983 world championship was won by Piquet in a turbocharged Brabham-BMW BT.52.

Turbocharged cars continued to dominate Formula One for the next five years. Niki Lauda of Austria won in a McLaren with

Above and right: The championship victory of Nelson Piquet in 1983 in the Brabham-BMW BT.52 was the first for a turbocharged car and ushered in five years when normally aspirated engines were overwhelmed by the dominant turbochargers. The popularity of Formula One racing grew worldwide as new Grands Prix were established, lengthening the racing season.

Right: Ayrton Senna followed Emerson Fittipaldi as a Brazilian world champion and became a sporting hero whose fame rivalled that of Brazil's footballers. His aggressive racing style won him few friends among his fellow-drivers, but secured for him a hat-trick of victories in the World Drivers' Championship: in 1988, 1990 and 1991.

a turbocharged TAG-Porsche engine in 1984, after a tense contest with his team-mate Alain Prost. Prost went on to win in 1985 and 1986; Piquet won in 1987 in a turbocharged Williams-Honda; and in 1988 Brazil's Ayrton Senna drove a turbocharged McLaren-Honda MP4/4B to victory, winning eight races to his team-mate Prost's seven.

A NEW FORMULA

The problem with turbocharged engines was that it was difficult to keep their power under control. In 1984, FISA had tried to do this by forbidding refuelling stops, and allowing each car only 48.4 gallons (220 litres) of fuel. This did not prevent wealthy teams from qualifying with enormously powerful engines that ran out of fuel in the closing laps, and it was agreed in 1987 that turbocharged engines would be phased out by the start of the 1989 season, with the introduction of a new Formula based upon a 3.5-litre normally aspirated engine.

The McLaren-Honda team remained in the forefront, with Prost winning four races and Senna six, but the rivalry between them had become increasingly bitter and after the 1989 season, Prost, who became that year's world champion, accepted an offer to join Ferrari.

CHAMPIONS OF THE 1990s

Senna won the championship in 1990, though his victory seemed hollow to many, as at the Japanese Grand Prix he had ended Prost's chances of the championship by driving him off the road. He also established a commanding lead early in 1991, winning the first four Grands Prix, and became world champion for the third time running.

In 1992, with his Williams-Renault FW14B in top form, Britain's Nigel Mansell won the world championship by a substantial margin, having set new records by winning nine Grands Prix in a single season, including the first five races. This was also the year when the young German driver Michael Schumacher won for Benetton in Belgium and managed an impressive third in the Drivers' Championship.

After a year's absence, Prost returned to Formula One in 1993. He joined Williams in place of Mansell, who had gone Indy Car racing. Prost won seven Grands Prix and his fourth championship before

Above: Britain's Nigel Mansell, a technically proficient if unimaginative driver, came close in the world championship several times before his victory in 1992. The following year he switched to Indy Car racing. Although he had some success, he never managed the level of excellence he had achieved in the Formula One Williams-Renault.

Right: Frenchman Alain Prost was perhaps the most durable driver of the 1980s, winning the world championship in 1985, 1986 and 1989. In 1993, after a year off, he joined the Williams team and clinched his fourth championship at Imola in the San Marino Grand Prix.

Above: Like his 1996 team-mate Damon Hill, Canadian Jacques Villeneuve was a second-generation Grand Prix driver, the son of Gilles Villeneuve. In 1997 he succeeded Hill as number one in the Williams team and then as world champion.

retiring to become a commentator for French television. He was commentating at Imola on the San Marino Grand Prix of 1994, when his great rival Senna died after a high-speed crash.

SAFER CIRCUITS

As a result of this tragedy, several racing circuits were redesigned to make them safer and to slow down the competing cars. Schumacher came through to win the 1994 world championship for Benetton, though the title was hotly contested by Britain's Damon Hill, who had joined the Williams team in 1993. In his first season with them, Hill – the

son of former world champion Graham Hill – had won three Grands Prix, and in 1994 he came within a point of the victorious Schumacher.

Schumacher won again in 1995 after the Williams cars suffered a bout of mechanical trouble, but in 1996 the championship soon turned into a battle between Hill and his new Williams team-mate, Canadian Jacques Villeneuve, as Schumacher abandoned Benetton for a new berth and a lucrative contract with Ferrari.

Although Schumacher won three races during the season, Villeneuve took four, and Hill seven. Hill was leading the championship going into the final race in Japan on 13 October; only Villeneuve could still catch him. The Canadian's hopes were finally dashed when his right rear wheel flew off, leaving Hill, who had been driving flawlessly, to win both the race and the 1996 world championship.

SCHUMACHER VERSUS VILLENEUVE

With Hill leaving Williams at the end of the season, Villeneuve became their number one driver. The 1997 championship soon became a two-way battle between Villeneuve, the man with the best car, and Schumacher, who was widely regarded as the best driver. Both men had their triumphs and failures, and neither of them was able to establish a telling advantage. The pair went to the final race of the season in Jerez

with Schumacher leading his rival by just one point. The championship was won and lost when the German drove into Villeneuve, apparently in an attempt to put both of them out of the race and so secure the title for himself. However, the gamble did not pay off: the Ferrari ran off the road into the gravel trap, while the Canadian raced on to take third place and the championship.

Right: Damon Hill's victory in the Japanese Grand Prix of 1996 made him world champion, emulating his late father, Graham.

Below: The German driver Michael Schumacher is generally regarded as the most technically gifted of Formula One drivers, although his apparent win-at-all-costs philosophy has led to conflicts with the sport's ruling body.

RALLYING WITH FOUR-WHEEL DRIVE

In another area of motor sport, rallying, one of the most significant developments came in 1981, when Audi introduced four-wheel drive to the World Rally Championship. Although the factory team's turbocharged, production-based Audi Quattro was larger and heavier than other rally cars, four-wheel drive gave it outstanding traction and braking, especially on loose or slippery surfaces.

During its first world series, the Quattro won three events, in one of which, the San Remo, Michele Mouton became the first woman ever to win a world championship rally. The following year, Mouton added to this success, winning the Portuguese, Brazilian and Acropolis rallies on her way to second place in the Drivers' Championship, while Audi won the manufacturers' title. In 1983, Hannu Mikkola of Finland became individual world champion in an Audi, and in 1984 the marque took its first manufacturers' and drivers' title double, with seven more victories, five of them won by the new champion, Stig Blomqvist of Finland.

By the early 1990s, rallying categories had been redefined, with Group A taking in cars with modified engines, transmissions, wheels, suspensions and tyres, and Group N for standard production cars with minor safety modifications. Mazda, who had won a number of World Rally Championships, scored a striking success in Group N in 1991,

Above: The Castrol Toyota team, in Celica Turbos, scored impressive wins in the world rallying championship in 1993 – when Juha Kankkunen (right) was top driver – and 1994.

Below: Michele Mouton and her co-driver F. Pons urging their Audi to victory in the Kenya Rally in 1983.

when Grégoire de Mevius of Belgium won the title in his Mazda 323 GTX. De Mevius won again in 1992, this time in a Castrol-lubricated Nissan Sunny GTIR.

In Group A, the outstanding achievement of the early 1990s was that of the Toyota Castrol team that won the manufacturers' and drivers' titles in both 1993 and 1994 with their turbocharged four-wheel-drive Toyota Celica Turbos, driven notably by Finland's Juha Kankkunen, champion in 1993; and Didier Auriol of France, who won in 1994.

WORLD RALLY CARS

In 1997 a new category of car – the World Rally Car (WRC) – was introduced in order to make it easier for manufacturers to enter the world championship. The new rules made it possible for teams to rally with modified production cars, provided at least 25,000 of the base model had been made.

The first WRC to appear was that of Subaru at the start of 1997. The Prodrive-run team had seen Colin McCrae win the championship in 1995, before Tommi Makinen captured the crown for Mitsubishi in 1996, and their WRC Impreza proved good enough to challenge the Finn all the way to the final round, even though McRae ultimately missed out on the crown by just one point.

Right and below: The first amateur hot-rod drivers customized production cars. This tradition is kept alive in funny-car races, a separate category of drag racing in which John Force of Team Castrol (below) was world champion six times in seven years and the first to break 4.9 seconds for the quarter-mile (400m).

Above and left: The fastest of all dragsters are in the Top Fuel class. These machines bear very little resemblance to production cars; they are basically pointed projectiles that are arrowed along the track by engines burning something resembling rocket fuel.

QUARTER-MILE STARS

Drag racing was established as a major international sport by the late 1980s, having travelled from the USA to as far afield as Australia, Sweden and Japan. Hot-rods had become increasingly specialized, and different classes had evolved, many of them aimed at the 21,000 amateur racers.

Among the few hundred professionals, 'Funny Car' dragsters such as John Force of Team Castrol drove highly exotic cars covered with a fibre-glass copy of a standard production model. From a standing start, these cars, running on nitromethane, could cover the standard quarter-mile (400m) in five seconds or less; as they accelerated away from the start, they subjected their driver to 4g of pressure.

Force won a record-breaking seven drag-racing victories in the 1990 season, and was crowned Funny Car Champion by the National Hot Rod Association (NHRA) six times in seven years. He also became the first Funny Car driver to break the 4.9-second barrier for the standing quarter-mile, setting a new record of 4.88 seconds. The fastest drag cars overall, though, are the 'Top Fuel' dragsters, so-called because of the highly volatile special mixtures on which they run. In March 1992, one of these cars reached 301.7kph (485.54kph) before completing the quarter-mile and they now often break the 300mph (480kph) barrier.

ON TWO WHEELS

In the more conventional world of top-level motorcycle racing, the late 1970s had seen an upsurge of factory involvement by Japan's leading manufacturers. In the 500cc world championship, Suzuki were dominant for many years. Britain's Barry Sheene won for them in 1976 and 1977, Kenny Roberts of the USA in 1978, 1979 and 1980, and Italians Marco Lucchinelli in 1981 and Franco Uncini in 1982. Then Honda returned to competition in 1979. Three years later, their 21-year-old American rider Freddie Spencer, who had started dirt-track racing at six years old, won three Grands Prix on their three-cylinder two-stroke NS500 – lubricated by Castrol A747.

In 1983 there was an exciting contest between Spencer and Kenny Roberts, then riding for Yamaha. The result was not settled until the twelfth and final round; both ended with six wins, but Spencer took the 500cc title with an overall lead of two points.

Above: Britain's Barry Sheene (inset) was twice 500cc world champion in the late 1970s. This shot shows him in action on his Suzuki in October 1977.

Left: Honda's emergence as a threat to Suzuki's dominance in the 1980s was spearheaded by the American rider Freddie Spencer, seen here on his three-cylinder, two-stroke Honda NS500 in 1982, the year before he took his first world championship.

Below: Kenny Roberts senoir (facing camera) and junior at the Dutch Grand Prix in 1996, Kenny junior's second 500cc season.

Right: Atop their Castrol-sponsored Lada (main picture), Nikonenko and Talantsev celebrate their victory in the 1995 Paris–Moscow–Beijing rally, in the Chinese capital. This gruelling event was contested by two-wheeled vehicles (right) and four-wheeled alike.

Below: Top trials rider Jordi Tarres won the World Trials Championship for the third time in 1991 on a purpose-built Beta Zero machine.

The following year Spencer was favourite to win on Honda's new V4-powered 140bhp Honda NSR500, but a series of unlucky accidents meant that he took part in only six Grands Prix – winning five of them – and the title went instead to Yamaha's Eddie Lawson.

However, Spencer more than made up for this in 1985 after Honda redesigned the NSR500 to make it easier to ride, and also built a 250cc vee-twin which, though not much more powerful than the opposition, was about 20lb (9kg) lighter. Spencer delighted in the smaller machine, on which he rode to victory in seven Grands Prix. With an equal number of 500cc wins, he became the first rider ever to achieve the 250cc and 500cc world championship double. Spencer would, however, never win another Grand Prix, and the 1986 season was dominated by the Castrol-lubricated Yamahas of Eddie Lawson, who won the 500cc championship, and Carlos Lavado, who took the 250cc title.

DOOHAN DOMINANT

The Japanese firms of Honda, Suzuki, Yamaha and Kawasaki, joined by Italy's Ducati and Bimota, dominated world championship motorcycling well into the 1990s. Michael Doohan was the top rider in the 1990s, breaking a number of records for consecutive wins, pole positions and fastest laps. The Australian, from Brisbane, took his Castrol-sponsored Honda to titles from 1994 to 1997.

A major motorcycle achievement passed almost unnoticed at the start of the decade; on 14 July 1990, American Dave Campos set a new world record speed for a motorcycle on Bonneville Salt Flats, averaging 322.15mph (518.45kph) on his 23ft (7m) streamlined machine.

HIGH-SPEED TRAINS

The quest for speed had also become a dominant theme of railway development. After numerous difficulties, the first French TGV *(Train à Grande Vitesse)* line opened between Paris and Lyon in September 1981. When it was fully commissioned in 1983, it would reduce the time for making that journey from three hours and 47 minutes to just two hours. In 1992, a TGV train recaptured the railway world speed record – which had briefly been held by a German Inter-City Express (ICE) train – by travelling at over 300mph (480kph).

The advent of high-speed trains had coincided with a worldwide renaissance in the fortunes of rail transport. This was the result partly of the 1973–74 oil crisis, which provided a strong economic argument for switching traffic from road to rail, and partly – at least in heavily industrialized and urbanized region – due to a growing realization that ever-increasing motor traffic led to both unacceptably polluted towns and cities and unacceptably clogged roads.

In the USA, Graham Claytor, Amtrak's Chairman from 1982 to 1993, almost single-handedly rescued the country's rail passenger service. He presided over the introduction of the moderately high-speed Metroliner passenger trains, which run successfully between New York and Washington, and set in motion ambitious schemes for its future. At the same time a number of the leading long-distance truck companies began to use the railway for hauls of more than 300 miles (480km).

NEW RAIL LINKS

Among exciting new developments in Europe, 1992 saw the completion of a new Spanish railway line between Seville and Madrid, while in 1994 France and Britain were linked by a rail tunnel under the English Channel, soon nicknamed the 'Chunnel'. Thanks to a new line on the French side known as the TGV-Nord, on which trains travelled at an average speed of 143mph (228kph), it became possible to travel by train from London to Paris in about three hours.

At the same time, the Italians were planning a high-speed line to run from Milan in the north to Naples in the south, and the Swiss had begun construction of a new set of Alpine rail tunnels. In 1995, China opened two sections of a railway intended to provide a high-speed train link

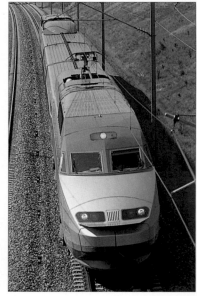

Above: The French TGV, one of the first of the modern generation of high-speed trains, came into service in the early 1980s, and soon took the world rail speed record.

Left: One of Eurostar's high-speed trains linking the UK with the European mainland via the Channel Tunnel is seen here just outside the Calais terminal in May 1994, the year in which the 'Chunnel' was opened.

Above: Introduced in the mid-1990s, Japanese Railways' JR500 locomotive *Nazomi* is the latest of the high-speed Bullet Trains.

Below: Japan's 'maglev' (magnetically levitated) train set a new world speed record for rail in early 1998 by reaching 321mph (517kph).

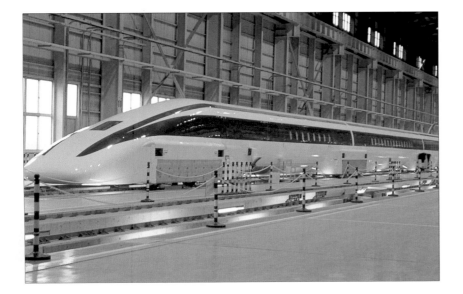

between Peking and Hong Kong; while in Japan in the late 1990s the average speed of wheeled trains stands at some 140mph (225kph).

THE MAGLEV REVOLUTION

By contrast, the absence of wheels characterizes a rail development which may well assume great importance if costs can be reduced. This is the high-speed, magnetically levitated passenger train system known as maglev. Introduced in the early 1990s, maglev trains exploit the electromagnetic reaction between a device in the track, or 'guideway', and another on board the train, in order to lift the train off the track.

Once the train is raised in this way, movement and braking depend on a reaction between magnets set in the train and a 'linear motor' built into the guideway. This reaction – and hence movement – is controlled by altering the current's voltage and frequency. Two main maglev systems have been developed. German trains are driven by magnetic attraction, while Japanese technology uses the principle of repulsion. The Japanese maglev train reached 249mph (401kph) on its test track, and it is believed that, with substantial upgrading of the electrical infrastructure, much greater speeds can be achieved.

In yachting, one of the chief events of the past two decades was the successful challenge made in 1983 by the Australian businessman Alan Bond in the America's Cup. This represented an astonishing reversal of fortune. There had been 25 competitions for the prize since it was established in 1851, and the New York Yacht Club had retained it on every occasion. However, Bond's *Australia II* boasted a revolutionary design, with a wing-shaped keel that improved its performance over that of the conventional keel of the American defender *Liberty*, and enabled it to win the series and the cup by four races to three.

NORTH AND SOUTH

Some of the most remarkable individual voyages were undertaken in the 39ft (12m) steel ketch *Northern Light*, crewed by Rolf Bjelke of Sweden and Deborah Shapiro of the USA. In June 1982, they sailed north from Sweden through the Barents Sea until the pack-ice became too thick for them to go any further. They then continued south-west through the Denmark Strait between Iceland and Greenland and ended their voyage in Boston, Massachusetts.

Later they sailed to Easter Island in the Pacific via the Panama Canal, and September 1983 found them cruising among the Polynesian islands. As the Southern summer began, they turned the prow of the *Northern Light* south-east, passed through the 'Roaring Forties' and sailed down the Patagonian coast past Cape Horn. By January 1984, they had reached Antarctica. Five months and around 8000 miles (13,000km) later, Bjelke and Shapiro were back in Boston. In recognition of their achievement, they were awarded the 1984 Blue Water Medal of the Cruising Club of America.

THREE TIMES AROUND THE WORLD

In just under two years – from 25 May 1986 to 13 March 1988 – an Australian, Jonathan Sanders, sailed single-handed around the world three times in his 46ft (14m) masthead sloop *Parry Endeavour*. Sanders had already made a double circumnavigation in 1981-82 in his 33ft (10m) sloop *Perie Banou*, but on that occasion he had taken on supplies during his voyage. This time, during his one westward and two eastward circuits, his only contact with the outside world (apart from his radio) came at the end of his first circumnavigation, when he had some newspapers dropped aboard and exchanged mail.

Left: In 1983, Alan Bond's yacht *Australia II* broke the longest winning streak in world sport, by ending the 132-year stranglehold of the New York Yacht Club over the America's Cup, the world's premier trophy for ocean-going yachts .

Right: One of the major factors in the success of the *Australia II* was its technical superiority, particularly its revolutionary new design of keel.

WOMEN AROUND THE WORLD

In 1988, Australian Kay Cottee became the first woman to sail solo around the world in *Blackmore's First Lady*. Her achievement was matched by Britain's Lisa Clayton, who set out on 17 September 1994 in her steel-hulled sloop *Spirit of Birmingham* in an attempt to become the first woman to achieve a solo, non-stop, unassisted global circumnavigation from the northern hemisphere.

As she had no major sponsor, she put more than £400,000 of her own money into the attempt. The first few weeks were uneventful, but from then on she contended with storms and gales. The *Spirit of Birmingham* capsized three times; once, Clayton was washed overboard and swept back on by the next wave. She lost much of her equipment, including her navigation lights, and was forced to stay on watch all night. Battling headwinds in the South Atlantic, she could advance just 30 miles (50km) a day, but on 29 June 1995, after 286 days, the rust-streaked *Spirit of Birmingham* returned to her home port of Dartmouth.

POWER ON THE WATER

Powerboat racing has become increasingly popular in the 1980s and 1990s, as the sport has split in two. The most prestigious racing takes place off-shore, where 50ft (15m) boats boasting two 1000hp engines and designs based as much on aero-engineering as nautical science hurtle across the water at top speeds of around 150mph (240kph). The only way to go this fast over water is to ride just above it, with only the

Above and right: Formula One powerboat racing has been dominated in the 1990s by the Italian Guido Cappellini, whose 'home-built' DAC/Laserline catamaran took him to several world championships, including an outstanding season with just one defeat in 1996.

bottom half of the twin propellers in the water – hence the aerodynamically designed boats. Class 1 off-shore boats have two drivers, one to work the throttle and keep the boat from taking off and flipping over, and the other to steer.

Although it is uniquely exciting for the drivers, off-shore racing makes a poor spectator sport as the sheer speed of the boats and the consequent length of the course makes the race difficult to follow; even helicopters have difficulty in keeping up with the action.

FORMULA ONE

This is not true of Formula One powerboat racing, which takes place over much tighter circuits on lakes and other inland waters. It can make good, exciting television and has, as a result, attracted a considerable following in the 1990s. From 1993, the world championship has been dominated by the Italian Guido Cappellini, whose DAC/Laserline hull powered by a 2-litre Mercury engine is among the most advanced circuit-racing catamarans ever seen in Formula One. Built by Cappellini and his partner Attilio Donzelli from wood and advanced composites, the vessel had features including variable-geometry running surfaces, transferable water ballast and radio telemetry.

Cappellini won the 1993 title easily, but the following year was closer. Welshman Jonathan Jones, who had won the world championship in 1986 and 1989, led at first, but the Italian eventually secured the championship with one win and five more top-three finishes. In 1995, Cappellini fended off the German veteran, Michael Werner, while 1996 was a truly remarkable season for him. He secured his fourth successive world title by winning every race except, ironically, the Campione d'Italia on Lake Lugano, where he had mechanical problems.

Right: Welshman Jonathan Jones, who pressed Cappellini all the way in the 1995 world championship, was twice champion in the 1980s. This shot shows him in his second championship season in 1989 racing in the Bristol Grand Prix.

Left and right: The Seacat *Hoverspeed Great Britain*, with Captain John Lloyd (above) at the controls, left New York City on 20 June 1993 at the start of the journey that won it the Blue Riband and the Hales Trophy for the fastest Atlantic crossing by a passenger vessel. The inset shows publicity material promoting Castrol's contribution.

NEITHER SHAKEN NOR STIRRED

Castrol meets yet another challenge supplying specialist lubricants to Hoverspeed Great Britain

SEACAT AND THE HALES TROPHY

By contrast with the ferocious competition seen in the first half of the century, most records for sea travel remained unchallenged for many years. The Blue Riband and the Hales Trophy for the fastest Atlantic crossing by a passenger vessel, had been held by the *United States* since July 1952, with a time of three days, ten hours and 40 minutes.

As the development of jet airline travel led inexorably to the decline of the ocean liner, little interest was shown in the record until the middle of the 1980s, when British businessman Richard Branson made two attempts on it. He and his crew failed to win back the Blue Riband in the *Virgin Atlantic Challenger*, but succeeded in 1986 in cutting two hours and nine minutes from the *United States*'s record in *Virgin Atlantic Challenger II*, which made the crossing in three days, eight hours and 31 minutes. However, as both *Atlantic Challengers* were basically speedboats rather than passenger craft, they were ineligible for the Hales Trophy.

REVOLUTIONARY DESIGN

It was not until 1990 that a genuine challenge came for the Hales Trophy. *Hoverspeed Great Britain*, a revolutionary catamaran also known as Seacat, was launched in Tasmania on 23 January that year. The world's largest wave-piercing catamaran, it measured 243ft (74m), twice as long as any previous craft of its type.

The Seacat had been designed for cross-English Channel passenger routes, and could carry 80 cars and 450 passengers. Its two long, narrow hulls each housed two Ruston 16RK 270 medium-speed diesel engines. Fitting medium-speed engines to a high-speed craft enabled the engines to be coupled directly to Riva Calzoni water jets. Two of these were used for manoeuvring and steering, and two to help the vessel reach its maximum speed of 42 knots (78kph) once it was clear of the harbour, thus eliminating the need for gearboxes.

RECORD ATTEMPT

The *Hoverspeed Great Britain* set out from New York on 20 June 1990. Despite strong headwinds and waves 20ft (6m) high, it reached the Bishop Rock lighthouse in the Scilly Isles at 8.25 a.m. on 23 June, having made the crossing in three days, seven hours and 25 minutes – at an average speed of 36.97 knots (68.47kph) – to take both the Blue Riband and the Hales Trophy.

On 14 August that year, the *Hoverspeed Great Britain* entered commercial service, with regular Portsmouth to Cherbourg crossings in two hours and 40 minutes, half the time of a conventional ferry. The Seacat is an excellent example of the way that technical advances first expressed in record-breaking eventually benefit the ordinary traveller.

Right: The Hales Trophy was introduced in the 1930s to supplement the purely notional prize of the Blue Riband.

AIR

FURTHER INTO THE UNKNOWN 1979–1999

At the dawn of the 1980s, just one great challenge remained for any would-be aviation pioneer: a non-stop flight around the world without refuelling. In 1980, two brothers, Dick and Burt Rutan, discussed the possibility of such a flight in a Californian café. Dick was a retired USAF Lieutenant Colonel, while Burt was an engineer who had revolutionized the market for home-built aircraft. That day, Burt made a quick sketch of a feasible round-the-world aircraft on a paper napkin.

Six years and $2,000,000 of sponsorship later, Burt had designed and built, with the help of John Roncz, a 'trimaran' light aircraft made of magnamite fibre stretched over a honeycomb paper core. *Voyager* was light, yet strong enough to carry five times its weight in fuel. There was room for 1489 gallons (6770 litres) of it in 17 storage tanks built into the wings, tailplane booms and fuselage.

The aircraft had a crew of two: Dick Rutan and his girlfriend Jeana Yeager, holder of nine aviation speed and endurance records. Just before eight o'clock in the morning of 14 December 1986, they made a worryingly rough take-off from Edwards Air Force Base in California. They were accommodated in a cramped, unpressurized fuselage pod 7½ ft (2.3m) long and 3½ ft (1.1m) wide between the front and rear engines, with a sleeping space on the left and the pilot's seat beneath a small canopy on the right. Behind the seat was storage space for oxygen, water and dried food. Keeping the weight down was crucial. Maps,

Below: Between 14 and 23 December 1986, *Voyager,* piloted by Americans Dick Rutan and Jeana Yeager (inset), made a remarkable 25,000-mile (40,000km) non-stop flight around the world without refuelling.

charts and manuals were on microfiche; two lightweight parachutes doubled as pillows; paint had been used only where *Voyager* needed protection from the sun, and Yeager had her hair cut short.

FIGHTING THE ELEMENTS

Two days out, they encountered Typhoon Marge above the Pacific. At first they used its winds as a boost, but were then forced south to New Guinea. The following evening they had crossed the Malay Peninsula and set out across the Indian Ocean. Over Africa they ran into weather so fierce that they were repeatedly thrown against the sides and roof of their compartment. They strapped on oxygen masks and took *Voyager* up to 18,000ft (5500m), where they found the tail winds which would help them over the Atlantic. By this time they were both exhausted, and nearly lost one of their engines in mid-Atlantic as they had forgotten to keep it topped up with oil.

On Monday 22 December they crossed Panama, and headed up the Pacific along the west coast of Mexico to complete the trip. Then, in the early hours of the next day, they came close to disaster. *Voyager*'s rear engine suddenly died as a result of a vapour lock and they plummeted earthwards for 90 terrifying seconds before they could restart it. Soon after, they landed at Edwards, having made a 25,000-mile (40,000km) non-stop flight lasting nine days, three minutes and 44 seconds.

HELICOPTER RECORD

Although the greatest aviation challenge had been overcome, the skies still offered scope for individual adventure and achievement. Over a period of 97 days, from 10 May to 15 August 1997, a 57-year-old grandmother, Mrs Jennifer Murray, and her erstwhile flying instructor, Quentin Smith, became the first people to circumnavigate the globe – a journey that took them through 26 countries – in a helicopter powered by a single-piston engine, a Robinson R44. Mrs Murray thus became the first woman to circumnavigate the world by helicopter, and the pair were the first Britons to make such a flight

COMMERCIAL ACHIEVEMENTS

As the scope for pioneer aviators narrowed, international flight – just a few decades earlier the exclusive preserve of the rich – became commonplace for people in the developed world, even those on comparatively modest incomes. Indeed, between 1980 and 1990 total world passenger journeys rose nearly 75 per cent to 1.176 million miles (1.893 million kilometres) – a good time for aircraft manufacturers.

Above: On its maiden flight the Airbus Industrie A320, as befitted this product of European collaboration, was flown by a British, French and West German crew, under Frenchman Captain Pierre Baud. The flight, from Toulouse, southern France, lasted three hours and 23 minutes.

Below: *Spirit of Australia,* a Quantas 747-400, set a new London–Sydney non-stop record of just 20 hours in August 1989.

On 22 February 1987, the twin-engined Airbus Industrie A320 made its maiden flight. This remarkable 150-seater had numerous computer-controlled safety systems ensuring that, for example, it was virtually impossible to stall the aircraft and that it could land safely with less than 900ft (275m) of visibility.

Then, in April 1988, Boeing launched the 747-400 'superjumbo', the world's heaviest commercial airliner. Its increased fuel capacity, combined with the reduced consumption of its four turbofan engines, allowed it to carry 400 passengers for more than 7500 miles (12,000km) non-stop. A Qantas 747-400, *Spirit of Australia*, made a record-breaking non-stop flight of 11,000 miles (17,700km) from London to Sydney in only 20 hours in August 1989.

AROUND THE WORLD IN 32 HOURS

Although there have been no serious attempts in the 1990s to break the outright air speed record, the fastest circumnavigation was achieved in 1995. The rules for this record state that the distance covered must be longer than a trip round either of the tropics, and on 15 and 16 August, an Air France Concorde flew from New York to Toulouse, Dubai, Bangkok, Guam, Honolulu and Acapulco, returning to New York in 32 hours, 22 minutes and 49 seconds.

THE SHUTTLE

The most dramatic developments in the history of flight were again associated with space. NASA had decided in the late 1960s to develop a new type of launch vehicle that would combine the characteristics of an aeroplane and those of a spacecraft to ferry people between earth and bases in space. This meant it would need to be able to return to earth and land on an extended runway and to be suitable for overhaul and reuse, perhaps as many as 50 times.

The technical difficulties involved in creating the Space Shuttle were considerable. Notably, there were problems with the main rocket engines and insulation against the heat of re-entry. Before this time, launch engines had been made to be used just once, and were required to last only a few minutes. The engines on the Space Shuttle, on the other hand, had to be built to survive more than 50 missions, and to run in eight-minute bursts for a total of around seven hours.

TAKING THE HEAT

The heat shield consisted of some 31,000 silicon tiles. Some of these were as thick as house bricks, which led to the first Space Shuttle, *Columbia*, being nicknamed the 'Flying Brickyard'. Although the tiles were excellent at dissipating heat, they were brittle, and the scientists had great difficulty getting them to bond to *Columbia*'s exterior.

These problems meant that it was not until 12 April 1981, some three years over schedule, that the first Space Shuttle was ready for launch. *Columbia* was a winged orbiting craft that contained the crew – in this case John Young of NASA, who had already flown two Gemini and two Apollo missions, and Captain Robert Crippen of the US Navy – any cargo, and the three main engines. It also had a massive external fuel tank holding the liquid hydrogen and the liquid-oxygen oxidizer for those engines, and was attached to two solid-fuel booster rockets. At the launch the booster rockets and the main engines were fired together.

Just over two minutes after lift-off, at a height of 30 miles (50km), the booster rockets were burned out and jettisoned. After six more minutes, with *Columbia* close to orbital speed, the main engines ceased firing; the external fuel tank was jettisoned, to burn up in the earth's atmosphere as small manoeuvring engines took the craft into orbit.

After 36 orbits at a height of 150 miles (240km), the manoeuvring engines were fired again in order to bring *Columbia* back into the Earth's

Left: The Space Shuttle *Columbia* is launched using the power of two huge booster rockets. Jettisoned soon after lift-off, the boosters parachuted down into the sea and were retrieved for use in future launches.

Left: John Young and Robert Crippen formed the crew for the first flight of the Space Shuttle *Columbia*. They are seen in the cockpit before the launch on 12 April 1982.

atmosphere. Friction raised *Columbia*'s external temperature to around 1500°C. This made it impossible for Mission Control to communicate for ten or eleven minutes, as radio signals could not pass through the ionized air around the craft. It was an anxious time, as the crew could see some of the heat shield's tiles had been lost in a non-critical area. However, *Columbia* and her crew survived. As the orbiter reached a lower and denser atmosphere it slowed and its wings began to produce lift. For the last part of its descent *Columbia* handled like a rather heavy glider, making a perfect landing at Edwards Air Force Base after a flight of some 54 hours.

THE SOYUZ T PROGRAMME

The USSR concentrated their efforts on the establishment of bases in space. In 1979, they introduced a new class of spaceships with improved propulsion, an automatic docking system and their own solar panels. The Soyuz T were designed to ferry cosmonauts – there was room for three people aboard – and supplies to and from orbiting Salyut space stations. The first manned flight of a Soyuz T took place in June 1980.

In April 1982 came the launch of *Salyut 7*, in which a team of cosmonauts set a new record for endurance of 211 days. When Svetlana Savitskaya visited the space station in August of that year, she became the

Below: Although it was launched on the back of a rocket, and used its own engines to achieve orbital speed and manoeuvre in space, the *Columbia* was piloted safely back to base in California as a glider.

Above: One of the most potent symbols of the end of the Cold War and the Space Race is the docking of the American Space Shuttle *Atlantis* and the Soviet Space Station *Mir* – 'Peace'.

people aboard, exploded shortly after take-off as a result of a fatal design flaw in the solid rocket boosters. The following month saw the launch of the advanced 'third-generation' Russian space station *Mir* ('peace'), in which Leonid Kizim became the first person to spend 365 consecutive days in space. The basic module – five others were added between December 1989 and April 1996 – was about 42ft (13m) long, weighed around 20 tonnes and had six docking ports.

Apart from four months in 1989, *Mir* has been continuously occupied since February 1987. When it was launched, its projected lifespan was just five to seven years, and the station is showing its age. In 1997, it was beset by fire, computer failure, generator breakdowns and a collision with an unmanned supply ship that resulted in the loss of more than half the station's power. *Mir* is due to return to earth and burn up in a controlled re-entry over the Pacific in late 1999, but might yet receive a reprieve.

SCIENCE IN SPACE

Other milestones in space travel since *Mir* blasted off are mainly concerned with carrying out scientific experiments in space. In April 1990, for example, the Hubble Space Telescope was carried into orbit, beyond Earth's obscuring atmosphere, by the Space Shuttle *Discovery*. Running repairs to the powerful telescope were successfully carried out in late 1993.

On 22 March 1995, Valery Polyakov, a 52-year-old doctor monitoring the physical and psychological effects of life in space aboard *Mir*, set a new record of 437 consecutive days, and a career total of 678 days, in space. Polyakov's record-breaking sojourn was not wholly intentional: a series of postponements and delays kept him aloft.

One of the largest space projects ever undertaken, the International Space Station (ISS), began in 1984, when NASA was directed to develop a permanent space station crewed by six to eight astronauts. It is due to come into use in 2003. Russia joined the ISS team in 1993, and Russians and Americans have frequently worked together in *Mir*, a vital training platform for ISS, learning about the problems of long-stay space flight. This collaboration led to several dockings of the American Space Shuttle *Atlantis* with *Mir*. On 15 May 1997, Eileen Collins became the first American woman to pilot a spacecraft when she blasted off in *Atlantis*.

Between 1998 and 2003 some 44 separate space flights using launch vehicles from the USA, Russia and Europe will carry equipment to be assembled in space to form ISS. When completed, the station will be manned by a permanent crew of seven astronauts – three from Russia and four from the USA, Canada, Japan and Europe – providing a base for scientific experiments, mainly in microgravity but also in biological and medical work on plants, animals and humans.

first woman to fly in space since Valentina Tereshkova in 1963. In another flight, in July 1984, she became the first woman ever to make a space walk. In February 1984, three more Soviet cosmonauts, Kizim, Solovyov and Atkov, embarked upon a long-term occupation of *Salyut 7*. They stayed there until October, setting a new record of 237 days in space, before returning safely to earth.

TRIUMPH AND TRAGEDY

A few months earlier, on 28 November 1983, the USA had launched Spacelab, the world's first reusable space workshop for scientific experiments. It took the form of a set of modules built by the European Space Agency and carried into orbit for up to ten days at a time inside the cargo bay of the Space Shuttle.

On 28 January 1986, however, the American space programme received a terrible setback. The Space Shuttle *Challenger*, with seven

Right: The Hubble Space Telescope has been one of the most successful of all the instruments put into space. By placing an astronomical instrument above the obscuring effects of the Earth's atmosphere, scientists have been able to see things much more clearly and peer much further into space, and hence time, viewing distant events that took place soon after the beginning of the universe. The telescope, seen here in 1997 in the bay of the Space Shuttle *Discovery*, is regularly serviced; early flaws that impaired its functioning were dealt with by astronauts.

Below: Russian cosmonaut Valery Polyakov looks out of the window of *Mir* during a rendezvous with the Space Shuttle *Discovery*.

THE FUTURE

In 1899 no one could have imagined the changes in technology that would take place over the dawning century and what impact these would have on the everyday lives of ordinary people. They could not have conceived that their own great-grandchildren could travel across the world and back, just for a two-week holiday, own their own car with built-in computer and regard space travel as almost commonplace. Technological advances are still continuing, bringing changes at an ever-faster rate. What does the future hold for our grandchildren? How will the transport that we use today evolve? Will we soon be driving any of the futuristic vehicles currently on the drawing board?

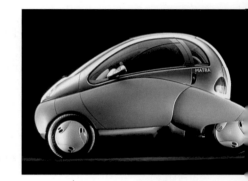

Among the many imaginative road vehicles undergoing evaluation as the century ends are Ford's Indigo (top left); Renault's Racoon (left) and Zoom (top and above); and BMW's C1 (below).

196

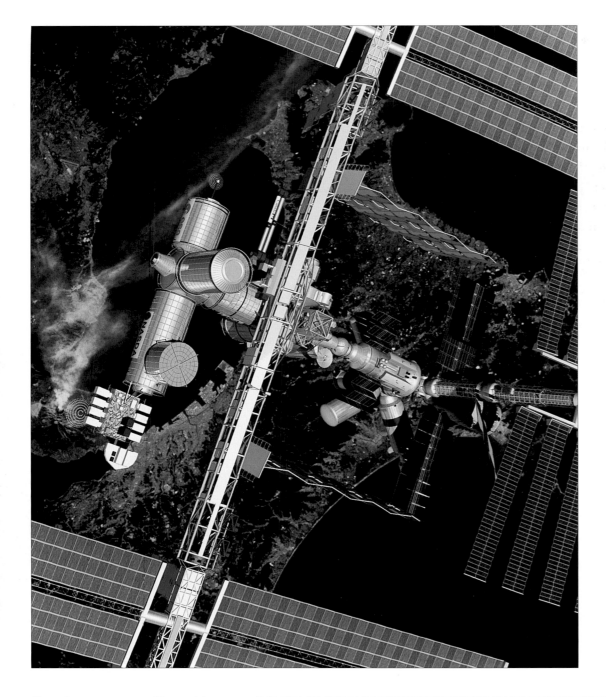

Above: America's Lockheed Martin X-33 Reusable Launch Vehicle is set to Revolutionize short-haul space travel.

Below: The US Navy's Stealth ship marks a significant advance in marine tactical warfare.

Above: A computer-generated image of the International Space Station's Phase III, heralding a future of co-operation in space.

Right: Japan's superconductive ship *Yamato1*, seen here at Kobe, points to a possible way forward in sea travel.

SELECTED ACHIEVEMENTS

1899–1997

1899

29 April Belgian Camille Jenatzy, in his electric-powered CITA No.25 car *La Jamais Contente*, sets a world land speed record at Achères, France, of 65.792mph (105.882kph). (Subsequent world land speed records are listed on pages 202–203.)

24 July Frenchman Chevalier René de Knyff in a Panhard 16hp wins the first Tour de France Automobile, begun on 16 July.

1900

23 April Start of the first Thousand Miles Trial, a road race organized by the Automobile Club of Great Britain (later known as the Royal Automobile Club). The winner is Briton the Hon. Charles Rolls in a 12hp Panhard.

14 June The first Gordon Bennett race, between Paris and Lyons, is won by Frenchman Fernand Charron in a 24hp Panhard Levassor at an average speed of 38.6mph (62.12kph). (Subsequent Gordon Bennett race winners are listed on page 202.)

1901

24 May The Paris–Bordeaux race is won by Frenchman Henri Fournier in a 60hp Mors at an average speed of 53mph (85.3kph).

27–29 June The Paris–Berlin race is won by Frenchman Henri Fournier in a 60hp Mors at an average speed of 44mph (71kph).

1902

26–29 June The Paris–Vienna race is won by Frenchman Marcel Renault in a 16hp Renault at an average speed of 38.9mph (62.6kph).

31 July The Circuit des Ardennes (53 miles/85.2km) in Belgium, the first major race on closed roads, is won by Briton Charles Jarrott in a 70hp Panhard at an average speed of 53.98mph (86.87kph).

March An unofficial world water speed record of 22.36mph (35.98kph) is set by an unknown skipper in the boat *Mercédès* at Nice, France. (Subsequent world water speed records are listed on page 204.)

1903

Germany's Siemens und Halske electric engine sets a rail speed record of 130mph (210.2kph).

The first British International Trophy for Motor Boats (also known as the Harmsworth Trophy) for motor boats is won at Queenstown, Ireland, by Briton S. F. Edge in his *Napier I* at an average speed of 19.53mph (31.43kph).

France's Poissy Sailing Club holds the first notable long-distance motor-boat race, from Poissy to Meulan (62 miles/100km). The winner is Frenchman M. Senot in the 24hp *Flore*.

17 December The first manned, powered, sustained and controlled flight, lasting 12 seconds, is made by American Orville Wright, in the *Flyer*, at Kitty Hawk, North Carolina, USA.

1904

25 September Russia's Trans-Siberian Railway opens a track around Lake Baikal, making it possible to travel by rail from Moscow to Vladivostok (5800 miles/9334km) without breaking the journey.

Briton George J. Churchward's *City of Truro* is claimed to be the world's first railway locomotive to reach 100mph (160kph) when it travels at an unverified speed of 102.3mph (164.6kph).

The first American Power Boat Association (APBA) Gold Challenge Cup is won by C. C. Riotte in *Standard* at a speed of 23.6mph (38kph).

1905

18 August The first Herkomer Trophy Rally in Bavaria, Germany, is won by German E. Ladenburg of Munich in a 40hp Mercedes.

The first international cup race for motorcyclists is held at Dourdan, France. The winner is Austrian Vondrich on a two-cylinder Laurin-Klement at an average speed of 54.5mph (87.7kph).

5 October American Wilbur Wright stays airborne in *Flyer III* for a record 38 minutes, 3 seconds, flying approximately 24 miles (39km).

1906

6 May The first Targa Florio race, on the Grande Madonie circuit in Sicily, is won by Italian Alessandro Cagno in an Itala at an average speed of 29.08mph (46.8kph).

26–27 June The first French Grand Prix, the forerunner of all national Grands Prix, is held near Le Mans, France. The winner is Frenchman François Szisz in a 90bhp Renault at an average speed of 62.88mph (101.19kph).

November The first Coupe de l'Auto, a six-day event for voiturettes, is held in France. The winner is Frenchman Georges Sizaire in his Sizaire-Naudin.

11 June Start of the first trans-Pacific race, which is won by the 86¼ft (26.3m) yacht *Lurline*.

The first Bermuda Race, from Gravesend Bay, Brooklyn, USA, to Bermuda (660 miles/1062km), is won by Day in the 38¼ft (11.6m) yacht *Tamerlane* with a time of 5 days, 6 hours and 9 minutes.

1907

28 May The first Tourist Trophy (TT) motorcycle races are held on the Isle of Man, UK. Rem Fowler wins the twin-cylinder prize on a Norton at 36.2mph (58.26kph). Charles Collier wins the single-cylinder prize on a Matchless at 38.2mph (61.48kph).

28 June The inaugural events are held at Brooklands motor-racing track, England. Briton S. F. Edge sets a world 24-hour distance record, travelling 1581 miles (2544km) at an average speed of 66mph (106kph).

13 November The first free helicopter flight, lasting 20 seconds and reaching a height of 1ft (30cm), is made by Frenchman Paul Cornu in a machine he created, at Lisieux, France.

1908

9 June Start of the 14,000-mile (22,530km) Prinz Heinrich Fahrt Rally, organized by the Imperial Automobile Club of Germany. There are 130 starters and the winner is German Fritz Erle, driving a 50hp Benz tourer.

1909

16 June W. E. Cook, on a 944cc NLG at Brooklands, England, sets a motorcycle world speed record of 75.92mph (122.16kph). (Subsequent motorcycle world speed records are listed on page 202.)

19 August The first race held at Indianapolis, Indiana, USA, is won by Louis Schwitzer in a Stoddard Dayton.

20 May Frenchman Paul Tissandier in a Wright biplane at Pau, France, sets an aviation world speed record of 34.03mph (54.77kph). (Subsequent aviation world speed records are listed on page 205.)

25 July Frenchman Louis Blériot, in a Blériot XI monoplane, makes the first powered aeroplane flight across the Channel from France to England and wins the £10,000 prize offered by the *Daily Mail*. He covers the 26 miles (42km) in under 37 minutes.

22 August The world's first international air show opens near Reims, France.

29 August At the Reims aviation meeting American Glenn Curtiss wins the first James Gordon Bennett International Aviation Cup race in his 50hp Curtiss Pusher biplane *Golden Flyer* at an average speed of 47.65mph (76.69kph). (Subsequent James Gordon Bennett International Aviation Cup results are listed on page 206.)

Also on 29 August at the Reims meeting, Briton Hubert Latham reaches an aviation world record height of 508ft (155m) in an Antoinette monoplane. (Subsequent aviation world altitude records are listed on page 204.)

15–26 October Britain's first air show is held at Doncaster, Yorkshire.

1910

The first Internationale Alpenfahrt Rally takes place in Austria.

27–28 April The £10,000 *Daily Mail* London–Manchester race is won by Frenchman Louis Paulhan in a Henri Farman III biplane powered by a 50hp Gnome rotary engine.

13 June American Charles Hamilton wins the *New York Times*'s $10,000 prize for the first return flight between New York and Philadelphia, USA.

23 September Peruvian Georges Chávez, in his Blériot monoplane, makes the first flight over the European Alps. However, tragically, he dies in a crash as he completes the flight.

1911

January The first Monte Carlo Rally is won by Frenchman Henri Rougier, who had set out from Paris in a 25hp Turcat-Méry.

30 May The first Indianapolis 500 is won by American driver Ray Harroun, in a single-seater 7-litre Marmon 'Wasp' at an average speed of 74.6mph (120kph).

May The first Isle of Man Senior Tourist Trophy motorcycle race to be held on the new, more demanding mountain circuit, is won by Oliver Godfrey on an Indian V-twin 500cc machine at an average speed of 47.63mph (76.65kph).

7 July Frenchman Lieutenant Jean de Vaisseau Conneau (flying as André Beaumont) wins the 1000-mile (1600km) Circuit of Europe, begun on 18 June, in a Blériot monoplane, with a flying time of 58 hours, 38 minutes.

27 July Lieutenant Jean de Vaisseau Conneau, in a Blériot XI monoplane, wins the *Daily Mail's* £10,000 Round Britain air race, begun at Brooklands, England, on 22 July.

10 December American Perry Calbraith Rodgers, in the Wright EX biplane *Vin Fiz*, completes an east-west flight across the USA in 84 days, landing at Long Beach, California, after setting out from New York City on 17 September.

1913

16 April The first Schneider Trophy contest, held at Monaco, is won by Frenchman Maurice Prévost in a Déperdussin seaplane at an average speed of 45.75mph (73.63kph). (Subsequent Schneider Trophy winners are listed on page 206.)

1916

Italian Dario Resta, in a Peugeot, wins the first American Automobile Association National Championship (see also 1956 and 1979).

1917

2 August Briton Squadron Commander E. H. Dunning of the Royal Naval Air Service, in a Sopwith Pup, makes the first aeroplane landing on a moving ship, landing on HMS *Furious* while it is steaming at 26 knots (48.2kph).

1919

16 January Britons Squadron Leader A. McLaren, Lieutenant R. Halley and others, in a Handley Page V/1500 heavy bomber, complete the first flight from England to India, landing in Delhi after setting out on 13 December 1918.

14–15 June Britons Captain John Alcock and Lieutenant Arthur Whitten Brown make the first non-stop transatlantic flight. The 1890-mile (3042km) journey from Canada to Ireland takes 16 hours, 12 minutes.

2–13 July The British R34 airship makes the first return journey by air across the Atlantic, from Britain to the USA and back.

25 August Britain's Aircraft Transport and Travel Ltd inaugurates the world's first scheduled daily international airline service, between Paris and London, using a de Havilland DH4A.

10 December Australians Ross and Keith Smith make the first flight from England to Australia, in 668 hours, 20 minutes, having set out from London on 12 November.

12 December Captain H. N. Wrigley and Lieutenant A. W. Murphy, flying a B.E.2e, reach Darwin and are the first men to fly across Australia, having set out from Melbourne on 16 November.

1920

20 March South Africans Lieutenant Colonel Pierre van Ryneveld and Squadron Leader Christopher Quintin Brand, flying first a Vimy and then (from Wadi Halfa) another Vimy, and finally (from Bulawayo) a de Havilland DH9, are the first men to fly from England to South Africa. They had set out on 4 February.

25 November The first Pulitzer Trophy Air Race is won by American Lieutenant Corliss C. Mosely over a closed circuit at Mitchell Field, Long Island, New York, flying his Verville VCP-R with a 638hp Packard engine at an average speed of 156.5mph (251.87kph).

1922

During the motorcycling TT week on the Isle of Man, UK, the first Lightweight Race is won by Geoff Davison on a Levis at an average speed of 49.89mph (80.29kph).

4 September American Lieutenant James Harold Doolittle, of the US Army, in a de Havilland DH4, makes the first coast-to-coast crossing of the USA, covering 2163 miles (3480km) in a single day, in a flight from Pablo Beach, Florida, to Rockwell Field, California, in 21 hours, 19 minutes' flying time.

1923

26–27 May The first Le Mans 24-hour Grand Prix d'Endurance is held in France. The winners are Frenchmen André Lagache and René Léonard, in a six-cylinder 2978cc Chenard et Walcker, who cover 1372.94 miles (2209.52km) at an average speed of 57.03mph (91.77kph).

1924

28 September The first circumnavigation of the world by air is completed by two US Army Air Service Douglas World Cruisers (open-cockpit, single-engined biplanes), the *New Orleans* and the *Chicago*. They take 175 days (flying time 371 hours, 11 minutes) and cover some 26,345 miles (42,152km), having set out from Seattle, Washington, USA, on 6 April.

1925

The Alfa-Romeo team wins the first Manufacturers' World Championship.

15 August The first Fastnet Race for yachts is won by the *Jolie Brise*, of French design and owned by Briton Lieutenant Commander E. Martin. The course is from Ryde, Isle of Wight, England, round the Fastnet Rock off south-west Ireland and back to Plymouth, England.

17 March Briton Alan Cobham becomes the first person to fly from England to India and back, in a de Havilland DH50 biplane fitted with a 230hp Siddeley Puma engine, having set out on 20 November 1924. For this feat he is awarded the Britannia Trophy by the Royal Aero Club.

1926

16 March American Dr Robert Goddard launches the world's first successful liquid-fuelled rocket at Auburn, Massachusetts, USA.

11–14 May The first flight over the North Pole is made by Norwegian Roald Amundsen in the airship *Norge*, accompanied by American Lincoln Ellsworth and Italian Umberto Nobile.

1927

26–27 March Italian Giuseppe Morandi wins the first Mille Miglia at Brescia, Italy, in an OM at an average speed of 48.27mph (77.68kph).

20–21 May American Captain Charles Lindbergh, flying from Long Island to Paris in the Ryan NYP monoplane *Spirit of St. Louis*, makes the first solo non-stop transatlantic flight, at an average speed of 107.5mph (173kph).

1928

7–22 February Australian Bert Hinkler makes the first solo flight from England to Australia, in an Avro Avian biplane. In doing so he sets a record for the longest solo flight of any kind in a light aeroplane.

9 June Australians Charles Kingsford-Smith and Charles Ulm, having set out on 31 May in their Fokker F.VIIB-3m *Southern Cross*, complete the first flight across the Pacific, from Oakland Field, California, to Brisbane, Australia, via Honolulu and Fiji in a flying time of 83 hours, 38 minutes.

1929

14 April The first Monaco Grand Prix is won by William Grover-Williams in a Bugatti Type 35 at an average speed of 50.23mph (80.84kph).

14 September The first International Motor Boat Meeting, held at Venice, Italy, is won by Briton Sir Henry Segrave in *Miss England*.

29 August The German airship *Graf Zeppelin* circles the world, having departed from New Jersey, USA, on 8 August.

28–29 November American Commander Richard Byrd, of the US Navy, and Bernt Balchen, Ashley McKinley and Harold June, in the Ford 4-AT Trimotor *Floyd Bennett*, make the first flight over the South Pole, in a flight of 1600 miles (2575km).

1930

5–24 May Briton Amy Johnson is the first woman to fly solo from London to Australia, in the de Havilland Moth light aeroplane *Jason*, powered by a Gipsy engine.

1 September In the National Air Races at Curtiss-Reynolds Airport, Chicago, USA, the first Thompson Trophy Air Race, over a closed circuit, is won by American Speed Holman in a 450hp Laird Solution at an average speed of 201.9mph (324.9kph).

1931

Belgium's Royal Motor Union of Liège holds the first true Marathon de la Route (a forerunner had taken place in 1927) over a 2800-mile (4500km) route. The winner is Toussaint in a Bugatti.

24 November American William Albert Robinson, in the Bermuda ketch *Svaap*, completes a 32,000-mile (51,500km) circumnavigation of the world, having set out from New York on 10 June 1928. Fellow American Willoughby Wright had accompanied Robinson from New York to Tahiti, where he was replaced by Etera, a Tahitian.

4–5 October Americans Clyde Pangborn and Hugh Herndon, in the Bellanca monoplane *Miss Veedol*, make the first non-stop flight from Japan to the USA, in 41 hours, 13 minutes.

1932

March In the first RAC Rally, held in Britain, the class for cars of over 1100cc is won by Briton Colonel A. H. Loughborough in a Lanchester 15/18, and the class for cars up to 1100cc class by Briton V. E. Leverett in a Riley Nine.

20–21 May American Amelia Earhart, in a Lockheed Vega monoplane, is the first woman to fly solo non-stop across the Atlantic. She flies from Harbor Grace, Newfoundland, Canada, to Londonderry, Northern Ireland.

18–19 August Scotsman James Mollison, in the de Havilland Puss Moth *The Heart's Content*, makes the first solo east-west crossing of the Atlantic, flying from Dublin to New Brunswick, Canada, in 31 hours, 20 minutes.

1933

3 April The Marquis of Clydesdale and members of a British team fly 100ft (30.5m) above Mount Everest (29,028ft/8848m) in two Westland (Bristol Pegasus) aircraft.

22 July American Wiley Post, in his Lockheed Vega *Winnie Mae*, completes the first solo round-the-world flight, in 7 days, 18 hours and 49 minutes.

1934

20–23 October The MacRobertson Race from England to Australia is won by Britons Charles W. A. Scott and Tom Campbell Black in the de Havilland DH88 Comet *Grosvenor House*, at an average speed of 158.9mph (255.7kph).

1935

27 September Briton Nigel Gresley's locomotive A4 No.2509 *Silver Link* sets a world record average speed for 25 miles (40km) of 107.5mph (173kph).

German Rudolf Caracciola of Mercedes wins the first European Drivers' Championship after winning the Tripoli, Eifel, French, Belgium, Swiss and Spanish Grands Prix.

1936

1 October Britons Charles W. A. Scott and Giles Guthrie, flying their Percival Vega Gull at an average speed of 116mph (186.7kph), win the Schlesinger Air Race, from Portsmouth, England, to Johannesburg, South Africa, begun on 29 September. The aircraft was the only finisher in the only occurrence of this race.

1938

3 July Sir Nigel Gresley's A4 No.4468 *Mallard* hauls his 'Coronation' train of seven coaches weighing 240 tons (244 tonnes) at 126mph (202.7kph) at Stoke Bank between Grantham and Peterborough, England, setting an all-time speed record for steam.

1941

February–March The first Southern Ocean Racing Conference (SORC) series of yacht races held off the coast of Florida, USA, is won jointly by the Sparkman and Stevens yawl *Stormy Weather*, sailed by William Labrot, and the 70ft (21.3m) *Gulf Stream*, sailed by Dudley Sharp.

15 May The Gloster-Whittle E28/39 experimental jet-powered aircraft begins its first trial flights.

13 August The first Messerschmitt Me.163A prototype makes its first flight under full rocket power at Peenemünde, Germany.

1942

3 October The first successful launch takes place, at Peenemünde, Germany, of the V-2 rocket.

1945

9 September The first postwar motor-racing event, the Coupe de Paris, takes place in the Bois de Boulogne, Paris, France.

26 December The first annual Sydney to Hobart race for sailing boats takes place, over a distance of 630 miles (1014km).

1947

During the motorcycling TT week on the Isle of Man, UK, the first Senior Clubman's race is won by Eric Briggs on a Norton at an average speed of 78.67mph (126.61kph).

The first Moto-Cross des Nations is won by Britons Nicholson, Rist and Ray.

28 April Norwegian Thor Heyerdahl and five others begin a 101-day, 5000-mile (8000km) voyage from Peru to the islands east of Tahiti on the balsa-wood raft *Kon-Tiki*.

14 October American Captain Charles 'Chuck' Yeager, of the USAAF, reaches 40,000ft (12,190m) in a Bell X-1 aircraft and is the first person to break through the sound barrier, with a speed of Mach 1.06 (700mph/1126kph).

1949

Spring The first Tulip Rally, organized by the Royal Automobile Club of the Netherlands, is won by British racing driver Ken Wharton.

13–15 June The first Motor-Cycle Grand Prix is held on the Isle of Man, UK. Briton Harold Daniell wins the 500cc race on a Norton at an average speed of 86.93mph (139.90kph); Briton Freddie Frith wins the 350cc race on a Velocette at 83.15mph (133.82kph); and Irishman Manliff Barrington wins the 250cc event on a Guzzi at 77.96mph (125.46kph).

In the first World Motor-Cycle Racing Championships, the 125cc World Champion is Italian Nello Pagani, on an FB Mondial; Italian Bruno Ruffo, on a Moto-Guzzi, takes the 250cc title; Briton Freddie Frith wins the 350cc championship; Briton Leslie Graham takes the 500cc title; and Briton Eric Oliver wins the title for 500cc machines with sidecar, on a Norton.

The Winston Cup, awarded by America's National Association for Stock Auto Racing (NASCAR), is contested for the first time. American Red Byron is the winner.

27 July The world's first jet airliner, the de Havilland DH106 Comet, makes its maiden flight at Hatfield, Hertfordshire, England.

1950

5 May Start of the first Carrera Panamericana, in Mexico, over a distance of 2178 miles (3504km). The winner is Hershel McGriff in an Oldsmobile 88 at an average speed of 77.43mph (124.58kph).

13 May Italian Giuseppe Farina wins the first Formula A (which became known as Formula One) race, in the British Grand Prix at Silverstone, driving an Alfa-Romeo T158 at an average speed of 90.95mph (146.37kph).

Giuseppe Farina, in an Alfa-Romeo wins the first Formula One World Championship, at Monza, Italy.

The first Rally of the Midnight Sun (later called the International Swedish Rally) is won in the summer by Cederbaum and Sohlberg, in a BMW 328.

The first Drag Racing World Record is set by American Harold Nicolson in a Ford Roadster at Santa Ana, California, USA, with a speed of 120mph (193kph) (see also 1955 and 1988).

Alfa-Romeo wins the first International Cup for Formula One Manufacturers.

1951

1 September Start of the first International Thousand Lakes Rally (Jyväskylan Suurajot) in Finland. The winners are Karlsson and Mattila in an Austin Atlantic.

1953

30 May–1 June The first East African Coronation Safari, passing through Kenya, Uganda and Tanganyika (now Tanzania), is won by A. N. Dix in a Volkswagen Beetle.

The first European Rally Championship for Drivers is won by H. Polensky in a Porsche.

The first Acropolis Rally is won by Nikos Papamichael/Sotiris Dimitracos in a Jaguar XK 120.

13 August Anne Davison reaches Miami, Florida, USA, in the 23ft (7m) sloop *Felicity Ann*, to become the first woman to sail the Atlantic single-handed, having left Plymouth, England, on 18 May 1952.

19 May American Jacqueline Cochran, flying over California in an F-86 Sabre jet, is the first woman to break the sound barrier, reaching Mach 1.01 (652.5mph/1050kph).

8–9 October The London to Christchurch (New Zealand) Air Race is won by Flight Lieutenants R. L. E. Burton and D. H. Gannon, flying an English Electric Canberra, at an average speed of 494.48mph (795.89kph).

November American Scott Crossfield is the first person to travel at twice the speed of sound when, in a Douglas D-558-II Skyrocket at Edwards Air Force Base, California, USA, he reaches Mach 2.01 (1327mph/2135kph).

1954

9 August Briton Captain R. T. Shepherd flies the Rolls-Royce Thrust-Measuring Rig, 'The Flying Bedstead', in the first step towards vertical flight.

1955

28–29 March Two French electric locomotives, the six-axle CC7107 and the four-axle BB9004, set, on succesive days, the same world speed record for railway trains of 205.6mph (330.9kph) on the Bordeaux–Hendaye line, breaking the 300kph (187mph) barrier for the first time.

American Lloyd Scott, in a Bustle Bomb, breaks the 10-second barrier in drag racing with a time of 9.44 seconds, at San Fernando, California, USA.

1956

November The first Tour de Corse, in Corsica, is won by Gilbert Thirion and Nadège Ferrier, in a Renault Dauphine.

The first USAC National Championship (from 1916 to 1955 known as the American Automobile Association National Championship) is won by American Jimmy Bryan in a Kuzma-Offenhauser.

27 September American Captain Milburn Apt is the first person to travel at three times the speed of sound when, in a Bell X-2 aircraft at Edwards Air Force Base, California, USA, he reaches Mach 3.2 (2094mph/3370kph). However, the aircraft then goes out of control and Apt is killed.

1957

September The first 500cc Moto-cross World Championship is won by Swede Bill Nilsson on an AJS 7R racing motorcycle.

Britain wins the first Admiral's Cup series (which includes the Channel Race and the Fastnet Race) of yachting races, organized by the Royal Ocean Racing Club (RORC).

11 April In the USA, the Ryan X-13 Vertijet completes a full transition from vertical take-off to horizontal flight and then back to the hover to make a successful tail-sitting landing.

4 October The USSR's modified two-stage R-7 missile lifts into orbit *Sputnik 1*, the world's first artificial satellite.

3 November The USSR's *Sputnik 2* carries the first living animal into space, the husky dog Laika.

1958

4 August The world's first nuclear-powered submarine, the *Nautilus*, captained by American Commander W. R. Anderson, of the US Navy, makes the first voyage under the North Pole's ice-cap.

October BOAC begins the first transatlantic passenger service by jet aircraft, between London and New York. In the same month Pan Am introduces the first daily passenger service by jet, flying Boeing 707s between New York and Paris.

1959

A permanent stock-car racing speedway opens at Dayton, Florida, USA, and American Lee Petty wins the first Winston Cup to be awarded there by the National Association for Stock Auto Racing.

25 July The SR.N1 Hovercraft, the brainchild of Briton Christopher Cockerell and the world's first practical air-cushion vehicle (ACV), leaves Calais, France, at 4.49 a.m. and reaches Dover, England, at 6.45 a.m. in the first crossing of the English Channel by ACV.

26 August Frenchwoman Jacqueline Auriol, flying a Dassault Mirage III, is the first woman flyer to reach a speed of Mach 2.

1961

The first San Remo Rally (originally known as the Rallye dei Fiori) is held in Italy and won by De Villa in an Alfa-Romeo Giulietta.

12 April The first man in space is the USSR's Yuri Gagarin, who orbits the earth in *Vostok I*.

1963

16 June The first woman in space is the USSR's Valentina Tereshkova, in *Vostok VI*.

1964

7 March The Hawker-Siddeley Kestrel, which in 1965 will be developed into the world's first operational VTOL fighter, makes its maiden flight.

1965

1 November Japanese National Railways, on its 'Tokaido' high-speed line between Osaka and Tokyo, begins the world's first scheduled railway service to travel at over 100mph (160kph).

18 March The USSR's Alexei A. Leonov takes the first space walk, from *Voskhod 2*.

1966

March The first docking of two spacecraft in orbit takes place during the USA's *Gemini 8* mission.

1967

The first Portugal Rally is won by Carpintero Albino and Silva Pereira in a Renault 8 Gordini.

28 May Briton Francis Chichester, in *Gipsy Moth IV*, completes a solo circumnavigation of the world, having set out from Plymouth, England, on 26 August 1966.

The first Crystal Trophy yacht race for cruising multihulls, from Cowes, Isle of Wight, via Cherbourg, France, and Wolf Rock Lighthouse to Plymouth (311 miles/500km), is won by K. Isted and G. Tinley in *Tomahawk*.

1968

8 December The first London–Sydney Rally, begun on 23 November, is won by Britons Andrew Cowan, Colin Malkin and Brian Coyle in a Hillman Hunter.

24 December The first manned orbit of the Moon is made by the USA's *Apollo 8*, launched on 21 December. Afterwards the craft returns to earth.

31 December The first flight by a supersonic transport aircraft is made by the USSR's Tupolev Tu-144.

1969

The first outright winners of the New Zealand Rally are Grady Thompson and Rick Rimmer, driving a Holden Monaro.

9 February The world's first wide-bodied commercial transport aircraft, the Boeing 747 'jumbo jet', makes it maiden flight.

21 July American Neil Armstrong, one of the three-man crew of *Apollo 11*, launched on 16 July, is the first person to walk on the Moon.

1970

April–May The first London–Mexico (World Cup) Rally is won by Hannu Mikkola and Gunnar Palm in a works Ford Escort Mk1.

In drag racing, the American Hot Rod Association's (AHRA) first Grand American Series is held at the Winter Nationals in Phoenix, Arizona, and is won by Don Garlits.

1971

6 August British yachtsman Chay Blyth is the first person to sail solo around the world against the prevailing winds, having set out on 18 October 1970 from Hamble, England.

19 April The USSR launches *Salyut 1*, the world's first space station, into Earth orbit.

1973

The first world speed record for diesel trains is established by a British Rail high-speed diesel train on the Darlington–York line, with a speed of 143mph (232kph).

1974

25 May The first London–Munich (World Cup) Rally, via Nigeria and Turkey, begun on 5 May, is won by Australians André Welinski, Ken Tubman and Jim Reddix in a Citroën DS23.

11 April Briton Chay Blyth, in *Great Britain II*, is the fastest yachtsman in the first Whitbread Round the World Race, after a voyage of 144 days, 10 hours. The handicap winner of the Whitbread Trophy is Mexican Ramón Carlin, in *Sayula II*, in 152 days, 9 hours.

1975

Briton Martin Lampkin wins the first Motorcycle Trials World Championship on a Bultaco.

1976

21 January The world's first scheduled supersonic air services for fare-paying passengers begin when a French Concorde leaves Paris for Rio de Janeiro and a British Concorde leaves London for Bahrain.

1977

The first FIA World Rally Championship Cup for Drivers is won by Sandro Munari.

1979

The first World Champion Driver in the FIA World Rally Championship is Swede Björn Waldegaard in a Ford Escort RS and a Mercedes 450 SLC.

The first Paris–Dakar Rally is won by Genestier, Lemordant and Tierbault in a Range Rover.

The first Rally of Argentina is won by Frenchmen Jean Guichet and Jean Todt in a Peugeot 504.

The first CART Indycar World Series (from 1957 to 1978 known as the USAC National Championship) is won by American Rick Mears in a Penske PC7-Cosworth and a Penske PC6 Cosworth.

1980

The first motorcycling World Endurance Championship is won jointly by Frenchmen Marc Fontan and Hervé Moineau, both on Hondas.

The first Sidecar World Moto-Cross Championship is won by West Germans Reinhardt Bohler and Siegfried Müller on a Yamaha.

January A world speed record for Hovercraft of 91.9 knots (170.2kph) is set on the Chesapeake Bay Test Range, Maryland, USA, by the US Navy test vehicle SES-100 B, built by Bell Aerosystems.

1981

12 April NASA's first Space Shuttle, *Columbia*, is launched from the Kennedy Space Center, USA.

1983

28 November The maiden flight takes place of NASA's Spacelab, the first reusable space workshop.

1985

5 December The French TGV (Train à Grande Vitesse) Atlantique No.325 achieves a speed of 300mph (482.4kph), the first time the 300mph barrier is broken.

The first Australian Safari, over a 3750-mile (6000km) course, is won by Andrew Cowan and Fred Gocentas in a Mitsubishi Pajero.

1986

A world speed record for outboard-powered vessels of 177.61mph (285.83kph) is set by P. R. Knight on Lake Ruataniwha, New Zealand, in his Chevrolet-powered Lauterbach.

14–23 December Americans Dick Rutan and Jeana Yeager make the first non-stop flight around the world without refuelling, in their 'trimaran' aircraft *Voyager*, covering 25,000 miles (40,000km)

1987

4 February A world speed record for a passenger-carrying train is set by Japanese National Railways' maglev test train MLU-001, which reaches 249mph (401kph) on an experimental track.

1 November A world speed record for diesel-electric trains is set by a British Rail Intercity 125 train with two power cars which reach 148.4mph (238.8kph) on the Darlington–York line, England.

March American Tom Gentry sets a world speed record for offshore boats of 154.438mph (248.537kph) in a 49ft (15m) catamaran powered by four turbo-charged V8 engines.

1988

6 April American Eddie Hall breaks the five-second barrier in drag racing, with a time of 4.99 seconds, at Dallas, Texas, USA.

1 May West Germany sets a railway world speed record for electric traction of 252.8mph (406.9kph) on the Fulda–Würzburg 'Neubaustrecke'.

American Fred Merkel, on a 750cc Honda VFR, wins the first World Superbike Championship in the final round in New Zealand.

The first Rally of Australia is won by Swedes Ingver Carlsson and Per Carlsson in a Mazda 323 4WD.

13 March Australian Jonathan Sanders, in his masthead sloop *Parry Endeavour* completes the first single-handed triple circumnavigation of the world, begun on 25 May 1986.

1989

November Briton Fiona Lady Arran, in her 15ft (4.57m) hydroplane *An Stradag* (Gaelic for 'The Spark') sets the first world speed record for an electrically-powered powerboat, reaching 51.973mph (83.64kph) at Holme Pierrepont, England.

1990

18 May A railway world speed record is set when a French high-speed TGV Atlantique (without passengers) reaches a speed of 320.2mph (515.3kph) between Courtalain and Tours, France.

1991

15 October Seacat's catamaran passenger ferry Hoverspeed France sets a record for the crossing from Dover to Calais, with a time of 34 minutes, 23 seconds and an average speed of 45mph (72kph).

1995

22 March Russian cosmonaut Valery Polyakov sets a record of 437 consecutive days, and a career total of 678 days, in space.

1997

15 October Briton Andy Green sets a new world land speed record in the jet-powered *Thrust SSC*, breaking the sound barrier for the first time on land. His average speed, over two runs within a specified time limit of 60 minutes at Black Rock Desert, Nevada, USA, is 763.035mph (1227.983kph).

15 May American Eileen Collins is the first woman pilot of a Space Shuttle, *Atlantis*.

SELECTED RECORDS

1899–1997

LAND

GORDON BENNETT RACE

YEAR	DATE	DRIVER	VEHICLE	COURSE	MPH	KPH
1900	14 June	Fernand Charron	24hp Panhard Levassor	Paris–Lyons	38.6	62.1
1901	29 June	L. Girardot	Panhard	Paris–Bordeaux	37	59.5
1902	26 June	S.F. Edge	35 hp Napier	Paris–Innsbruck	31.8	51.2
1903	2 July	Camille Jenatzy	9.2 litre Mercedes *The Red Devil*	Kildare–Naas, Ireland	49.2	79.2
1904	17 June	Léon Théry	Richard-Brasier	Homburg Course	54.5	87.7
1905	5 July	Léon Théry	Richard-Brasier	Auvergne, France	48.6	78.2

MOTORCYCLE WORLD SPEED RECORD

YEAR	DATE	DRIVER	MACHINE, CC	LOCATION	MPH	KPH
1909	16 June	W.E. Cook	NLG, 994	Brooklands, UK	75.92	122.16
1910	20 July	Charles Collier	Matchless	Brooklands, UK	80.24	129.13
	August	Charles collier	Matchless	Brooklands, UK	84.89	136.62
1911	July	Jake de Rosier	Indian, 994	Brooklands, UK	85.38	137.41
	July	Jake de Rosier	Indian, 994	Brooklands, UK	88.87	143.02
	4 August	Charles Collier	Matchless	Brooklands, UK	89.48	144.00
	19 August	Charles Collier	Matchless	Brooklands, UK	91.37	147.05
1914	2 May	Sidney George	–	Brooklands, UK	93.48	150.44
1920	14 April	Ernest Walker	Indian, 994	Daytona, USA	104.12	167.67
1923	6 November	Claude Temple	British Anzani, 996	Brooklands, UK	108.41	174.58
1924	6 July	Herbert Le Vack	Brough Superior-JAP, 867	Arpajon, France	119.07	191.59
1926	5 September	Claude Temple	OEC-Temple, 996	Arpajon, France	121.30	195.33
1928	25 August	Oliver Baldwin	Zenith JAP, 996	Arpajon, France	124.62	200.56
1929	25 August	Herbert Le Vack	Brough Superior, 995	Arpajon, France	128.86	207.33
1930	31 August	Joseph Wright	OEC-Temple, 994	Arpajon, France	137.23	220.99
	September	Ernst Henne	BMW, 735	Ingolstadt, Ger.	137.58	221.54
	October	Joseph Wright	OEC Temple JAP, 995	Cork, Ireland	150.65	242.59
1932	3 November	Ernst Henne	BMW, 735	Tat, Hungary	151.77	244.40
1934	28 October	Ernst Henne	BMW, 735	Gyon, Hungary	152.81	246.069
1935	Autumn	Ernst Henne	BMW, 735	Frankfurt–Munich autobahn, Germany	159.01	256.046
1936	12 October	Ernst Henne	BMW, 495	Frankfurt–Munich autobahn, Germany	168.92	272.006
1937	19 April	Eric Fernihough	Brough Superior-JAP, 995	Gyon, Hungary	169.68	273.244
	21 October	Piero Taruffi	Gilera, 492	Brescia autostrada, Italy	170.27	274.181
	November	Ernst Henne	BMW, 495	Frankfurt–Munich autobahn, Germany	173.57	279.503
1951	12 April	Wilhelm Herz	NSU, 499	Ingolstadt, Ger.	180.29	290.322
1955	2 July	Russell Wright	Vincent HRD, 998	Swannanoa, NZ	184.83	297.64
	July*	Johnny Allen	Triumph, 650	Bonneville, USA	193.72	311.7
1956	4 August	Wilhelm Herz	NSU, 499	Bonneville, USA	211.40	338.092
	August*	Johnny Allen	Triumph, 650	Bonneville, USA	214	344
1962	5 September	William Johnson	Triumph, 667	Bonneville, USA	224.57	361.41
1966	23 August	Robert Leppan	Triumph Special, 1298	Bonneville, USA	245.60	395.28
1970	17 September	Don Vesco	Yamaha, 700	Bonneville, USA	251.66	405.25
		Calvin Rayborn	Harley-Davidson, 1480	Bonneville, USA	251.66	410.37
	16 October	Calvin Rayborn	Harley-Davidson, 1480	Bonneville, USA	265.49	426.40
1975	28 September	Don Vesco	Yamaha, 1496	Bonneville, USA	302.92	487.515
1978	25 August	Don Vesco	Kawasaki, 2032 *Lightning Bolt*	Bonneville, USA	318.598	512.733
1990	14 July	Dave Campos	USA streamliner *Easyriders*	Bonneville, USA	322.150	518.450

* Not an official record, because it was not timed according to the requirements of the Fédération Internationale Motocycliste (FIM).

WORLD LAND SPEED RECORD (WHEEL-DRIVEN)

YEAR	DATE	DRIVER	VEHICLE	LOCATION	MPH	KPH
1899	29 April	Camille Jenatzy	CITA No.25 (electric powered) *La Jamais Contente*	Achères, France	65.792	105.882
1902	13 April	Léon Serpollet	Steam Gardner-Serpollet *La Baleine*	Nice, France	75.065	120.79
	5 August	William Vanderbilt	9.2l. Mors Z	Ablis, France	76.086	122.499
	5 November	Henri Fournier	9.2l. Mors Z	Dourdan, France	76.607	123.287
	17 November	M. Augières	9.2l. Mors Z	Dourdan, France	77.136	124.138
1903	7 March*	Charles Rolls	9.2l. Mors Z	Clipstone, UK	82.849	133.333
	17 July	Arthur Duray	13.5l. Gobron-Brillié	Ostend, Belgium	83.468	134.328
	July*	Baron de Forest	Mors 'Dauphine'	Dublin, Ireland	84.095	135.338
	October*	Charles Rolls	Mors 'Dauphine'	Clipstone, UK	84.732	136.363
	5 November	Arthur Duray	13.5l. Gobron-Brillié	Dourdan, France	84.732	136.363
1904	12 January**	Henry Ford	16.7l. Ford *The Arrow*	L. St Clair, USA	91.371	147.047
	27 January	William Vanderbilt	11.9l. Mercedes-Simplex 90	Daytona, USA	92.308	148.555
	31 March	Arthur Duray	13.5l. Gordon-Brillié	Nice, France	88.767	142.857
	31 March	Louis Rigolly	13.6l. Gobron-Brillié	Nice, France	93.206	150.00
	31 March	Louis Rigolly	13.6l. Gobron-Brillié	Nice, France	94.705	152.542
	25 May	Pierre de Caters	11.9l. Mercedes Simplex 90	Ostend, Belgium	97.258	156.522
	21 July	Paul Baras	11.3l. Darracq	Ostend, Belgium	101.679	163.636
	21 July	Louis Rigolly	13.6l. Gobron-Brillié	Ostend, Belgium	103.561	166.666
	13 November	Paul Baras	11.3l. Darracq	Ostend, Belgium	104.530	168.224
1905	24 January**	Arthur Macdonald	15l. Napier L48	Daytona, USA	104.651	168.419
	30 December	Victor Hémery	22.5l. Darracq V8	Arles, France	108.589	174.757
1906	23 January	Victor Hémery	22.5l. Darracq V8	Daytona, USA	115.306	185.567
	25 January	Louis Chevrolet	22.5l. Darracq V8	Daytona, USA	117.647	189.334
	26 January	Fred Marriott	Steam Stanley Steamer *Rocket*	Daytona, USA	121.573	195.652
1909	8 November	Victor Hémery	21.5l. Benz No.1	Brooklands, UK	125.946	202.691
1910	23 March**	Barney Oldfield	21.5l. Benz No.1	Daytona, USA	131.275	211.267
1911	23 April	Robert Burman	21.5l. Benz No.1	Daytona, USA	141.732	228.096
1914	24 June	L.G. Hornsted	21.5l. Benz No.3	Brooklands, UK	124.095	199.711
	12 February**	Ralph de Palma	14.8l. Packard '905'	Daytona, USA	150.534	242.261
1920	27 April**	Tommy Milton	5l. Twin Duesenberg	Daytona, USA	156.047	251.133
1922	17 May	Kenelm Lee Guinness	18.3l. Sunbeam	Brooklands, UK	133.708	215.182
	23 June	Malcolm Campbell	18.3l. Sunbeam *Bluebird*	Fano, Denmark	137.720	221.639
1924	19 June	Malcolm Campbell	18.3l. Sunbeam *Bluebird*	Saltburn, UK	145.255	233.766
	6 July	René Thomas	10.6l. Delage DH *La Torpille*	Arpajon, France	143.312	230.638
	12 July	Ernest Eldridge	21.7l. Fiat Special *Mephistopheles II*	Arpajon, France	146.01	234.987
	25 September	Malcolm Campbell	18.31l. Sunbeam *Bluebird*	Pendine, UK	146.163	235.217
1925	21 July	Malcolm Campbell	18.31l. Sunbeam *Bluebird*	Pendine, UK	150.76	242.8
1926	16 March	Henry Segrave	4l. Sunbeam *Ladybird*	Southport, UK	152	245.149
	27 April	J.G. Parry Thomas	26.9l. Higham-Thomas Special *Babs*	Pendine, UK	169.298	272.459
	28 April	J.G. Parry Thomas	26.9l. Higham-Thomas Special *Babs*	Pendine UK	171.019	275.229
1927	4 February	Malcolm Campbell	22.1l. Napier-Campbell *Bluebird*	Southport, UK	174.88	281.447
	29 March	Henry Segrave	22.5l. Sunbeam	Daytona, USA	203.79	327.98
1928	19 February	Malcolm Campbell	22.3 1. Napier-Campbell *Bluebird*	Daytona, USA	206.96	333.06
1928	22 April	Ray Beech	26.9l. Packard Liberty powered *White Triplex Special*	Daytona, USA	207.55	334.02
1929	11 March	Henry Segrave	26.9l. Irving Napier Special *Golden Arrow*	Daytona, USA	231.446	372.340

YEAR	DATE	DRIVER	VEHICLE	LOCATION	MPH	KPH
1931	5 February	Malcolm Campbell	26.91. Napier-Campbell *Bluebird IV*	Daytona, USA	246.088	396.04
1932	24 February	Malcolm Campbell	26.91. Napier-Campbell *Bluebird IV*	Daytona, USA	253.968	408.722
1933	22 February	Malcolm Campbell	36.51.Campbell-Rolls-Royce *Bluebird*	Daytona, USA	272.465	438.489
1935	7 March	Malcolm Campbell	36.51.Campbell-Rolls-Royce *Bluebird*	Daytona, USA	276.8	443.2
	3 September	Malcolm Campbell	36.51. Campbell-Rolls-Royce *Bluebird*	Bonneville, USA	301.128	484.6
1937	19 November	George Eyston	36.51. Rolls-Royce powered *Thunderbolt*	Bonneville, USA	312	501.374
1938	27 August	George Eyston	36.51. Rolls-Royce-powered *Thunderbolt*	Bonneville, USA	345.49	555.92
	15 September	John Cobb	26.91. Railton Special	Bonneville, USA	350.20	563.471
	16 September	George Eyston	36.51. Rolls-Royce-powered *Thunderbolt*	Bonneville, USA	357.5	575.217
1939	23 August	John Cobb	26.91. Railton Special	Bonneville, USA	369.74	591.6
1947	16 September	John Cobb	26.91. Railton Mobil Special	Bonneville, USA	394.196	634.398
1964	17 July	Donald Campbell	Gas-turbine Campbell-Norris *Bluebird-Proteus CN7*	L. Eyre, Australia	403.135	648.783
	12 November	Bob Summers	6.91. Chrysler–powered *Goldenrod*	Bonneville, USA	409.277	658.667

* Not officially recognized

** Not recognized by the Association internationale des Automobile-Clubs Reconnus (AIACR).

† Officially recognized by the newly formed Fédération Internationale de l'Automobile (FIA), even though it was slower than speeds previously achieved at Daytona, as it accorded with the FIA's requirements, which averaged the speed of two runs over a 1-mile (1.6km) timed course.

†† Not recognized by the AIACR, but recognized by the American Automobile Association (AAA).

WORLD LAND SPEED RECORD (JET- AND ROCKET-POWERED)

YEAR	DATE	DRIVER	VEHICLE	LOCATION	MPH	KPH
1963	5 August*	Craig Breedlove	Jet-engined *Spirit of America*	Bonneville, USA	428.4	689.4
1964	2 October	Tom Green	Jet-engined *The Wingfoot Express*	Bonneville, USA	413.199	664.977
	5 October	Art Arfons	Jet-engined *Green Monster*	Bonneville, USA	434.022	698.491
	13 October	Craig Breedlove	Jet-engined *Spirit of America*	Bonneville, USA	468.719	754.331
	15 October	Craig Breedlove	Jet-engined *Spirit of America*	Bonneveille, USA	526.277	846.961
	27 October	Art Arfons	Jet-engined *Green Monster*	Bonneville, USA	536.712	863.755
1965	2 November	Craig Breedlove	Jet-engined *Spirit of America Sonic 1*	Bonneville, USA	555.127	893.391
	7 November	Art Arfons	Jet-engined	Bonneville, USA	576.553	927.873
	15 November	Craig Breedlove	Jet-engined *Spirit of America Sonic 1*	Bonneville, USA	600.601	966.573
1970	23 October	Gary Gabelich	Rocket-powered RDI *The Blue Flame*	Bonneville, USA	622.407	1001.666
1983	4 October	Richard Noble	Jet-engined *Thrust 2*	Black Rock Desert, USA	633.468	1019.468
1997	15 October	Andy Green	Jet-engined *Thrust SSC*	Black Rock Desert, USA	763.035	1227.983

* Not officially recognized by the Association Internationale des Automobile-Clubs Reconnus (AIACR).

Note: On 17 December 1979 Stan Barrett of the USA became the first man to drive a wheeled vehicle faster than the speed of sound in his rocket-propelled Budweiser Rocket at Edwards Air Force Base, California, USA. Barrett achieved 739.666mph (1190.374kph), but the achievement was not officially recognized as a record, as this speed was not the result of averaging two runs over a 1-mile (1.6km) timed course.

SEA

BLUE RIBAND

YEAR	DATE	SHIP	DIRECTION	TIME	AVERAGE SPEED	
					KNOTS	KPH
1897	September	*Kaiser Wilhelm der Grosse*	E to W and then	5 days 22h 45m	22.36	41.41
			W to E	5 days 15h 10m	–	–
1900	July	*Deutschland*	E to W and then	5 days 20h 20m	22.42	41.52
			W to E	5 days 7h 38m	22.46	41.59
	August	*Kaiser Wilhelm der Grosse*	W to E	–	22.89	42.39
	September	*Deutschland*	W to E	5 days 7h 15m	23.36	43.26
1901	July	*Deutschland*	E to W and then	5 days 16h 5m	23.06	42.71
			W to E	–	23.51	43.54
1902	April	*Kaiser Wilhelm der Grosse*	E to W	5 days 15h	22.84	42.29
	September	*Kronprinz Wilhelm*	E to W	5 days 11h 57m	23.09	42.76
1904	April	*Kaiser Wilhelm II*	E to W	5 days 12h 45m	23.12	42.82
1906	September	*Kaiser Wilhelm II*	W to E	5 days 8h 17m	23.57	43.65
1907	October	*Lusitania*	E to W and then	4 days 19h 52m	23.99	44.43
			W to E	4 days 22h 53m	23.61	43.73
	December	*Mauretania*	W to E	4 days 22h 33m	23.69	43.87
1908	May	*Mauretania*	E to W	4 days 20h 15m	24.86	46.04
	July	*Lusitania*	E to W	–	25.85	47.87
1909	February	*Mauretania*	W to E	4 days 20h 27m	25.16	46.59
	September	*Mauretania*	E to W	4 days 10h 50m	26.06	48.26
1929	July	*Bremen*	E to W and then	4 days 17h 42m	27.83	51.54
			W to E	4 days 14h 30m	27.95	51.76
1930	March	*Europa*	E to W	4 days 17h 6m	27.92	51.71
1933*	March	*Bremen*	E to W	–	28.51	52.80
	August	*Rex*	E to W	4 days 13h 58m	28.92	53.56
1935	May	*Normandie*	E to W	4 days 3h 2m	29.98	55.52
	June	*Normandie*	W to E	4 days 3h 25m	30.35	56.21
1936**	August	*Queen Mary*	E to W and then	4 days 27m	30.14	55.82
			W to E	–	30.63	56.73
1937	March	*Normandie*	W to E	4 days 6m	30.99	57.39
	July	*Normandie*	E to W	3 days 23h	30.58	56.63
	August	*Normandie*	W to E	3 days 22h 7m	31.20	57.78
1938	August	*Queen Mary*	E to W and then	3 days 21h	30.99	57.39
			W to E	3 days 20h 42m	31.69	58.69
1952	July	*United States*	W to E and then	3 days 20h 40m	35.59	65.91
			E to W	3 days 12h 12m	34.51	63.91
1986†	27–30 June	*Virgin Atlantic Challenger II*	W to E	3 days 8h 31m	37	68.52
1989††	July	*Gentry Eagle*	W to E	62h 7m 17sec	45.7	84.64
1990	20-23 June	*Hoverspeed Great Britain*	W to E	3 days 7h 25m	36.97	68.47

* In this year Harold Hales, a British Member of Parliament, commissioned a trophy, to be known as the Hales Trophy, which was to be awarded to winners of the Blue Riband. The first winner was the Rex.

** Although the Queen Mary *achieved a superior speed in 1936 (and in 1938), the Hales Trophy was retained by the owners of the* Normandie, *Compagnie Générale Transatlantique, because Sir Percy Bates, chairman of the Cunard line, which owned the* Queen Mary, *decided that his company should not claim it.*

† Although Hales did not stipulate that competing vessels should be merchant ships, the American Merchant Marine Museum in the King's Point Naval Academy, Long Island Sound, USA, declined to relinquish the Hales Trophy on the grounds that the Virgin Atlantic Challenger II *(owned by Richard Branson of the UK) was not a merchant ship. As a result, Branson won the Blue Riband but did not receive the Hales Trophy.*

†† The Gentry Eagle *(owned by Tom Gentry of the USA) was not a merchant ship and therefore won the Blue Riband but not the Hales Trophy.*

WORLD WATER SPEED RECORD (UNOFFICIAL)

YEAR	DATE	SKIPPER	VESSEL (ENGINE)	LOCATION	MPH	KPH
1902	March	Unknown	*Mercédès* (Daimler)	Nice, France	22.36	35.98
1903	12 July	Campbell Muir	*Napier* (Napier)	Cork Harbour, Ireland	24.9	40.1
1904	11 April	M. Théry	*Trèfle-à-Quatre* (Brasier)	Monaco	25.1	40.4
1905	February	Proctor Smith	*Challenger* (Simplex)	Palm Beach, USA	29.3	47.2
	Unknown	Tucker	*Napier II* (Napier)	R. Thames, UK	29.93	48.17
	11 June	Marius Dubonnet	*Dubonnet* (2 Delahayes)	Juvissy, France	33.82	54.43
1906	1 February	Unknown	*Legro-Hotchkiss* (Hotchkiss)	R. Seine, France	34.17	54.99
1908		Clinton Crane	*Dixie II* (Crane)	Bayonne, USA	36.6	58.9
1910	April	Noel Robbins	*Ursula* (2 Wolseleys)	Monaco	43.6	70.2
1911	September	Fred Burnham	*Dixie IV*	Huntingdon Bay, USA	45.21	72.76
1912	July	Ton Sopwith	*Maple Leaf* (2 Austins)	Solent, UK	46.51	74.85
1914	April	Victor Despujols	*Santos-Despujols* (Unknown)	Monaco	59.964	96.503
1915		C. Smith	*Miss Minneapolis* (Unknown)	Putin Bay, USA	66.66	107.28
1919	9 September	C. Baldwin	*Hydrodome IV* (2 Liberty Aeros)	Beinn Bhreagh, Ireland	70.86	114.04
1920	18 September	Gar Wood	*Miss America*	L. George, USA	77.89	125.35
1921		George Wood	*Miss America II*	–	80.57	129.66
1924	9 November	Jules Fischer	*Farman Hydroglider*	R. Seine, France	85.56	137.69

WORLD WATER SPEED RECORD (UNOFFICIAL) (REGULATED BY THE IMYU)

YEAR	DATE	SKIPPER	VESSEL	LOCATION	MPH	KPH
1928	4 September	Gar Wood	*Miss America VII*	Indian Creek, USA	92.834	149.402
1930	13 June	Henry Segrave	*Miss England II*	L. Windermere, UK	98.76	158.01
1931	2 April	Kaye Don	*Miss England II*	R. Paraná, Brazil	103.49	165.58
	9 July	Kaye Don	*Miss England II*	L. Garda, Italy	110.223	177.387
1932	5 February	Gar Wood	*Miss America IX*	Indian Creek, USA	111.712	179.783
	18 July	Kaye Don	*Miss England III*	Loch Lomond, UK	119.81	192.81
	20 September	Gar Wood	*Miss America X*	Detroit, USA	124.91	201.02
1937	1–3 Sept.	Malcolm Campbell	*Bluebird K3*	L. Maggiore, Italy	126.33	203.31
			then		129.5	208.4
1938	17 September	Malcolm Campbell	*Bluebird K3*	Hallwiler See, Switzerland	130.94	210.726
1939	19 August	Malcolm Campbell	*Bluebird K4*	Coniston Water, UK	141.7	225.6
1950	26 June	Stanley Sayres	*Slo-Mo-Shun IV*	L. Washington, USA	160.32	258.01
1952	7 July	Stanley Sayre	*Slo-Mo-Shun IV*	L. Washington, USA	178.497	287.263
1955	23 July	Donald Campbell	*Bluebird K7*	Ullswater, UK	202.32	325.6
	16 Nov	Donald Campbell	*Bluebird K7*	L. Mead, USA	216.2	347.9
1956	20 Sept	Donald Campbell	*Bluebird K7*	Coniston Water, UK	225.63	363.12
1957	7 November	Donald Campbell	*Bluebird K7*	Coniston Water, UK	239.07	384.75
1958	September	Donald Campbell	*Bluebird K7*	Coniston Water, UK	248.62	400.12
1959	14 May	Donald Campbell	*Bluebird K7*	Coniston Water, UK	260.35	418.99
1964	31 December	Donald Campbell	*Bluebird K7*	L. Dumbleyung, Australia	276.30	444.66
1967	30 June	Lee A. Taylor Jr.	*Hustler*	L. Guntersville, USA	285.21	459
1977	20 November	Ken Warby	*Spirit of Australia*	Blowering Dam L., Australia	288.60	464.45
1978	8 October	Ken Warby	*Spirit of Australia*	Blowering Dam L., Australia	317.186	510.461

AIR

AVIATION WORLD ALTITUDE RECORD

YEAR	DATE	PILOT	LOCATION	AEROPLANE	FEET	METRES
1909	22 August	Hubert Latham	Reims, France	Antoinette	508	155
	18 October	Comte Charles de Lambert	Paris, France	Wright	984	300
	1 December	Hubert Latham	Châlons, France	Antoinette	1486	453
1910	7 January	Hubert Latham	France	Antoinette	3281	1000
	12 January	L. Paulhan	Los Angeles, USA	Henry Farman	3966	1209
	14 June	W. Brookins	Indianapolis, USA	Wright	4380	1335
	7 July	Hubert Latham	Reims, France	Antoinette	4540	1384
	10 July	W. Brookins	Atlantic City, USA	Wright	6234	1900
	11 August	A. Drexel	Lanark, UK	Blériot	6601	2012
	3 September	Léon Morane	Deauville, France	Blériot	8471	2582
	8 September	Georges Chávez	Issy-les-M., France	Blériot	8488	2587
	1 October	H. Wynmalen	Mourmelon, France	Henry Farman	9120	2780
	October	A. Drexel	Philadelphia, USA	Blériot	9449	2880
	31 October	R. Johnston	Long Island, USA	Wright	9711	2960
	8 December	G. Legagneux	Pau, France	Blériot	10,170	3100
1911	8 July	M. Loridan	Châlons, France	Henry Farman	10,423	3177
	9 August	Capt. Félix	Étampes, France	Blériot	10,466	3190
	4 September	Roland Garros	St-Malo, France	Blériot XI	12,828	3910
1912	6 September	Roland Garros	Houlgate, France	Blériot XI	16,076	4900
	17 September	G. Legagneux	Corbeaulieu, France	Morane-Saulnier	17,880	5450
	11 December	Roland Garros	Tunis, Tunisia	Morane-Saulnier	18,405	5610
1913	11 March	M. Perreyon	Buc, France	Blériot XI	19,291	5880
	28 December	G. Legagneux	St-Raphael, France	Nieuport	20,079	6120
1920	27 February	Maj. R.W. Schroeder	Dayton, USA	Lepere	33,113	10,093
1921	18 September	Lt J.A. MacReady	Dayton, USA	Lepere	34,508	10,518
1923	5 September	Joseph Sadi-Lecointe	Villacoublay, France	Nieuport	35,242	10,742
	30 October	Joseph, Sadi-Lecointe	Issy-les-M., France	Nieuport-Delage	36,565	11,145
1927	25 July	Lt C. Champion	Washington DC, USA	Wright Apache	38,418	11,710
1929	8 May	Lt Apollo Soucek	USA	Wright Apache	39,140	11,930
	26 May	W. Neuenhofen	Dessau, Germany	Junkers W34	41,795	12,739
1930	4 June	Lt Apollo Soucek	Washington DC, USA	Wright Apache	43,166	13,157
1932	16 September	Capt. C.F. Ewins	Filton, UK	Vickers Vespa	43,976	13,404
1933	28 September	G. Lemoine	Villacoublay, France	Potez 50	44,820	13,661
1934	11 April	Cdr R. Donati	Rome, Italy	Caproni 161	47,352	14,433
1936	14 August	G. Détré	Villacoublay, France	Potez 50	48,698	14,843
	28 September	Sqn Ldr S.R. Swain	Farnborough, UK	Bristol 138	49,944	15,223
1937	8 May	Lt Col M. Pezzi	Montecelio, Italy	Caproni 161	51,362	15,655
	30 June	Flt Lt M.J. Adam	Farnborough, UK	Bristol 138	53,937	16,440
1938	22 October	Lt Col. M. Pezzi	Montecelio, Italy	Caproni 161 *bis*	51,362	15,655
1948	23 March	J. Cunningham	Hatfield, UK	de Havilland Vampire 1	59,445	18,119
1953	4 May	W.F. Gibb	UK	English Electric Canberra	63,668	19,406
1955	29 August	W.F. Gibb	UK	English Electric Canberra	65,889	20,083
1957	28 August	M. Randrupp	UK	English Electric Canberra	70,308	21,430
1958	18 April	Lt Cdr G.C. Watkins	USA	Grumman F11 F-1 Tiger	76,932	23,449
	2 May	R. Carpentier	France	SO9050 Trident	79,452	24,217
	7 May	Maj. H.C. Johnson	USA	Lockheed F-104A Starfighter	91,243	27,811
1959	14 July	Maj. V. Ilyushin	USSR	Sukhoi T431	94,659	28,852
	6 December	Cdr L Flint	USA	McDonnell Douglas F-4 Phantom II	98,556	30,040
	14 December	Capt. B. Jordan	USA	Lockheed F-104C Starfighter	103,389	31,513
1961	28 April	Col. G. Mosolov	USSR	Mikoyan E-66A	113,891	34,714
1973	25 July	A. Fedotov	USSR	Mikoyan E-266	118,898	36,240
1977	31 August	A. Fedotov	USSR	Mikoyan E-266M	123,524	37,650

AVIATION WORLD SPEED RECORD

YEAR	DATE	PILOT	LOCATION	AEROPLANE	MPH	KPH
1909	20 May	Paul Tissandier	Pau, France	Wright biplane	34.03	54.77
	23 August	Glenn Curtiss	Reims, France	Herring-Curtiss biplane	43.34	69.75
	24 August	Louis Blériot	Reims, France	Blériot monoplane	46.17	74.39
	28 August	Louis Blériot	Reims, France	Blériot monoplane	47.84	76.99
1910	23 April	Hubert Latham	Nice, France	Antoinette monoplane	48.20	77.57
	10 July	Léon Morane	Reims, France	Blériot monoplane	66.18	106.50
	29 October	Alfred Léblanc	Long Island, USA	Blériot monoplane	68.18	109.73
1911	12 April	Alfred Léblanc		Blériot monoplane	69.46	111.79
	11 May	Édouard Nieuport		Nieuport biplane	74.40	119.74
	12 June	Alfred Léblanc		Blériot monoplane	77.67	124.99
	16 June	Édouard Neuport	Châlons, France	Nieuport biplane	80.80	130.04
	21 June	Édouard Neuport	Châlons, France	Nieuport biplane	82.71	133.11
1912	13 January	Jules Védrines	Pau, France	Déperdussin monoplane	90.18	145.13
	22 February	Jules Védrines	Pau, France	Déperdussin monoplane	100.21	161.27
	29 February	Jules Védrines	Pau, France	Déperdussin monoplane	100.99	162.53
	1 March	Jules Védrines	Pau, France	Déperdussin monoplane	103.64	166.79
	2 March	Jules Védrines	Pau, France	Déperdussin monoplane	104.32	167.88
	13 July	Jules Védrines		Déperdussin monoplane	106.10	170.75
	9 September	Jules Védrines	Chicago, USA	Déperdussin monoplane	108.16	174.06
1913	17 June	Maurice Prévost	France	Déperdussin monoplane	111.72	179.79
	27 September	Maurice Prévost	Reims, France	Déperdussin monoplane	119.22	191.87
	29 September	Maurice Prévost	Reims, France	Déperdussin monoplane	126.66	203.85
1920	7 February	Joseph Sadi-Lecointe	Villacoublay, France	Nieuport-Delage	171.01	275.22
	28 February	Jean Casale	Villacoublay, France	Blériot monoplane	176.12	283.43
	9 October	Baron de Romanet	Buc, France	Spad biplane	181.83	292.63
	10 October	Joseph Sadi-Lecointe	Buc, France	Nieuport-Delage 29	184.51	296.94
	20 October	Joseph Sadi-Lecointe	Villacoublay, France	Nieuport-Delage 29	187.95	302.48
	4 November	Baron de Romanet	Buc, France	Spad biplane	191.98	308.96
	12 December	Joseph Sadi-Lecointe	Villacoublay, France	Nieuport-Delage 29	194.49	313.00
1922	20 September	Joseph Sadi-Lecointe	Villesauvage, France	Nieuport-Delage 29	205.20	330.23
	21 September	Joseph Sadi-Lecointe	Villesauvage, France	Nieuport-Delage 29	211.89	341.00
	13 October	Brig-Gen. William Mitchell	Detroit, USA	Curtiss Racer HS D-12	222.93	358.77
1923	15 February	Joseph Sadi-Lecointe	Istres, France	Nieuport-Delage 29	233.00	374.95
	29 March	Lt R.L. Maughan	Wright Field, USA	Curtiss R-6	236.54	380.67
	2 November	Lt A Brown	Mitchell Field, New York, USA	Curtiss HS D-12	255.40	411.04
	4 November	Lt Alford Williams	Mitchell Field, New York, USA	Curtiss R-2 C-1	267.16	429.96
1924	11 December	Adj Chef A. Bonnet	Istres, France	Ferbois V-2	278.47	448.15
1927	4 November	Mario De Bernardi	Venice, Italy	Macchi M-52	297.83	479.21
	22 October	Mario De Bernardi	Venice, Italy	Macchi M-52bis	300.931	484.304
1928	30 March	Mario De Bernardi	Venice, Italy	Macchi M-52bis	318.57	512.69
1931	29 September	Flt-Lt George H Stainforth	Ryde, UK	Vickers Supermarine S6B	406.94	654.90
1933	10 April	W/O Francesco Agello	L. Garda, Italy	Macchi-Castoldi MC.72	423.82	682.078
1934	23 October	Lt Francesco Agello	L. Garda, Italy	Macchi-Castoldi MC.72	440.60	709.07
1939	30 March	Flugkapitan Dieterle	Oranienburg, Germany	Heinkel He 100V-8	463.82	746.45
1939	26 April	Flugkapitan Fritz	Augsburg, Germany	Messerschmitt Me.209	469.22	755.138
1945	7 November	Group-Capt. H.J. Wilson	Herne Bay, UK	Gloster Meteor F4	606.25	975.67
1946	7 September	Group-Capt E.M. Donaldson	Rustington, UK	Gloster Meteor F4	615.65	990.79
1947	19 June	Col. Albert Boyd	Muroc, USA	Lockheed P-80R Shooting Star	623.61	1003.60
	20 August	Cdr T.F. Caldwell	Muroc, USA	Douglas D-558 Skystreak	640.60	1030.95
	25 August	Maj. M.E. Carl USMC	Muroc, USA	Douglas D-558 Skystreak	650.78	1047.33
1948	15 September	Maj. R.L. Johnson USAF	Muroc, USA	North American F-86A Sabre	670.84	1079.61
1952	19 November	Capt. J. Slade Nash USAF	Salton Sea, USA	North American F-86D Sabre	698.35	1123.89
1953	16 July	Lt Col W.F. Barnes USAF	Salton Sea, USA	North American F-86D Sabre	715.60	1151.64
	7 September	Sqn Ldr Neville Duke	Littlehampton, UK	Hawker Hunter 3	727.48	1170.76
	25 September	Lt Cdr M. Lithgow	Libya	Supermarine Swift4	735.54	1183.74
	3 October	Lt Cdr J.B. Verdin USN	Salton Sea, USA	Douglas F4D-1 Skyray	752.78	1211.48
	29 October	Lt Col F.K. Everest USA	Salton Sea, USA	North American YF-100A Super Sabre	754.99	1215.04
1955	20 August	Col H.A. Hanes USAF	Edwards Air Force Base, USA	North American F-100C Super Sabre	822.09	1323.03
1956	10 March	Lt Peter Twiss	Chichester, UK	Fairey Delta 2	1131.76	1821.39
1957	12 December	Maj. Adrian Drew USAF	Edwards Air Force Base, USA	McDonnell F-101A	1207.34	1943.03
1958	16 May	Capt. W.W. Irvin USAF	Edwards Air Force Base, USA	Lockheed F-1041AStarfighter	1403.79	2269.18
1959	31 October	Col. G. Mosolov	Sidorovo, USSR	Mikoyan E-66	1483.51	2387.48
	15 December	Maj. J.W. Rogers USAF	Edwards Air Force Base, USA	Convair F-106A Delta Dart	1525.93	2455.74
1961	22 November	Lt Col R.B. Robinson	Edwards Air Force Base, USA	McDonnell F4H-1F	1606.51	2585.43
1962	7 July	Col. G. Mosolov	Sidorovo, USSR	Mikoyan E-166	1665.89	2681.00
1965	1 May	Col. R.L. Stephens	Edwards Air Force Base, USA	Lockheed YF-12A	2070.10	3331.51
1976	28 July	Capt. Eldon Joersz Maj. George Morgan	Edwards Air Force Base, USA	Lockheed SR-71 Blackbird	2193.167	3529.56
1981	12 April	Robert I. Crippen		Space Shuttle Orbiter Columbia	16,600.00	26,715

AIR-LAUNCHED AVIATION WORLD SPEED RECORD

YEAR	DATE	PILOT	LOCATION	AEROPLANE	MPH	KPH
1941	2 October	Heini Dittmar	Peenemünde, Germany	Bf163 Komet	623.8	1004
1947	14 October	Capt. Chuck Yeager*	Edwards Air Force Base, USA	Bell X-1	700	1127
1953	November	Scott Crossfield**	Edwards Air Force Base, USA	Douglas D-558-II Skyrocket	1327	2135
	12 December	Capt. Chuck Yeager	Edwards Air Force Base, USA	Bell X-1AA	1612	2595
1956	27 September	Capt. Milburn Apt†	Edwards Air Force Base, USA	Bell X-2	1094	3370
1961	7 March	Maj. R.M. White	Edwards Air Force Base, USA	North American X-15	2905	4675
1967	3 October	Maj. William J. Knight	Edwards Air Force Base, USA	North American X-15 A-2	4534	7297

Having reached Mach 1.015, Yeager was the first person to break the sound barrier.

**Having reached Mach 2.01, Crossfield was the first person to travel at twice the speed of sound.*

†*Having reached Mach 3.2, Apt was the first person to travel at three times the speed of sound.*

JAMES GORDON BENNETT INTERNATIONAL AVIATION CUP
(COUPE INTERNATIONALE D'AVIATION)

YEAR	DATE	LOCATION	PILOT	AEROPLANE (ENGINE)	MPH	KPH
1909	22 August	Reims, France	Glenn Curtiss	Curtiss Pusher 50hp biplane *Golden Flyer*	47.56	76.54
1910	29 October	Long Island, USA	Claude Grahame—White	Blériot XI *bis* 100hp Gnome	61.3	98.65
1911		Eastchurch, UK	Charles Weymann	Nieuport 100hp Gnome	78	125.53
1912	9 September	Chicago, USA	Jules Védrines	Déperdussin 160hp Gnome	105.5	169.79
1913	29 September	Reims, France	Maurice Prévost	Déperdussin 160hp Gnome	124.5	200.36
1920	28 September*	Étampes, France	Joseph Sadi-Lecointe	Nieuport Hispano-Suiza V-8	168.5	271.17

This was the third French victory in a row, so the Cup remained permanently in France.

SCHNEIDER TROPHY

YEAR	DATE	LOCATION	PILOT	AEROPLANE	MPH	KPH
1913	16 April	Monaco	Maurice Prévost	Déperdussin	45.75	73.63
1914	20 April	Monaco	Howard Pixton	Sopwith Tabloid biplane	86.78	139.66
1920	21 September	Venice, Italy	Luigi Bologna	Savoia S.12	109.77	176.66
1921	7 August	Venice, Italy	Giovanni di Briganti	Macchi M.7	117.90	189.74
1922	12 August	Naples, Italy	Captain Henry Biard	Supermarine Sea Lion II	145.7	234.48
1923	28 September	Cowes, UK	Lt David Rittenhouse	Curtiss CR-3	177.38	285.46
1925	26 October	Baltimore, USA	Lt James H. Doolittle	Curtiss R3C-2 Racer	232.57	374.28
1926	13 November	Hampton Roads, USA	Mario De Bernardi	Macchi M.39	246.5	396.70
1927	26 September	Venice, Italy	Flt-Lt S.N. Webster	Supermarine S.5	281.65	453.28
1929	7 September	Spithead, UK	Flt-Lt H.R.D. Waghorn	Supermarine S.6	328.63	528.87
1931	13 September	Spithead, UK	Flt-Lt J.N. Boothman	Supermarine S.6B	341.08	547.31

ACKNOWLEDGEMENTS

William H. Longyard, author *Who's Who in Aviation History*; Peter Boyd Smith, Cobwebs (ocean-liner and aviation memorabilia), Southampton, UK; Julie Canavan, National Boat Museum, Basildon, Essex, UK; Andrew Renwick, RAF Museum, Hendon, London, UK; John Pulford, Brooklands Museum, Weybridge, Surrey, UK; Shuttleworth Collection, Biggleswade, Bedfordshire, UK; Ken Norris, Bournemouth Airport, Dorset, UK; Sea Containers, London, UK; Toby Wilson, Sotheby's, London, UK; Michael Ware, Beaulieu Motor Museum, Hampshire, UK; Librarian and staff, Shrewsbury Reference Library, Staffordshire, UK; Librarian and staff, Cork Public Library, Ireland; Librarian and staff, Royal Aeronautical Library, UK; Librarian and staff, Royal Automobile Club Library. UK; Librarian and staff, Science Museum Library, UK.

PICTURE CREDITS

Abbreviations: t – top, m – middle, b – bottom, l – left, r – right.

All photographs in this book were supplied by the Castrol Photographic Archives except for the following:

Front cover m, 188tl, 189: Seaco Picture Library; front cover r, 5b, 11m, 163, 164 both, 165 both, 166, 167, 168, 192, 193 both, 195r, 197tl: NASA/BKR; 5m, 33, 66t, 67tr, 70t, 71, 184, 185: Beken of Cowes; 9t, 15t, 52bl and br, 103b, 112 both, 113, 115tr, 150, 170b, 182r, 190 both: Topham Picturepoint; 9m, 12, 26, 29b, 30–31, 31tm and tr, 35tl, 36t, 48, 62tl and tr, 62bl, 63m and b, 64tl, 65 all, 67bl, 74t, 74–75, 80tr, 81bl, 83tl, 89t and br, 94t, 95b, 97b, 98, 116, 120: Science and Society Picture Library; 9b, 18bl, 19t, 21m, 25 all, 32m, 52t, 81br, 89bl, 101 both, 105 both, 106m, 107r, 108 both, 109b, 111tl, 124br: Derek Forsyth & Partners; 10b, 36b, 37t, 38 both, 39b, 40br, 44t, 46, 78t and bl, 79br, 81t, 82t, 83tm, 86, 92, 93bl, 95tr, 126, 127, 130 both, 131 both, 154t and b, 155t, 157, 158, 161: Philip Jarrett; 11t, 64tr and bl, 66b, 100r, 104, 115tl, 136t, 141, 143t and m, 147r: Popperfoto; 11b, 162m, 194: Science Photo Library; 14t, 15bl, 16m, 17br, 23l, 24, 36m, 45t, 69tr, 72t, 73 both, 74br, 76b, 77t, 78br, 79bl, 82m, 160 both: Brooklands Museum; 14m, 17t and bl, 19bl and br, 23r, 29tl, 54 both, 56t, 57t and m, 58mr, 59t, 66m, 67m and br, 72ml, 109t, 140l, 144tl, 151m: Philip Sayer; 14b, 15br, 16t and b, 20b, 59b, 100l, 110 both, 114t, 115b, 140r, 142, 143b, 152b: Ludvigsen; 18t and br, 21t and b, 44b, 117l: Roger Viollet/Frank Spooner Pictures; 19b, 22 both, 27b, 28b, 29tr, 30t, 31tl, 39r, 40bl, 45b, 47 all, 50 all, 56ml, 57b, 58bl, 67tl, 69tl and m, 70b, 74bl, 77b, 84t and b, 85, 94b, 95tl, 96, 102t, 103t, 121t and b, 124t and bl, 128, 132, 144b, 151t and b, 153l and r, 154m, 156t: Hulton Getty Collection; 20t, 51, 88, 118–119, 147l: Corbis/Bettmann; 27t: Tom Donovan; 28t: Chris Kaye; 32t: Napier Heritage Trust; 32b, 155b, 177b, 178b, 181 both, 182l, 183b, 188tr, 195l, 197tr, mr and b: Frank Spooner Pictures; 34 all, 35tr and b, 90br, 145, 148bm, 156t: BKR; 37b, 43, 191b: Aviation Picture Library; 42, 97t: Smithsonian National Air & Space Museum; 55t and b, 123b: Quadrant Picture Library; 62br, 63t, 64br, 183t: Milepost 92½; 74m: Mary Evans Picture Library; 80tl, 82b, 83m: American Aviation Historical Society; 92b: TWA; 93t and br: Adrian Meredith Photography; 117r: Union Pacific/BKR; 119: Marine Art Posters; 133 all, 162t and b: Novosti Photo Library; 134: Telegraph Colour Library; 148t and m, 149b, 174t: Phipps Photographic; 148br: Beaulieu National Motor Museum; 149t and m, 174b, 175t, 177t, 180 both: Allsport; 159 both: Solo Syndication; 179t and ml: Neil Smith; 191t: Airbus Industrie/BKR; 196tl: Ford UK/BKR; 196ml and tr: Renault UK/BKR; 196br: BMW/BKR.

INDEX